*Northern Money, Southern Land*

# Northern
# MONEY *Southern*
# LAND

The Lowcountry
Plantation Sketches
*of* Chlotilde R. Martin

*Edited by*

ROBERT B. CUTHBERT
*and* STEPHEN G. HOFFIUS

THE UNIVERSITY OF SOUTH CAROLINA PRESS

© 2009 University of South Carolina

Published by the University of South Carolina Press
Columbia, South Carolina 29208

www.sc.edu/uscpress

Manufactured in the United States of America

18  17  16  15  14  13  12  11  10  09    10  9  8  7  6  5  4  3  2  1

*Library of Congress Cataloging-in-Publication Data*
Martin, Chlotilde R., 1895–1991.
    Northern money, southern land : the lowcountry plantation sketches of Chlotilde R. Martin / edited by
Robert B. Cuthbert and Stephen G. Hoffius.
        p. cm.
    Includes bibliographical references and index.
    ISBN 978-1-57003-822-8 (cloth : alk. paper)
    1. South Carolina—History, Local—Anecdotes. 2. Plantations—South Carolina—History—20th
century—Anecdotes. 3. South Carolina—Social life and customs—20th century—Anecdotes. 4. Social
change—South Carolina—History—20th century—Anecdotes. 5. Shooting preserves—South Carolina—
History—20th century—Anecdotes. 6. Natural areas—South Carolina—History—20th century—
Anecdotes. 7. Vacation homes—South Carolina—History—20th century—Anecdotes. 8. Rich people—
Northeastern States—Biography—Anecdotes. 9. Northeastern States—Biography—Anecdotes. 10. South
Carolina—Biography—Anecdotes. I. Cuthbert, Robert B. II. Hoffius, Stephen G. III. Title.
    F270.M35 2009
    307.1'41209757—dc22
                                2009004273

# CONTENTS

# ILLUSTRATIONS

**Maps**

# ACKNOWLEDGMENTS

WE HAVE BOTH BEEN HUMBLED by the number of people who have gone out of their way to provide us with assistance as we have worked on this project. The idea for the book began at the South Carolina Historical Society (SCHS) when library assistant Pat Kruger passed to Robert B. Cuthbert a number of brown and disintegrating newspaper clippings of articles by Chlotilde R. Martin, thinking that he might want them for his own files. Lo and behold, a book was born! Other helpful staff at the SCHS, where Robert has conducted research for more than thirty years and where Stephen Hoffius once worked, included Jane Aldrich, Mike Coker, Lisa Hayes, Faye Jensen, and Karen Stokes.

At the South Caroliniana Library in Columbia, Allen Stokes, Beth Bilderback, and Graham Duncan provided valuable assistance. At the South Carolina Department of Archives and History, we were aided by David Kelly, Brad Sauls, and Steve Tuttle. At the Historic Beaufort Foundation, Maxine Lutz and Evan Thompson always greeted us warmly when we arrived unexpected in their offices. Cynthia Jenkins, once of the Lowcountry Council of Governments and the Historic Beaufort Foundation and now director of the Preservation Society of Charleston, gave us early encouragement. Grace Cordial at the Beaufort County Public Library always seemed able to find books or clippings or maps that we needed. Ginny Kozack of the Lowcountry Council of Governments sent us in the right directions, both figuratively and literally, when we were lost. Nicholas M. Butler at the Charleston County Public Library was never too busy to help, despite the dozens of projects on which he always seemed to be working. Charles Philips and Josh Fletcher of Brockington and Company in Mt. Pleasant were very considerate, even when we—well, Steve—misplaced a disc of photos. Fellow researchers Bill Behan, Dan Vivian, and Sarah Fick shared their knowledge with us.

We have spent more time than we ever expected in the government offices of Beaufort, Jasper, Hampton, Colleton, and Berkeley counties, especially in the Registers of Mesne Conveyance. The staffs of those offices have been unfailingly helpful as we stumbled through volumes and computers that baffled us to no end.

Dr. Lawrence S. Rowland, Beaufort County's leading historian, shared a copy of one chapter of his upcoming second volume of *The History of Beaufort County*, which was most helpful, and he was a marvelous source of information and insights. Two hours with Larry seemed to pass in just minutes as we discovered someone else as fascinated as we are by Kate Gleason and others. In the same way, Calvert Huffines and Budd Price helped us improve our chapter on Colleton County. Dr. Alexander Moore, who co-authored volume 1 of *The History of Beaufort County*, grew excited by the idea of this book as soon as we mentioned it to him, and he shepherded it through the publishing process at the University of South Carolina Press. He nudged us when he could have demanded, for which we are eternally grateful.

The *Post and Courier* of Charleston, descendant of the *News and Courier*, granted permission to reprint Chlotilde R. Martin's original articles. We thank Paul F. Rossmann, who deciphered our handwriting in order to design the five maps.

Among the individuals associated with individual pieces of property who gave us much-needed assistance, we would like to recognize Al Altman, David Bormes, John M. Bryan, Jocelyn Clark, Julian Clark, Priscilla Merrick Coleman, Hank Cram, Peter Cram, John Dixon, Harry Hanna, Joe Hanna, Paula Hickman, Bobby Hood, Daniel and Katherine Huger, Hal Marvin Hunter, Rita and John D. Igleheart, Alice Jepson, Michael Kusaj, Wofford E. Malphus, Cecily McMillan, Mrs. Jack Rhodes, Joe Shuman, Gerry Spaulding, Grady Strange, John M. Trask Jr., Ernie P. Wiggers Jr., and the staff of the James W. Webb Wildlife Center.

Of special value has been the chance to hear the memories of Chlotilde R. Martin's daughter, Chloe Martin Pinckney, and grandson, Roger Pinckney, himself a prolific author. We never met Mrs. Martin, and they knew her well. The task of comparing the woman we were discovering to the one they had known and loved was intriguing. Sometimes we were talking about the same woman, sometimes not, but the conversations helped us learn who she was.

Finally, we must thank Susan Dick Hoffius, who has generously shared lunch with us every week for all the years we have been working on this project, and longer. In that time she has rarely complained when we jabbered on about properties on which we had recently trespassed or arcana we had uncovered in a visit to a library or government office. Instead she twirled her spoon in her coffee cup and wondered when we would ever tire of searching out plantation lore. She is twirling still.

# INTRODUCTION

IN 1932 A GROUP of almost fifty sportsmen and their companions gathered at the Hamilton Ridge Club in Hampton County, South Carolina. They flushed many quail, but they never fired a shot because they were interested in their dogs, not the birds. According to a newspaper article about the event, almost all of them had double addresses, one in the North and the other in South Carolina, such as "George D. Widener, of New York and Mackey's Point."[1] The winning dog was Gravel Hill Bob, owned by "Robert Huntington, of Garnet [*sic*] and New York." The dog took its name from the plantation owned by Huntington, a compound of shingle-sided buildings that would have looked more appropriate in the Adirondack Mountains than in a lowcountry pine forest. Huntington, whose firm designed some of the most prestigious office buildings in New York City, drew up the plans for the Gravel Hill structures, as he did for the clubhouse of the hunt club to which he belonged, the Palachucola Club. (Another lowcountry clubhouse was designed by Stanford White, better known for Fifth Avenue mansions than hunt clubs.) Huntington's fellow club members included some of the most important businessmen from New York and Boston. Back home he lived at Hopeland House in Staatsburg, New York, a residence so grand that it suggested royalty. His neighbors were Astors; his daughter married one.

Almost everyone at the field trials moved in the highest social circles of New York, but in the winter months they lived a very different life in South Carolina. For many the schedule was to rise early in the morning for a hunt (after black servants had crept into their bedrooms before dawn to light the fireplaces that were the only sources of heat), eat breakfast on the run, move to another field in the afternoon to hunt a different prey, bathe (often with water transported by servants since some of the places had no plumbing), dine in tuxedo jackets (though perhaps with boots and rough pants under the table), and end the day with cigars and after-dinner drinks. This was South Carolina plantation life of the 1930s, and it bore few similarities to the activities on these same plantations a century before. A working plantation in the 1830s demanded a large crew of enslaved workers, most of whom tilled fields of rice; a century later a fraction of that number of workers was needed to wait on the northern owners during their four or five months of residence.

Chlotilde R. Martin, circa
World War II. *Photograph
courtesy of Chloe M. Pinckney*

The 1932 article about the field trials was a rare glimpse of northerners' South Carolina lives. "The guests assembled at the club house, transferred from automobiles to horses—and some to mules—and the trials were on." During the rest of the year the plantation owners were written up frequently in the society pages of newspapers in New York, Philadelphia, and Boston. In South Carolina they were largely anonymous. Nonetheless they were transforming South Carolina, and local people noticed.

In October 1930 William Watts Ball, editor of the *Charleston News and Courier*, wrote to the journalist Chlotilde Martin in Allendale, South Carolina, asking if she would be interested in "temporary work provided you have an automobile and can take pictures."[2] When she responded positively, he spelled out his proposal: "a series of illustrated stories about the estates in coastal South Carolina purchased and improved by wealthy men, from the Savannah river to Georgetown." In addition, he wanted her to write other stories, essentially offering full-time temporary employment for sixty dollars a week, no benefits or expenses except film developing. It was the Depression; she accepted at once. About the same time Ball gave a similar assignment to the reporter Chalmers Murray, asking him to write a series of articles on plantations owned by northerners in the Georgetown area and, eventually, on Edisto Island.[3] Other reporters tackled other plantations.

For the previous three years Mrs. Martin had been working for a group of weekly newspapers in the southern part of South Carolina. Before that, however, she had been employed by the *State* newspaper in Columbia, where Ball had been her editor, and she had established a strong reputation for her work. She may have been the first female full-time news reporter in South Carolina. Ball must have considered publishing such a series for several years, and he seems always to have had her in mind. In 1928, after he moved to the *Charleston News and Courier*, he hired Mrs. Martin to write a freelance article about White Hall plantation in Beaufort County (Jasper County after border changes) in the exact style she would use later for her series.

Ball never used the word "Yankee" when he wrote to her, and he went out of his way to describe the "newcomers" in positive terms.[4] He wrote her a letter of introduction that explained: "The News and Courier is convinced that these purchases are fortunate for South Carolina and its wish is to fortify this impression among South Carolinians. The further aim is to promote the development of the coastal region, which The News and Courier believes must follow eventually as a by-product of the coming of men of means." Even in a personal letter to her he was no less boosterish, suggesting that she work with a Beaufort realtor who was developing a lucrative business selling plantation properties to northern sportsmen: "I think if you will see Niels Christensen, taking this letter, explaining to him that at the core of these articles is the aim to advertise the coastal region, to promote its further development, to attract population, he will not only extend you every courtesy but give you much intelligent help."

Mrs. Martin wrote that she could start on November 10; on November 16 she explained to Ball that she had already visited twenty of the thirty northern-owned estates that she had targeted in Beaufort County: "I traveled about the county the whole of every day and spent each evening reading books or parts of books and articles which I thought would help me. In addition, I visited many people in an effort to obtain as much information as possible. I took pictures of nearly every place I visited. However, it rained every day and some of them, I fear, will not be good. However, I was able to borrow a number of pictures with the promise that they would be returned." A week later, on November 23, the first of her plantation articles, on Tomotley in Beaufort County, appeared. (On November 27 Ball ran an article by Mrs. Martin entitled "Baronial Homes Returning to Coastal South Carolina," which introduced the theme of the series.) She attacked her assignment with great energy: sixteen different articles were published before the end of the year, one almost every other day. For the following six months she published slightly fewer than one a week.

Many people wanted more of the articles. The *Beaufort Gazette* reprinted some of them, and Mrs. Martin was asked almost from the beginning to gather them into book form. Until now that has never happened, and outside of Beaufort, Chlotilde Martin is largely unknown.

The subject of Mrs. Martin's assignment—northerners buying South Carolina coastal plantations—was a phenomenon of which many people in South Carolina were aware. It had been going on for decades. Of the almost eighty estates that she described in more than fifty articles, seven properties had been bought before 1900, and they were almost all extensive. William Bradley of Massachusetts came to the state within five years of the end of the Civil War, purchased land, and invested in phosphates; his son eventually would own sixteen thousand acres in Colleton County. Before the end of the century tens of thousands of acres were gathered up for clubs to serve northern hunters. Mrs. Martin claimed that the first of them, the Pineland Club in Jasper County, was started about 1877, though no deeds have been found to document that. (In another article she suggested that the Pineland began in 1887.)

Whatever the year, six club members living in Philadelphia, New York, Boston, and Baltimore bought more than thirteen thousand acres of land that previously had been part of Cotton Hill plantation. Other investors and other hunt clubs were soon to follow. J. P. Clyde of the Clyde Line shipping fleet bought up most of Hilton Head Island in 1889. Two years later U.S. senator J. Donald Cameron from Pennsylvania purchased Coffin Point on St. Helena, and New York banker Harry B. Hollins Sr. acquired Good Hope in Jasper County, including White Hall, the former home of Thomas Heyward Jr., signer of the Declaration of Independence. In 1893 a group of sportsmen from New York, New Jersey, and Pittsburgh completed a deal for thirty-five thousand acres of Jasper County land that would become the Okeetee Club.

Each purchase seemed to encourage others, and the speed of these land transactions must have seemed bewildering to the locals. By the time Ball gave his assignment to Mrs. Martin, several purchases were taking place every year. Indeed she could have continued her column for years to come, though only a few such articles appeared in print after 1931. Mrs. Martin's articles do not exhaust the subject by any means—she covered only a few estates near Charleston and none north of that city—but they begin to address the wide range of questions that such purchases raise: Who were these purchasers? Why did they buy South Carolina land? What impact did they have on local development?[5]

As her articles make clear, the northerners came from many different communities—Philadelphia, Boston, Cleveland, Cincinnati—but primarily from the New York area. They were among the most successful businessmen of their day. The only business-woman among them was the remarkable Kate Gleason, who became one of the largest property owners in Beaufort County. A number of them had ties to Standard Oil or DuPont. Many of their names are familiar to us still—Doubleday, DuPont, Hutton, Kress, Vanderbilt—though most are not. However, the vast majority were familiar to those who read the financial or social pages of 1930s newspapers.

Almost all of them said that they were coming for sport, especially hunting (usually birds, not deer), though no doubt the cheap land prices were also attractive. They were responding to a major campaign initiated by Charleston business and cultural leaders to market the area for its history. A 1932 article in *Country Life* entitled "The Renaissance of the Plantation" described the properties in terms almost guaranteed to appeal to the "Wall Street planters," as the architect Albert Simons referred to them: "There is no part of America more remote from the pressure salesmanship and its philosophy of hurry and shove; there is no place where the sound of a stock ticker would seem so ill-suited to the surroundings."[6] The relative privacy must have been especially appealing. Some of Mrs. Martin's accounts allude to wild parties, with crowds of young women who were often called Broadway or New York "showgirls." Harry Cram's affairs at Foot Point are now familiar lowcountry legends, and many people still remember tales of Arthur Barnwell of Cuthbert Point (which he renamed Pleasant Point). However, the activities of Paul and Roy Rainey of Hilton Head and Don Cameron of Coffin Point are mostly forgotten. There were no paparazzi hanging out in 1930s Bluffton or Ridgeland, and Mrs. Martin was about the only journalist who disturbed the vacations. For the most part, what happened in Yemassee stayed in Yemassee.

However, many of the sportsmen also decided to try to make some income from their land. They sold off timber, raised cattle, or planted "truck crops" (fruits and vegetables that could be trucked to northern markets). Claude W. Kress at Buckfield raised paperwhite narcissus bulbs, which he sold through his family's nationwide chain of stores. Kate Gleason of Dataw was planning residential developments not significantly different from those that now cover many of the Sea Islands. Most of those business enterprises failed.

Few of the new owners stuck around. They were not coming to set down roots. Those who did—Cram, Mr. and Mrs. William Copp (Spring Island), Gertrude Legendre (Medway), Benjamin Kittredge (Dean Hall), several members of the Clark (Spring Hill) and Hollins families—were the exceptions. In fact many of the properties changed hands before the Depression ended. Some, such as Hilton Head Island, were sold almost before Mrs. Martin could record the owners. A decade later the scene was different, but the pattern she described stayed true for the time being.

The articles provide good reading. Though Mrs. Martin was churning out journalism quickly, she did so with a flair, capturing scenes, describing the colors of interior decorations or landscaping, retelling stories that were shared with her, and making little jokes. At times her prose became poetic. "Caretakers at White Hall," she wrote, "planted the ground beneath these oaks several weeks ago and just now it is like an emerald carpet for the feet, while far overhead the beautiful old trees form three perfect arches, like softly-stirring green canopies. On sunny days, the blue of the sky slips through, exquisitely patterned, and the sunshine touches the gray moss into shining scarfs, tossed in the wind. When a moon is in the heavens, the green canopies are like great sieves distilling liquid silver over the world."

The assignment by the *News and Courier* was an important one, but it was also fun. It allowed Mrs. Martin to drive around the countryside of South Carolina's southernmost counties, poking into properties, asking questions of caretakers and farmworkers, snooping with a purpose. Some of the people she described clearly fascinated her, especially independent women such as Kate Gleason and Emma Wines (Lady's Island). The first was fabulously wealthy and invested heavily in Beaufort; the second was a recluse who helped build her own home and rowed her boat across the Beaufort River to pick up supplies. Mrs. Martin loved the stories of wealthy young playboys, the first nudist colony in America (though the residents denied their plans to her), and black farmworkers who wanted to travel to New York City to see their bosses' homes, which they had been assured were piled high with gold and silver. She reveled in stories of lowcountry men such as Arthur Barnwell and Legare Sanders (Chisolm Island), who made fortunes in the North but chose to return home to the joys of the southern coast.

She was in hot water about the articles almost from the beginning. One reason for the interest in this topic was that the plantations were rich in history. Many had been occupied for at least two centuries by some of the state's leading political, economic, and social figures, and Mrs. Martin had to share the histories or she would not be true to the sites. On the other hand, the *News and Courier* was not paying her to spend her days poring over tax-office record books. On December 10, 1930, Mr. Ball wrote her, "I have had complaint from a person in Beaufort about the historical data in some of the Beaufort articles. I expected this. I do not think that it would be practicable for a newspaper correspondent to obtain the detailed history of a plantation. Only a lawyer can do that by going deep into the records in the public offices." Historical events could be addressed, he suggested, but "it would be well not to undertake to recite successive ownerships." Mr. Ball was pinpointing a problem that for years would bother Mrs. Martin, as well as other writers to this day. Who owned individual properties? Sure it was Mr. Elliott—or Mr. Heyward or Mr. Cuthbert—but which Mr. Elliott? Her informants made mistakes. Often the spellings in the deed books were inaccurate. Some individuals were identified only by initials. Families handed down the same names for several generations, so which William Elliott was this?

Mrs. Martin sent Mr. Ball a letter of apology and explained that many of the new plantation owners were requesting the inclusion of historical information, but the problem followed her throughout her coverage of the assignment. Often she recorded the information told to her but got the spellings wrong: *Mr. Lawrence* instead of the correct *Mr. Lawrance, Major Scriven* instead of *Major Screven.* (The editors of this volume have silently corrected those errors.) Mr. Ball wrote back almost immediately to say that in that day's article she had misidentified Senator J. Donald Cameron, who owned property on St. Helena Island. She had been told that his name was Senator J. M. Cameron. Senator Cameron had been a major figure before his death in 1918: bank and railroad president, secretary of war under President Ulysses S. Grant, as well as U.S. senator for twenty years. No doubt Mr. Ball, who had served as an editor for decades and was the first dean of journalism at the University of South Carolina, was very familiar with him, while Mrs. Martin yearned for a copy of *Who's Who.* (Senator Cameron's name has also been corrected.)

One of the earliest articles included here, about Retreat plantation, includes the captivating tale of a "French hermit" named "Lagay," who in the eighteenth century was murdered by his enslaved servants. The perpetrators were captured, and at least one was quartered, his head stuck on a post as a warning to others. It was a great story, and no doubt she recorded it as she heard it, but she combined two tales. Retreat was owned by a Frenchman named John DelaGaye, but the murder was of a man of Swiss descent named Charles Purry.

Mr. Ball often tried to put her in touch with local people who were familiar with the plantations, especially in areas distant from Beaufort. He directed her to E. T. H. Shaffer (who in 1939 would write the book *Carolina Gardens*), James E. Padgett, and W. W. Smoak (editor of the *Walterboro Press and Standard*) in Colleton County. The architect Albert Simons of Charleston identified ten northern plantation owners for whom his firm of Simons and Lapham had worked, and she wrote up some of them. However, several were too far away from Beaufort for her to take on. She had two small children and wanted to be home whenever possible.

CHLOTILDE ROWELL was born on July 23, 1895, in Aiken, South Carolina, the daughter of Melvin Leander Rowell and Eva Randall Rowell.[7] She was the oldest of four siblings, who also included Melvin Leander Rowell Jr., a member of the U.S. Merchant Marine; Evelyn Pundita Rowell, who married Archibald Edward O'Neil (a career U.S. Marine who was promoted to general); and Thomas Randall Rowell (another career U.S. Marine). In 1911, when she was a teenager, her family moved to Beaufort, so her father, a member of the "Governor's Constabulary Force," as she described it, could take on the "blind tigers" (illegal bars). The streets then were covered in "dazzling white crushed oyster shells," but "the odor was something awful for a time after the oyster shell treatment," she remembered.[8] In 1917 she graduated from Winthrop College, and two years later she started work as a reporter for William Watts Ball and the *State*.

Mrs. Martin often boasted to family and friends of her journalistic exploits. When she worked at the *State*, she explained, she covered the aviator Eddie Rickenbacker's visit to Columbia and went up for a flight, complete with barrel rolls and loops. None of the other reporters would enter the open cockpit with him. One fellow reporter who paid attention was Thomas Seaborn Martin, a University of South Carolina graduate who was especially noted in the newspaper office for his speedy typing on a double keyboard, although he had lost his right arm in a cotton-gin accident when he was fourteen years old. Martin was the son of Ernest Cliff Martin, an Anderson County farmer. He and Miss Rowell were married in 1923.

They moved to their hometown of Beaufort and the *Beaufort Gazette* later that year, then to Greenwood, South Carolina, and the *Greenwood Index-Journal* (she was society editor, he telegraph editor), and then to Asheville, North Carolina, and the *Asheville Citizen* (she was associate editor, he state news editor). In the North Carolina mountains, Mr. Martin discovered that he had Hodgkin's disease. Though he traveled to the Mayo Clinic in Minnesota, he died on March 15, 1927, leaving his widow with two small children to raise: Chloe, born in 1924, and Thomas Jr., born in 1926. His obituary read, "He had been seriously ill for about one month and in bad health for some time." He was thirty-two years old.

Soon after that, Mrs. Martin and her children moved to Allendale, South Carolina. There she ran three weekly newspapers owned by Eugene B. McSweeney: the *Allendale County Citizen*, the *Hampton County Guardian*, and the *Jasper County Record*. By late 1930 she and her children were back in Beaufort, near her parents, and she was traveling the lowcountry for Ball and the *News and Courier*. It was a short-term assignment, though, so on June 17, 1931, she proposed writing for Ball "a daily column of the doings of lowcountry people with a generous mention of names, etc.," which would pay her a steady (though small) income and possibly generate subscriptions for the paper. Ball agreed to a weekly column, and she began writing "Lowcountry Gossip," which she continued for several decades.

The column included her observations from her travels around the area—flowers then in bloom, fashions in style, funny stories she had just heard, some references to the plantations she had earlier reported on, and the cute things that her children, and eventually her grandchildren, did and said. The children, of course, were mortified. Chloe remembers demanding that her mother stop writing the column so that she could avoid embarrassment; her mother suggested that she stop eating so that they would not need the income. Readers of the paper, however, responded enthusiastically; whenever she asked for information (a recipe, the lyrics of a song, the origins of obscure names), dozens of people responded. Some people in Beaufort still remember when she stopped at "the smallest church I've ever seen" on St. Helena Island and, lacking a ruler, determined that the building measured six umbrellas by twelve umbrellas.[9]

For the rest of her life, Mrs. Martin, who never remarried (in one column she wrote, "The longer I live the more firmly convinced I am that men and women are not constitutionally fitted to live together"[10]), pieced together income as she could. A few years after she finished the plantation series, she was employed as a field representative for the Federal Writers' Project of the Works Progress Administration. She was exactly what FDR was looking for: a low-income, trained writer who was familiar with her local area. She became the main Beaufort County researcher for the volume on South Carolina published by the WPA and provided much information on Jasper County as well.

She turned in manuscripts on Beaufort-area literature, imports and exports, museums, drama, music, manufacturing and industry, and much more. Among her contributions were lively descriptions that were cut by the government editors, including her claim that Beaufort's "residents often know an existence as the rest of the world can only envy." The editors suggested that this was "over the top."[11] In another account she claimed that the area hunt clubs "paved the way for the reception of Yankees (before that time being spelled 'damnyankee') into this section of the country where feeling about them had been very bitter."[12] That parenthetical phrase was also removed. She interviewed a number of people who had lived under slavery; she prepared a guide to Beaufort and the Sea Islands (published in 1938); and she contributed to many other WPA publications. Among the manuscripts she prepared was a 286-page bibliography of newspaper articles about the Beaufort area.[13]

After the end of the New Deal, she interviewed people on outlying islands to determine if they qualified for the welfare department's services, and she worked as clerk and registrar for the Selective Service System. During World War II she and some friends published a mimeographed newsletter, *The Beaufort News*, every month for local men and women serving in the military overseas. For Kate Gleason, who owned Colony Gardens on Lady's Island, Mrs. Martin served as a local rental agent and was given the use of one unit for free in the summer. She retired as a social worker in 1959, soon after her home was battered by Hurricane Gracie, but she continued to write her column.

Throughout her life she wrote about local history. In January 1944 she delivered "An Account of the Towns of Radnor and Edmundsbury" to the Beaufort County Historical Society. (Radnor ceased to exist before the American Revolution, Edmundsbury in 1815.) She wrote a history of St. Helena's Episcopal Church, created a brochure for the four hundredth anniversary of the landing of Jean Ribaut on what is now Parris Island, and prepared the text to accompany Carl Julien's photos of state landmarks in the book *Sea Islands to Sand Hills* (University of South Carolina Press, 1954).

Chlotilde Martin lived the rest of her life in Beaufort, most of it in her pre–Revolutionary War house at 712 New Street, which she bought from the wife of the African American attorney J. I. Washington. Years later Mrs. Martin remembered that the previous owner "had inherited it from her former slave mother, who, in turn, had bought it at one of those United States Tax Commission sales during and after The War Between the States." The previous owners moved out when they "built a much larger and finer house at the opposite end of the block on property that he also owned."[14]

Mrs. Martin was one of the first volunteers who campaigned to save the Lafayette House (now known as the Verdier House), helping to develop Beaufort's preservation ethos and the Historic Beaufort Foundation. She also worked to protect Retreat plantation. For years she served as the secretary and treasurer of the Beaufort Museum. In 1980 she was named Woman of the Year by the Sertoma Club. Four years later Beaufort mayor Henry Chambers presented her with a resolution approved by the city council honoring her for outstanding civic achievement and historic preservation. The Beaufort County Historical Society awarded her a commendation.

In addition to her preservation and history work, in the 1960s she volunteered her time with the right-wing Minute Woman organization and staffed the anticommunist Freedom Library Reading Room in the basement of the Verdier House. Her grandson has explained that she shared many of the beliefs of the John Birch Society, especially around the questions of the power of the U.S. government (though she would be employed much of her life by the federal bureaucracy). According to her daughter, Mrs. Martin considered Martin Luther King Jr. a communist.

Inevitably one must wonder about her views on race. She interviewed "Becky Frazier, ancient black crone" at Clay Hall, who said, "It was jest like slavery time when Mr. [Geraldwyn L.] Redmond was livin'." Mrs. Martin made clear that Ms. Frazier meant that slavery was a good thing: the happy time when white folks took care of blacks, giving them Christmas gifts. Martin told the story of "'Daddy Scipio,' an aged negro" at Laurel Spring, later described as an "old darkey" who could not recall his age but said, "We bin so busy dose days we couldn't keep score of chillun's age, but I bin big niggah den." She described the "wide-eyed piccaninnies" at Cuthbert Point. Few whites in Beaufort at the time—and perhaps not many blacks either—would have considered those descriptions insulting.

Most remarkable is how few African Americans appear in her plantation articles. At one time blacks far outnumbered whites on these plantations; in her 1930s articles they are almost invisible. Some of that, of course, was because of her assignment. She was supposed to write about the owners of the properties, not the full-time residents.

Occasionally Mrs. Martin just could not resist going beyond her assignment. Like many lowcountry whites, she loved Gullah stories, collected them, and shared them. The stories present wisdom as well as humor. After 1971 she prepared a book of her experiences with "the Gullah Negroes" entitled *Winds of Change in Gullah Land*, but she was unable to publish it during her lifetime. It includes a number of descriptions taken from her research for the *News and Courier* and whole chapters that repeat her writings for the WPA. After her death in 1991, her daughter, Chloe Martin Pinckney, prepared and distributed it in her honor.

WILLIAM WATTS BALL and Chlotilde Martin could not have known the results of the new ownership pattern of their day. We are still trying to figure it out today. Often the northern sportsmen bought up multiple plantations to make a single property of five thousand acres or more—sometimes many more. If not for them, no doubt the lands would have been sold off in small plots of perhaps twenty acres. That is what the Reconstruction politician Thomas Miller did, helping Beaufort-area blacks own their first homes. If such a pattern had been widespread, the result might have been a huge increase in road building, tree cutting, further division into even smaller lots, and demands for sewage and electrification. Perhaps all the counties that Mrs. Martin wrote about—Beaufort, Jasper, Hampton, Colleton, and Berkeley—would now be covered with endless tract housing. On the other hand, maybe, as has been the case with St. Helena Island, the land would have been divided into so many small plots, with complicated ownership patterns, that developers would not have bothered to try to build suburban subdivisions or resorts. Easier to buy 5,000 acres from one owner than twenty acres each from hundreds of feuding families. And maybe with the land ownership, low-income South Carolinians might have gained pride, self-confidence, and independence and been incorporated into county leadership much more than they were.

The northern ownership stopped or delayed the denuding of South Carolina fields and woods, but it also hindered local governments. In all her plantation articles, Mrs. Martin described well over 300,000 acres of unimproved lowcountry land. Some of the plantations were vast. Mrs. Martin described nine individuals or clubs who controlled more than 10,000 acres apiece, for a total of more than 160,000 acres. The author James Kilgo has written that in Hampton County the average antebellum plantation contained about 2,000 to 3,000 acres. According to Mrs. Martin, the Okeetee Club alone controlled 42,000 acres, and it grew by more than 20,000 beyond that. Such lands were barely taxed. How could the county provide services with such a shrunken tax base?

Niels Christensen of Beaufort, the realtor to whom Mr. Ball directed Mrs. Martin, came up with one solution in 1917 when he served in the state senate. He introduced a bill that would have raised taxes specifically on these vast expanses—kind of a tax on Yankees. The proposal was first developed by "economic boosters and political leaders from Beaufort, Jasper, Hampton and Colleton counties," who joined together to form the Southern Carolina Association. They wanted to levy taxes of two cents per acre for estates of more than five thousand acres, four cents per acre over thirty thousand acres, and five cents per acre for property above fifty thousand acres. The bill was never passed.[15]

However, if the northern ownership hurt social services, it was a godsend for land preservation. The new owners wanted most of their land left exactly as they found it: open woods, fields protected for the birds, waters undammed and unpolluted. They were true conservationists, if not environmentalists.

Mrs. Martin was writing at a time of great change. Her friend Kate Gleason, of Rochester, New York, and Dataw Island, was showing the way, for better or worse. After buying Dataw, Gleason began to prepare it for residential development, constructing causeways across two islands to get there and seawalls on the island. On Lady's Island her Colony Gardens project included a number of residences built around a swimming pool and golf course, the first such development in the area.

Most of the properties that Mrs. Martin visited near Hilton Head and Beaufort have been converted to residential neighborhoods and golf courses since Hilton Head's transformation in the late 1950s and 1960s. Some of the peaceful islands of the 1930s are entirely suburban today. When Mrs. Martin wrote about Hilton Head, she estimated that there were only about fifty white residents on the island and nearby Jenkins Island. She described beaches so wide and empty that people landed private planes between the waves and the dunes. The northerners saved the land, but only for thirty to fifty years. When the acres of pineland were converted to paved streets and private homes, southerners such as Hilton Head's Charles Fraser were responsible, along with northern investors. The story of South Carolina coastal development is not just what Yankees did to southerners; it was all business, and South Carolinians profited too.

Today developers have been forced to find open lands further and further from the centers of Beaufort or Hilton Head (or Charleston or Georgetown). They have been remarkably successful. A drive through the countryside reveals new subdivisions and shopping strips on lands where forests spread not long ago. Ridgeland and Hardeeville are now bracing for massive development.

Few of the properties described by Mrs. Martin have ended up in public hands: the lands of the Palachucola Club (Jasper County) are part of a wildlife management area; Fort Fremont (Beaufort County) is being developed as a park; and Cypress Gardens (Berkeley County) has long been a popular attraction, with wooden boats rented for tours of the cypress swamps. Considering the number of properties involved, that is not many. The alternatives for those properties not yet built on can probably be seen in two examples, Bindon in Beaufort County and Hope in Colleton County.

Bindon plantation in 2005 contained about the same acreage as it did in 1931. Developers must have looked at the unspoiled land covetously. The twenty-five miles that separate it from Beaufort once seemed like a considerable distance; now it lies within commuting range. Beaufort County had zoned it as a rural area—it has no sewage system—appropriate for one unit every three acres, fewer than four hundred in all. Unsatisfied, developers appealed to the town of Yemassee, whose town council agreed to annex the rural area, allowing thirteen hundred residential units and 450,000 square feet of commercial property. Since Bindon and Yemassee are not contiguous, a requirement for annexation, the town annexed a twenty-foot-wide strip of land two miles long down Highway 17 and through marshland. Suddenly Bindon was contiguous and about to become a major community requiring massive new infrastructure: highways, schools, police and fire departments, water and sewage. In this instance the annexations are being challenged. However, even if Yemassee's plans are denied, almost four hundred new homes will be built on land nearly as protected today as when Mrs. Martin described the approach this way: "one comes upon the gates that lead through a grassy meadow, then through a forest of oaks, pines, and holly trees."

Another possible model of rural development may be seen at Hope plantation, now owned by Ted Turner and his family, modern equivalents of the moguls who bought so much of the land in the 1930s. The Turners have placed conservation easements on their acreage, limiting the number of buildings that can ever be constructed. Many other land owners, especially in the ACE Basin, have done the same. The land here was originally put together by northern men whose fortunes were made from fine stationery, back in the days of letter writing. The land will now be protected permanently thanks to the farsightedness of the southerner who dreamed up CNN. However, the land will remain inaccessible to the public, and while it is taxed at a rate far higher than Niels Christensen could have imagined when he yearned to hammer the Yankees at two cents an acre, it is hardly a major profit center for Colleton County.

Land development is always about trade-offs: taxes versus open space, industry versus recreation, homes versus highways. Decisions made in the 1930s affect us still, and they help us choose how we would like our counties to look in the future. Chlotilde Martin chronicled one transformation almost eighty years ago. In 1932 she interviewed Henry W. Corning of Cleveland at his Clarendon plantation. He talked of the important political and economic issues of the day—the Depression, unemployment, Prohibition—but she could not pay attention. "Somehow," she wrote, "under the spell of January sunshine slanting through brown woods, these things did not seem to matter particularly. They were not real. They were like the fire breathing dragons of fairy tales kept away from the enchanted forest by a kind godmother with a magic wand." Ultimately that was how Chlotilde Martin seems to have considered her assignment from William Watts Ball: she was to describe the enchanted forest of the southern South Carolina coast in which she lived. It was a subject of which she never tired.

Stephen G. Hoffius

## Notes

1. *Charleston News and Courier*, February 25, 1932.

2. Correspondence between Ball and Mrs. Martin can be found in the News and Courier collection (23-377, folders 9–11), South Carolina Historical Society, Charleston.

3. See, for instance, his articles on Hasty Point and other properties owned by Jesse Metcalf, March 22, 1931; Ponemah, owned by Willis E. Fertig, April 26, 1931; Dirleton, owned by three Upton brothers of Virginia, May 3, 1931; Hobcaw Barony, owned by Bernard Baruch, originally from South Carolina, May 17, 1931; an unnamed, one-hundred-year-old house moved from Newberry to Belle Isle gardens, owned by Henry M. Sage, May 24, 1931; Annandale, owned by Mrs. Susan B. Reeves, May 31, 1931; Atalaya (then unnamed, now at Huntington Beach State Park), owned by Archer M. Huntington, June 7, 1931; Rice Hope, owned by Joseph S. Frelinghuysen, June 14, 1931 (and another article, South Carolina Historical Society copy undated); Arcadia, owned by Isaac E. Emerson, June 21, 1931; Kinloch, owned by members of the DuPont family, John Philip Sousa, and R. R. M. Carpenter, July 10, 1931; Waverly Mills, owned by the Reverend Dr. J. D. Paxton of Virginia, July 26, 1931; Spring-

field, owned by Dudley L. Pickman, July 27, 1931; Friendfield, owned by Radcliffe Cheston, August 2, 1931; Chicora Wood, owned by D. C. Waddell Jr. of Asheville, N.C., August 9, 1931; Willbrook, owned by William S. Ellis, August 16, 1931; Leitchfield, owned by Dr. Henry Norris, August 16, 1931; Nightingale Hall, owned by J. S. Holliday, August 30, 1931; Springwood, owned by C. W. Coker of Hartsville, S.C., September 11, 1931; Harrietta, owned by H. S. Shonnard, September 13, 1931; the Wedge, owned by E. G. Chadwick, September 20, 1931; Wedgefield, leased by W. Winchester Keith, September 27, 1931; and Wee-Nee Lodge, owned by Charles L. Amos and H. B. Mebane, October 4, 1931. Another article about Frelinghuysen's holdings in the Georgetown area appeared on August 9, 1931. On Edisto properties, see, for instance, articles on Cow-Pen's Point, owned by Mr. and Mrs. James Hathaway Kidder, July 5, 1931; and the Lafayette House (the old William Seabrook plantation), then owned by Donald Dodge, July 19, 1931.

4. He had written earlier to a friend that "the odor of genteel Yankee wealth, while not suffocating, is pervading Charleston" (quoted in Stephanie E. Yuhl, *A Golden Haze of Memory: The Making of Historic Charleston* [Chapel Hill: University of North Carolina Press, 2005], 177).

5. For some reason (other reporters took the assignments or she had a full schedule?), Mrs. Martin did not write about several prominent plantations owned by northerners in the counties she covered, including Airy Hall, Belmont, Cherokee, Hamilton Ridge, Poco Sabo, and Turkey Hill.

6. Simons quoted in Yuhl, *Golden Haze of Memory*, 177; *Country Life* quoted in ibid., 178.

7. For biographical information on Mrs. Martin, see William H. Whitten, "Chlotilde Martin, 1895–1991, Was Beaufort's Long-time Columnist," *Lowcountry Ledger*, November 24, 1991; and the biographical introduction to Chlotilde Rowell Martin, *Winds of Change in Gullah Land* (Beaufort, S.C.: Chloe M. Pinckney, 2003). The editors are grateful for the opportunity to interview Mrs. Martin's daughter, Mrs. Chloe M. Pinckney, in Beaufort, S.C., and Mrs. Martin's grandson, Roger Pinckney, on Daufuskie Island, S.C.

8. Martin, *Winds of Change*, 36.

9. Chlotilde Martin, "Lowcountry Gossip," *Charleston News and Courier*, March 1, 1959.

10. Ibid., October 26, 1958.

11. Mrs. Martin's contributions may be found in the Works Progress Administration papers at the South Caroliniana Library, University of South Carolina, Columbia. This draft is in cabinet C, drawer 2, folder 3.

12. Ibid., cabinet C, drawer 3, folder T1-b.

13. Ibid., cabinet D, drawer 4, folder 60.

14. Martin, *Winds of Change*, unnumbered p. 5 of the foreword. The historian Lawrence Rowland identifies the attorney as J. I. Washington.

15. For more on this proposal, see the forthcoming *History of Beaufort County, South Carolina*, vol. 2, by Lawrence S. Rowland. The editors of this volume thank Dr. Rowland and the editors at the University of South Carolina Press for sharing this manuscript before its publication.

*Northern Money, Southern Land*

# *Prologue*

By the fall of 1932 Chlotilde Martin had published almost all of the articles in her series. She wrote the following for the *News and Courier* to mark the beginning of the season when the northern sportsmen came south, and she summarized information about many of the plantations she had already documented. In addition she mentioned other northern-owned properties elsewhere on the coast, suggesting just how extensive this movement was.

Yankees in the "nawth," worn out with their battle against depression and constant watching of the stock market, are beginning to feel the tug of coastal South Carolina once again. The sharp chill of northern mornings conjure up before their mind's eye the blue and gold of October days down on the plantation, the glint of sunshine upon the little winding coastal rivers, the pungent odor of dead leaves burning, the deep baying of favorite hounds.

The uncertainty of the financial world and the approaching election will keep a large number of them reluctantly at their listening posts up there "where things go 'round" for a little while longer, but the annual hunger for the lowlands of South Carolina is getting in its work.

The yankees will be coming south before long now.

Already, the plantations, where weeds and underbrush have been having a riotous time all summer and where houses have been barred and shuttered and silence has reigned for many months, are beginning to snap out of their lassitude.

### Things "Redded Up"

Wide, rolling lawns are being clipped and spruced up, repairs and renovations are being made to homes and outhouses. Things are being "redded up" in anticipation of the return of the owners for the hunting season.

Original title: "Low-Country Plantations Stir as Air Presages Coming of New Season. Caretakers Spruce Up Big Houses for Northern Guests. Some Come to Hunt, Others to Rest and Sun on Their Large Coastal Estates. Election Will Delay Arrivals. Baronial Homes of Northern Winter Colonists along South Carolina Coast." Publication date: October 16, 1932.

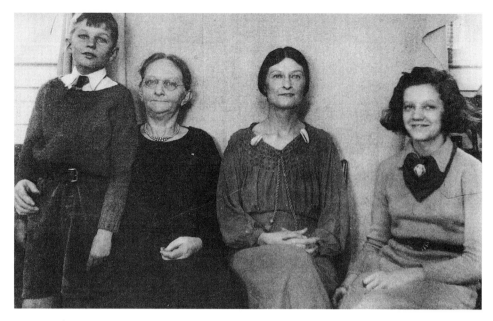

Chlotilde R. Martin (second from right), circa late 1930s, with her son, Thomas Martin Jr., her mother, Eva Randall Rowell, and her daughter, Chloe Martin. *Courtesy of Chloe M. Pinckney*

Even the dogs have caught the spirit. They perk up their long ears and sniff the new tang in the air. They know it won't be long now and they frisk and frolic in their kennels, eager to be at the good times they know are in store for them.

And not the least of those anticipating the arrival of the yankees are the negroes who live in the little cabins scattered here and there about the lands.

The word "yankee" in lower South Carolina used to be synonymous with a monstrous creature with horns and a pitchfork. The word had a colorful prefix—"damn"—and the older generation had a habit of running the two together with such a nicety of pronunciation that its children grew up thinking it was all one word.

Even many of the negroes, whose condition was the bone of contention, called them "damnyankees."

But the descendants of these slaves—and a scattering of the ex-slaves themselves—feel differently towards these Yankees who have bought up the old coastal plantations and re-built the "big houses" of that romantic "befo' de war" time.

**Create Big Preserves**

These may be children of the yankees who laid the south in ashes, reason these darkies, but they themselves have brought back the old days with their benevolent and paternal attitude to those negroes they found living upon the lands which they purchased for hunting preserves.

Plantation life is enjoyed to the fullest by the new owners of the various tracts of land, which range in extent from forty thousand acres down to just a few hundred. It means different pleasures to the different owners.

Some of them, like the W. R. Coes at Cherokee, overlooking Combahee, the R. G. Elberts' Airy Hall on the Ashepoo river in Colleton, the Bayard Dominicks on the Tullifinny, the George D. Wideners on the Pocotaligo at Mackay Point, Joseph S. Frelinghuysen at Rice Hope on the Cooper river, G. D. B. Bonbright at Pimlico in Berkeley county, Percy K. Hudson on the Combahee, the Harry Payne Binghams at Cotton Hall in Beaufort county, the H. K. Hudsons, of New York, at The Delta on the Savannah, Arthur Corlies of New York near Bluffton, Charles L. Lawrance of Long Island, designer of the motor of the Lindbergh ship, The Spirit of St. Louis, at White Hall in Colleton, Edward F. Hutton of New York at Laurel Spring, A. H. Caspary's Bonnie Doone in Colleton and others, have preferred to build homes of varying degrees of ornateness and grandeur, equipped with every modern comfort and convenience upon their recently acquired plantations. Some of these homes are fashioned after the old coastal colonial style, others after the New England type of architecture and still others are palatial affairs of brick and stone, carrying out their respective owners' tastes.

To these the owners come at intervals during the winter seasons, bringing groups of friends for house parties, hunting, resting or riding through the woods which are ever green and pleasant with the mellow winter sunshine.

Other northern property owners in this section prefer to erect hunting clubs or lodges or merely plain frame buildings to house them from the elements. Some of the quaintest of the lodges are those of R. P. Huntington at Gravel Hill, near Garnett; Dr. A. W. Elting of Albany, at Pine island; Paul and Dalton on the Combahee, remodeled from an old house by Charles L. Lawrance and Jack Hollins, of Long Island; the lodges owned by Landon K. Thorne and Alfred L. Loomis, of New York, at Hilton Head; Strawberry Hill in Jasper, where John F. Harris of Chicago comes to hunt; the colony of log cabins at Good Hope camp in Jasper owned by Herbert L. Pratt; and Bindon, near Yemassee, owned by E. E. Lorillard of tobacco fame.

Henry W. Corning, of Cleveland, has a simple white cottage on the Broad river in Beaufort county. The Frederic Pratts, of Long Island, have two small white houses at Chee-ha-Combahee plantation at Wiggins.

There are the sportsmen pure and simple. They prefer to "rough it" when they come south, spending their entire days in the woods or streams and having very little need for the niceties of living at their sleeping or eating quarters.

## Large Hunting Clubs

In addition to the private hunting lodges there are several big hunting clubs with large memberships where sportsmen may come and be cared for while enjoying the hunting season. One of these is the Chelsea club in Jasper county, which escaped Sherman's flames. This has been renovated and is used by the club members on their hunting trips over the twenty thousand-acre game preserve.

Okeetee club with a forty-two thousand acre game preserve was one of the first hunting clubs formed in this section. It has a fifty-room clubhouse and employs between thirty and forty people.

Pineland club, the oldest of them all, was formed in 1877 with the purchase of nearly fourteen thousand acres of land. The membership in this club was fifteen at the beginning but when a member dies, the others buy his share so that the 1931 membership list included only: J. S. Clark, Philadelphia attorney; Walter E. Clark, Philadelphia banker; E. J. Baetjer, Baltimore attorney; Dr. L. R. Morris, retired, of New York; Arthur Lyman, lawyer and real estate man of Boston; and Mr. Getties, of New York.

Rice Hope hunting plantation in Georgetown is another club, housed in the old Lucas home and the members listed this year were William N. Beach, George C. Meyer, William J. Knapp and Clarkson Cowl, all of New York.

Another hunting club is Palachucola at Garnett, of which R. P. Huntington is president.

**Houses Renovated**

There is still another group of northerners who have renovated the old plantation houses which they found upon their properties, furnished them fittingly and make their homes there while here, thus carrying out the spirit of the old south.

Among these are the J. Fritz Franks, of the Bluff plantation, overlooking the Cooper river in Berkeley; Henry Laurens' home, Mepkin, on the Cooper, now the property of the J. W. Johnson family of New York, manufacturers of the surgical supplies; Z. Marshall Crane, of the Crane Paper company, at Hope plantation in Colleton; Wappaoolah on the Cooper, owned by W. H. Barnum and Owen Winston, of New York; the famous and handsome Oaks in Berkeley county, property of Mr. and Mrs. Charles H. Sabin, once the home of Arthur Middleton, signer of the Declaration of Independence; the Cameron estate on St. Helena island, one of the first of the game preserves; the LaFayette house on the Edisto, property of Donald Dodge of Maine; Dean Hall and the beautiful Cypress Gardens in Berkeley, property of Mr. and Mrs. Benjamin R. Kittredge of New York and South Carolina; Mansfield in Georgetown, property of Robert M. Montgomery, Philadelphia banker; Mulberry Castle, in Berkeley, rich in romance and history, owned by the C. E. Chapmans; Medway, historic home of Landgrave Smith, now the home of Mr. and Mrs. Sidney J. Legendre of New York; and the home of A. Felix du Pont on the Combahee. On this plantation is a landing field used by air-minded Du Pont guests.

The William Copps occupy their Spring island home the year around, farming and raising cattle. Belfair, near Bluffton, built of tabby by its artist-owner, W. Moseley Swain, is also occupied by the Swain family the entire year. Spring Hill plantation in Jasper county, owned by Mr. and Mrs. J. B. Clark of New England, is actually the Clark home, Mr. Clark making his more than 3,000 acres of land a self-supporting venture. Harry Cram, young scion of a wealthy Tammany hall leader, and his young wife live all year in their little white frame cottage at Foot Point, below Bluffton. James H. Kidder lives at Green Point, Beaufort county, all the year.

Buckfield plantation, better known as the Kress Narcissus farm, near Yemassee, property of C. W. Kress, is the winter home of the Kress family as well as a money-making venture in the raising of bulbs for the Kress stores.

Gippy in Berkeley county, winter home of Nicholas G. Roosevelt, of New York and Philadelphia, is a self-supporting dairy project.

Harold Ashton Richardson, Canadian inventor, lives simply in a small frame cottage at Long Brow plantation in Colleton county, during his visits here.

Archer M. Huntington and his sculptor wife occupy a fortress-like house on Magnolia beach in Georgetown county, where they are developing gardens to preserve the native wild flowers of this state.

Among the other interesting and beautiful plantation estates of the northern property owners are Bernard M. Baruch's (native South Carolinian) Hobcaw Barony near Georgetown; Tomotley, owned by Edward Thorne, Sr., of New York; the Dewees island estate of C. B. D. Huyler; Harrietta, near McClellanville, owned by Horatio S. Shonnard; Arcadia, near Georgetown, owned by George Vanderbilt; Fenwick Hall, on John's Island, estate of Victor Morawetz; Willbrook, near Summerville, property of William S. Ellis; Pierate House, across the Cooper from Charleston, owned by Dana Osgood, of Hopedale, Mass.; Bonny Hall, near Yemassee, owned by Arthur Lyman; Arthur Barnwell's magnificent swimming pool at Cuthbert Point; Dawn plantation, in Colleton, owned by G. V. Hollins; Myrtle Grove, in Colleton, owned by J. W. Stevens; Twickenham, near Yemassee, owned by R. J. Turnbull; Castle Hill, Beaufort county, property of John S. Williams; Brewton Hall, nearby, owned by John R. Todd, of New York; Peter B. Bradley's vast acreage, which includes several old plantations down in Colleton and Charleston counties. Solomon Guggenheim owns a hunting preserve on Lady's island. And there are others.

These large preserves are well stocked with wild game, including deer, turkey, quail, duck, marsh hen, and fox. The salt water rivers or "cricks," as the Gullah negroes term these little back water streams, are teeming with fish to tempt the sportsmen.

Since the duck season does not open this year until November 16, some of the Yankees will doubtless postpone their coming until around that time. The quail addicts will be down in good time for the opening of the season on Thanksgiving day.

Many extensive duck ponds have been built on these coastal plantations in recent years, so great has the interest been in duck shooting. And these new plantation owners have bred quail by the thousands in pens and turned them loose on their preserves so that the stock of wild game will not be depleted.

Another experiment in preservation being conducted by several of these wealthy landowners is that of reforestation and the lessening of the danger of forest fires in the coastal section.

The organization of the Carolina plantation society last season, following the first plantation field trials, is expected to aid in cultivating a more neighborly friendliness among plantation owners. ✄

Chlotilde Martin wrote a similar article, also naming dozens of northern property owners, which appeared in the *Charleston News and Courier* on June 28, 1936. Near the beginning of this article, Mrs. Martin alludes to subjects that she rarely mentions in the bulk of her articles: the political and economic situation of the day, which of course at the time was grave. Approaching was the first presidential election since the 1929 stock market crash, when Franklin D. Roosevelt challenged the incumbent president Herbert Hoover. As the editors' comments following each of the plantation articles in this book make clear, a remarkable number of northern plantation owners held on to their properties through the Depression. The plantation society that she mentions at the end of the article still survives and still provides the "neighborly friendliness" that was intended, though now the bulk of the members live in South Carolina and Georgia.

# *Beaufort County* PROPERTIES

Belfair

Bray's Island (also the Old Means' Farm,
Cunningham's Bluff, Hall's Island,
Grays Hill, Laurel Bay)

Callawassie Island

Cat Island

Chisolm Island

Clarendon

Clay Hall, Nieuport (also Green Point)

Coffin Point

Cotton Hall

Cuthbert Point (Pleasant Point)

Dataw Island

Foot Point

Fort Fremont

Hilton Head Island (Part 1)

Hilton Head Island (Part 2)

Lady's Island

Orange Grove (also Fripp [Seaside])

Palmetto Bluff

Pine Island

Polawana Island

Retreat

Rose Hill

Spring Island

Tomotley, Brewton, Bindon, and Castle Hill

Twickenham, Bonny Hall, and Hobonny

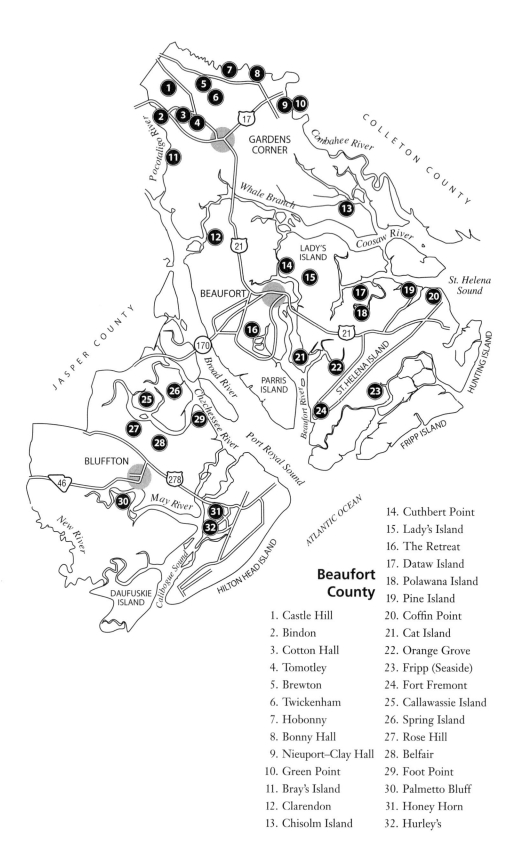

**Beaufort County**

1. Castle Hill
2. Bindon
3. Cotton Hall
4. Tomotley
5. Brewton
6. Twickenham
7. Hobonny
8. Bonny Hall
9. Nieuport–Clay Hall
10. Green Point
11. Bray's Island
12. Clarendon
13. Chisolm Island
14. Cuthbert Point
15. Lady's Island
16. The Retreat
17. Dataw Island
18. Polawana Island
19. Pine Island
20. Coffin Point
21. Cat Island
22. Orange Grove
23. Fripp (Seaside)
24. Fort Fremont
25. Callawassie Island
26. Spring Island
27. Rose Hill
28. Belfair
29. Foot Point
30. Palmetto Bluff
31. Honey Horn
32. Hurley's

# *Belfair*

W. Moseley Swain, artist, has perhaps more truly recaptured the spirit of the old homes of Coastal South Carolina than any of the other northerners who have bought lands and built large estates in this section.

Perhaps it is because he is an artist and, therefore, capable of a keener sense of the fitness of things than the average person. However that may be, Mr. Swain has achieved the atmosphere of the old south in his magnificent tabby home, which is situated on a bluff overlooking the Colleton river about four miles from Bluffton, in Beaufort county.

Mr. Swain's plantation is called Belfair, the original name of the old plantation being retained in practically every instance where these old low-country estates have come into the hands of wealthy men from the north.

Belfair is entered through high white wooden gates just off a country road between Hardeeville and Bluffton. At the left of the entrance is the small white cottage of the superintendent of the estate and at the end of a long white shell road is Belfair.

## Four Stories High

This beautiful home is four stories high and is fashioned of a combination of three-fourths oyster shell and one-fourth cement. The old tabby was made of oyster shell and lime.

The material for the home was made up at the site, the oyster shell being obtained from a nearby oyster factory. The house was designed by Mr. Swain himself.

The approach is made to the rear of the building, although, in this case, the rear is so lovely that one can scarcely believe the front is more so.

The walk that leads to the wide high stairs, which mount to the great porch, is bordered with Satsuma oranges. The low bushes in December were heavy with fruit, glowing golden through the green foliage. These bushes have been growing only a year and a half.

Original title: "Belfair—Designed by Artist Owner. W. Moseley Swain, 'A Citizen of South Carolina,' He Says, Builds Magnificent Tabby Home Overlooking Colleton River in Beaufort County." Publication date: January 18, 1931.

Belfair. *Courtesy of the Bluffton Historical Preservation Society*

In fact, the home was built only two years ago, but so perfectly did Mr. Swain carry out his ideas that the building seems aged already.

The house fronts the river with its wide concrete porch, great white columns and curving railed stairs which lead down over a flagged walk to the water's edge.

### Four Windows to River

The immense reception hall has a double stair, which leads to the sleeping apartments above. On one side of the hall is a large, bright living room and on the other the dining room. These rooms have three exposures each, with four windows which overlook the river.

Upon the walls hang interesting family portraits, exquisite tapestries and paintings. Above the mantel in the dining room is a full-length portrait of Mr. Swain in his uniform during the World war.

On the second floor are bedrooms and one small sitting room. All of these rooms, with one exception, command a splendid view of the river, glinting in the sunshine or winding grayly to sea, according to the moods of the weather.

On the fourth floor are three of the coziest attic rooms that could be imagined. The big center room has its oddly shaped walls lined with books and magazines. On either side of this is a big dormitory room with many single beds. This floor is used for hunting parties.

Peeping out of the quaint little attic windows is to be seen the Swains' white yacht, riding gracefully at anchor. It sways there proudly, like a swan.

### Two Daughters and Son

There are Mr. Swain, his two daughters, Louise and Phyllis, the latter being just out of Smith college, and W. Moseley Swain, Jr., a tall fair youth with a warm, friendly smile, known to his family as "Bill."

Phyllis, who was in khaki breeches and shirt, just in from a "gunning" trip, is boyish and athletic and is the housekeeper. Mrs. Swain died suddenly just after the home was finished and the family make their home at Belfair, although they come and go as the notion strikes them.

"But this is our home," Mr. Swain waxed enthusiastic. "This is how well we like your coastal country. We used to live in Haverford, Pa., but I am now a citizen of South Carolina."

And, here, tucked away from the stir of the world, yet within easy reach of the glitter of bright lights, is everything that the heart could desire. Still, Louise and Phyllis and Bill are young, and when asked what they did to amuse themselves, Phyllis' bright eyes crinkled with laughter. She dashed off somewhere and returned with a picture. "This is what we do, mostly—pushing ourselves out of the mud. Oh, yes, and we also help fight forest fires. Did you ever do it? It's lots of fun."

They are very versatile, these young people. They speak with equal casualness of trips to Europe and of deep sea fishing. On one wall hangs a huge tarpon weighing 99 ¾ pounds, which was caught by Louise Swain, off the coast of Florida. Had the fish weighed a quarter pound more, she would have received a medal. Down in the basement is another fish weighing 147 pounds which her father caught in the same place.

**Pictures in Basement**

Down in the basement, too, are hung some of Mr. Swain's pictures. His work features nude women, although there are some still life scenes. Mr. Swain has exhibited at the Art club in Philadelphia and received two honorable mentions, one nude and one still life. He never seriously studied art until he was a grown man with children, but his pictures show a rarely delicate touch.

Mr. Swain comes of a newspaper family, his grandfather Swain being one of the founders of the *Philadelphia Ledger* and the *Baltimore Sun*. During the Confederate war, his partner, who was running the *Sun*, was a Secessionist, while Mr. Swain, who ran the *Ledger*, could not agree with him. So they dissolved their partnership.

Belfair plantation is located at what is known as Wigg's Point and comprises about two thousand acres, including what were formerly the old Barnwell and Glover plantations. Part of this property is also known as the old H. A. M. Smith place. It is said that the name Belfair was a combination of the names Bell and Telfair, which families at one time owned some of the property.

Mr. Swain and his children like to shoot birds, but not deer. Asked why he did not like deer hunting, Mr. Swain looked slightly embarrassed, but Phyllis rushed to his rescue. "Oh, who could shoot a beautiful deer!"

Her father's eyes warmed upon her. "I couldn't get a kick out of killing a deer—it would be like cold-blooded murder."

Eager, responsive, likable people are the Swains. Their beautiful, expensive tabby home was a happy thought for Coastal South Carolina, but they themselves are the richer acquisition. ⁓

Judging from Mrs. Martin's enthusiastic description of Belfair, the Swain family must have given her a cordial welcome when she made her visit in 1931. The family had been living there since 1928.

William Moseley Swain's grandfather, who shared the same name with his grandson, founded the newspapers mentioned by Mrs. Martin. His son Charles Moseley Swain, a prominent lawyer and financier in Philadelphia, left a fortune of $1.8 million in 1904 but no will. In addition to his painting career, William Moseley Swain was president of the Williamson Motor Company.

The Belfair property had been part of Devil's Elbow, or Okeetee Barony, the twelve-thousand-acre grant to Sir John Colleton in 1718. It was rich, productive land on the Colleton River, and the family had kept it intact until sometime after Sir John's death in 1777. It had never been the family seat, however. That was always Fairlawn Barony in Berkeley County. Later, in the nineteenth century, Belfair was owned by William Wigg Barnwell and sometimes was called Barnwell. Wigg Point, where Mr. Swain built his house, takes its name from that ownership.

The Swain house was a striking residence, as Mrs. Martin says, of tabby construction, a material used along the coast for the raised foundations of plantation houses as well as for local fortifications. Its reputation was that the composition strengthened with age.

Mr. Swain was his own engineer, but unfortunately he had not mastered the art of preparing tabby. Over time the excessive saline content of the mixture began to leach out, causing the walls to crumble—a distressing end to a house built to last for the ages. His "magnificent tabby home" fell to pieces after Mr. Swain's 1940 death in Savannah at age sixty-seven. W. Moseley Swain Jr., the "tall fair youth with a warm, friendly smile," was murdered in Beaufort County in December 1948, a crime that remains unsolved and is still discussed locally. Belfair Plantation, five miles from the bridge to Hilton Head Island, is now a residential golf development.

# Bray's Island

(also the Old Means' Farm, Cunningham's Bluff,
Hall's Island, Grays Hill, and Laurel Bay)

Bray's Island, one of the many interesting sea islands surrounding Beaufort, has been purchased by J. K. Hollins, of New York. The island was at one time owned by the McKee family and at another by the Cuthberts. How the name Bray was acquired is not clear. This name is not indicated in a 130-year old map of the island which is still in existence.

The house on Bray's Island has an aged, weather-beaten appearance, but it belies its looks. It is only about thirty or forty years old, having been brought here by schooner from New York ready cut about that long ago. Just now it is unoccupied.

Probably the most interesting object to be found on Bray's Island is a monstrous live oak tree. This tree is famous for miles around and many people go to see it. It has a spread of 125 feet and is 28 feet in circumference at the smallest part of its trunk. There are four branches, each as large as an ordinary tree, growing out of the great trunk. The tree has an enormous network of roots, much of it above ground. This tree is said to be the oldest and largest in this part of the county, its age being variously estimated at from 150 to 2,000 years old.

The island contains 989 acres, including marsh, and about 200 acres are under cultivation. A large per cent of the island is in marsh. Mr. Hollins has been engaged in developing a number of duck ponds and in preparing the high land for quail shooting.

The present causeway by which the island is reached is about twenty years old, but before the Confederate war the island was approached from another direction. A federal gunboat came up the Pocotaligo river and went aground near Bray's Island. Although it remained there for a week, the Confederate troops, because of bad roads, were unable to bring their cannon from Yemassee in order to sink it.

Original title: "Largest Tree along Coast Found on Beaufort Island. Famous Live Oak Measures 28 Feet in Circumference at Smallest Part of Trunk and Lifts Four Branches Big as Ordinary Tree." Publication date: December 9, 1930.

The Davis house at Bray's Island. *Photograph by Ned Brown, courtesy of Barton and Barton*

Bray's Island is an ideal place for a beautiful home. The home site is reached over the causeway from Sheldon and thence over a sandy road across the island. It stands in a grove of great, aged live oaks, all draped with the familiar Spanish moss. The island slopes down to the very water's edge and is as lovely and romantic a spot as one could wish to make a home.

In this section of the county there are several other large tracts of land owned by rich northerners, who are interested mainly in hunting on this acreage.

### Means' Farm Now Owned by Carroll

Continuing on down the mainland, after coming off Bray's Island, one comes to the tract known as the old Means' farm. This place is now owned by Phillip A. Carroll, New York attorney.

This farm contains 1,640 acres of land and only a small frame cottage. This cottage is occupied by L. J. Williams, who is Mr. Carroll's superintendent. Mr. Williams farms some of the land, but the great majority of it is used for hunting.

### Hollins Properties

Still farther down the road is the property of Harry B. Hollins, Jr., who owns Cunningham's Bluff, a lovely home site, and Hall's Island, which, together, contain about 2,000 acres.

There is only a small cottage on Mr. Hollins' property and the land is used almost entirely for hunting. Horace Davis looks after the property for Mr. Hollins.

### Corning Estate

Not far from these lands, about three miles from Grays Hill, is a tract of 2,617 acres owned by Warren H. Corning. Mr. Corning is from Cleveland, Ohio, and is a retired sewing machine manufacturer.

This land was formerly the property of N. M. Polk.

On his estate, Mr. Corning has erected an interesting group of buildings. There are a handsome clubhouse and three attractive bungalows.

Mr. Corning also owns a tract of land on Broad river. This is Laurel Bay, the history of which dates far back before the Revolutionary war.

**William Barnwell Home**

At the end of a long avenue of oaks is the site of the old William Barnwell home. This house was destroyed by the British forces during the Revolutionary war and the last home to be built on this site was burned about forty years ago. ༈

An Indian trader named William Bray was in the Pocotaligo area as early as 1704 but was killed in the Yamassee uprising of 1715 with a number of other traders and their families. While no document connects Bray to this particular property, it is reasonable to assume, considering his presence in the region, that the island bears his name.

A handsome 1798 plat by John Goddard shows the island of 404 acres as the property of Thomas Bowman. The Bowmans had owned it as far back as 1763, when it was a 1,239-acre tract bought from Richard Clark.

In 1831, to settle the estate of James Bowman, the court of equity ordered Bray's Island sold at public auction. It was then 930 acres, and the buyer was Mary B. Stuart of Beaufort, who made the purchase for her son, William H. Cuthbert, though the deed was never registered in his name. The Cuthberts owned it until after the Civil War, when economic ruin forced the family to borrow a substantial sum to reestablish itself. The property was offered as collateral, and when the family was unable to regain the mortgage, Bray's Island was lost to foreclosure. The Union gunboat mentioned by Mrs. Martin may have been the one that is said to have destroyed the main house that stood near the river.

J. K. Hollins, the owner when Mrs. Martin wrote her article (and brother of Harry Hollins Jr. of Cunningham's Bluff), was a son of Harry B. Hollins, who had banking and brokerage associations in New York and was also vice president of the Central Railroad and Banking Company of Georgia. He had come to the Beaufort area about 1890 and was involved with establishing the Okeetee, Good Hope, and Chelsea hunting clubs.

Bray's Island was bought in 1937 by F. B. Davis Jr. (1883–1962). Mr. Davis told a family member that his father had served on a federal warship off the southeastern coast and advised his son, "New York is a good place to earn a living, but if you want to live, go to South Carolina."

A farm boy and an orphan from Fort Edward, New York, with ambition and a degree from Yale's Sheffield Scientific School, Davis went to work for the DuPont Company as a construction engineer in 1909, and for the next fifty years he built a career in service to the company. DuPont was run by Irénée and Pierre du Pont, who were among America's preeminent industrialists; they held controlling interests in a number of enterprises beyond the parent company. Sensing Davis's managerial talents, the Du Ponts steadily advanced him from technical to administrative positions in businesses in which they held majority shares: DuPont Chemical (1919), General Motors (1921), Viscoloid and Celastic (1925), and

Pittsburgh Safety Glass (1928). Davis's greatest business opportunity came in 1929. The Du Ponts had acquired large holdings in the faltering U.S. Rubber Company, which was once the largest rubber manufacturer in America but had fallen behind its three domestic rivals. Davis's successful approach was to institute a close attention to financial performance, to decentralize management as Alfred P. Sloan had effectively done at General Motors, and to place operating and service divisions under tight financial control. Davis retired as president and chairman of U.S. Rubber in 1949, but he remained an advisory director for another decade. He died in Savannah, Georgia, in 1962.

Davis built the present house in 1938 from a design by Willis Irvin of Augusta, Georgia, and he and his wife took up permanent residence at Bray's in 1959. A *Beaufort Gazette* article claimed he spent more than $3.5 million fixing up the plantation. In addition he added several surrounding properties (including the Means Farm, which he bought from Philip A. Carroll in 1939, ten years after Carroll purchased it), bringing the acreage up to about four thousand. He and Mrs. Davis made it a working plantation, known internationally for a prize stock of Aberdeen-Angus cattle. For some years the Davises made annual trips to Scotland to secure new bloodlines for their stock. Davis's neighbor and friend Jocelyn Clark of Spring Hill plantation has said not disparagingly, "Davis had the best of everything at Bray's Island—and he died broke."

At Mr. Davis's death, the estate was said to have had a mortgage claim against it in excess of seven hundred thousand dollars. The Bray's Island property was offered for sale at auction, and in the initial bidding it was clear that the plantation would have to be broken up into smaller tracts. Mrs. Davis, then living in Virginia, requested that the property stay intact, so the early bids were rejected in favor of a competitive offer from a neighboring plantation owner, Mr. Sumner Pingree Jr., who agreed not to divide it. Bray's Island was maintained as a working plantation until 1987, when Mr. Pingree converted it to a privately owned community focused on hunting and outdoor life. Two hundred of the fifty-two hundred acres have been given to building lots, while the remainder is open land and a hunting preserve.

In *The Story of Sea Island Cotton,* Sarah Fick writes that Laurel Bay was in the Barnwell family "long before the Revolution." It was a Sea Island cotton plantation fronting the Broad River on Port Royal Island. The Barnwells' brick house at Laurel Bay was burned by the British during the Revolution, leaving the thick-walled lower story standing. After the war a second house was built above this old lower story, but during the Union occupation of Port Royal Island it suffered the same fate as its predecessor.

# Callawassie Island

Callawassee island, on the Colleton river, is one of the romantic sea islands off the Carolina coast, which add to the glamour and interest of the coastal country.

This island, which retains its old Indian name, was owned by Clarence Kirk and purchased about thirteen or fourteen years ago by B. C. and J. L. Kuser, of Trenton, N.J.

B. C. Kuser liked it so well that he spent nearly all of his winters there until his death this year.

Callawassee island consists of about three thousand acres of land, about half of which is marsh land. The island was used by the Kusers mainly as a hunting preserve and it is said to be plentifully stocked with game of all kinds. Mr. Kuser at one time tried raising cattle, but eventually abandoned this work. He raised pheasants and peacocks and the island was full of wild turkeys.

**Veteran Winter Visitors**

The Kusers have been coming to Coastal South Carolina for about thirty-five years and were formerly members of Chelsea club.

B. C. Kuser had planned to build a handsome home on the bluff overlooking the river at Callawassee island, but the death of his wife caused him to change his plans and he contented himself with remodeling and enlarging the small house which had been built for the caretaker.

This house has finally developed into a rather large place, consisting of nine bedrooms, five baths, two large halls, a large living room, dining room, sun parlor, kitchen, pantry, laundry and servants quarters.

On this island there are the remains of some interesting old tabby walls. Who built them and why seems to be a matter of conjecture among local people. Some think they were built by Indians.

Original title: "Callawassee, Beaufort Sea Island. Northerners Develop Place Once Very Profitable as Producer of Sea Island Cotton, into Game Preserve and Ideal Retreat for House Parties." Publication date: May 10, 1931.

The photograph of the Kuser home on Callawassie Island that accompanied the original *Charleston News and Courier* article. *Courtesy of the Charleston County Public Library*

Callawassee was very profitable before the war, a high grade of sea island cotton being raised there. After the war, the value of the place declined and Mr. Kirk sold it. He himself was said never to have lived there, but managed the large farm there through an overseer who lived on the island.

Mr. Kirk lived in Bluffton. He is said to have been a Southerner, highly educated, who taught school, both as a private tutor and in the public schools. He is said to have been considered one of the best educators in this entire section.

B. C. Kuser was widely known locally and liked for his friendliness and generosity. He was lavish in his hospitality and his home was always open to his friends. He entertained house parties a great deal and delighted in having his friends around him. Many people in Jasper county have feasted off wild turkeys and other game brought to them by Mr. Kuser from Callawassee island.

Since his death, the island is owned by his brother, J. L. Kuser, who is prominently identified with a number of New Jersey concerns, among them being a pottery company, a brewing concern and a coal company.

Callawassee island is in Beaufort county, but nearer Ridgeland. A telephone connects the island with the outside world and a trim yacht makes pleasant traveling between the island and the mainland. ❧

In New Jersey, Benedict Kuser expanded on his family's wealth with investments in ice and coal distribution and a Trenton hotel. He was an avid outdoorsman—a hunter, especially of rattlesnakes, and fisherman—and president of the New Jersey Fish and Game Commission. After the death of his wife in 1911, "he became a bit hedonistic and enjoyed life," according to William A. Behan's *A Short History of Callawassie Island, South Carolina*. Part of that life included the purchase of Callawassie (the present spelling) in 1917, where he hosted many parties both at his home and on his sixty-five-foot yacht.

After his death in September 1930, the island was inherited by Benedict's older brother John Kuser, a New Jersey businessman involved with car, beer, power, and film companies. John Kuser owned the island only until March 1937, five months before his death.

After one intermediate owner, the island was bought by Anthony J. Drexel III of the Philadelphia banking family, whose sister Edith was married to Harry Cram of Foot Point. Through Cram, Drexel became close to Billy Swain of Belfair and Roy Rainey of Hilton Head. "The four men," writes Behan, "had identical interests: sports, hunting, fishing, alcohol and women, not necessarily in that order."

The Drexels tore down Kuser's home before they sold the property in 1946 and bought Wappaoola in Berkeley County. After their departure, the island passed through a number of hands, most of them corporations seeking to profit from the island's timber or, later, from real estate schemes. In 1985 those plans succeeded and the island became a residential development.

Mrs. Martin included none of the island's early history, though it was widely repeated, with or without accuracy, as the property was owned by several prominent families. Callawassie was first settled by James Cochran in 1711. Daniel Heyward purchased it in 1756, and, until the end of the eighteenth century, the Heyward family controlled the property. For thirty years it was managed by Thomas Heyward Jr. (1746–1809), who lived at White Hall plantation. Thomas's granddaughter Elizabeth Heyward inherited the island, though her husband, James Hamilton Jr., sold it in 1819. Later governor and a congressman of South Carolina, he purchased many other properties in the area, including Pennyworth Island and Rice Hope. He had a tabby sugar mill built near the marsh on what is now Sugar Mill Drive, the ruins of which are still extant.

James B. Kirk, a Beaufort County cotton planter, bought the island about 1845. Kirk's story—or legend, as there is little documentation outside Heyward family "tradition"—is the kind of tale Mrs. Martin would have loved. As an infant, and during the American Revolution, he and his family were targeted for death by a local Tory planter and officer. Kirk's father, who fought under Francis Marion, was killed, but Kirk, his mother, and his siblings were sneaked out of their home on the Savannah River. James supposedly was dropped from an upper-story window into the waiting arms of a loyal slave woman, who carried the child eight miles through the woods, where she and the surviving Kirk family members were given safety by the Heyward family. Later the family was moved to the Heyward settlements on Callawassie until the threat passed. Fifty years later, after starting work as a plantation overseer, Kirk became a wealthy planter in his own right, and he purchased Callawassie Island.

Considering all the research Mrs. Martin conducted in the area, she must have come across the legend, but perhaps she was growing wary of plantation stories that seemed too good to be true. She certainly swallowed enough fallacies about Callawassie. The Kusers bought the island not from the Kirks but from the Burns family in 1917. Clarence Kirk, son of James B., sold the island soon after the end of the Civil War to a Union commissary general named William Burns; Kirk was on the verge of losing it to debt anyway. According to

Behan's *Short History of Callawassie Island,* Kirk did live on the island. He ran local schools and had a good reputation as an educator, though he had enjoyed virtually no formal education. When Mrs. Martin estimated the island to measure about three thousand acres, she may have tripled its actual size.

# Cat Island

The handful of folk who have just purchased Cat island, one of the sea coast islands of South Carolina, near Beaufort, for the purpose of earning their livelihood by farming are aghast at the startling publicity which their innocent adventure has brought them. Busily engaged from dawn until dark in the laborious work of getting their water pump in operation, scrubbing down walls and floors, persuading their new cow to allow herself to be milked and their new hens to lay, they blissfully were unaware that they have been the objects of great curiosity as members of an alleged love cult, band of nudists, health fanatics and whatnot until they were shown newspaper clippings to this effect.

They seemed stunned at the sensation they have been causing. One of them, a German girl, put her hand to her mouth in horror. "Oh, but dat is awful!" she exclaimed.

Another, an Englishman, looked a little uneasy when he considered the nudist report. "Well, er—it was very hot the other day and I was fishing on the dock with my shirt off—and the little girl here, she isn't very well, and she gets her daily sun bath off by herself—maybe somebody saw us."

His audience, a native one, laughed heartily. He seemed to feel better when he learned that fishermen in these parts often fish without their shirts and that sun baths are very popular also.

**"Back to the Farm"**

"And as for the love cult—bah!" the lone man of the party, so far, who is slight in physique, exclaimed. "If there were anything to that I tell you frankly, I believe they would have picked a bigger man than I."

Then he grew serious. "It is very simple," he said. "We are merely a group of people—who knew each other with varying degrees of friendship in New York and discovered that we all had one common ambition—that of getting away from New York and back to a farm. And here we are."

Original title: "Colony from New York City Buys Beaufort Island Farm. Handful of People Putting Houses in Order in Back to the Land Movement. Study South Carolina Methods." Publication date: May 8, 1932.

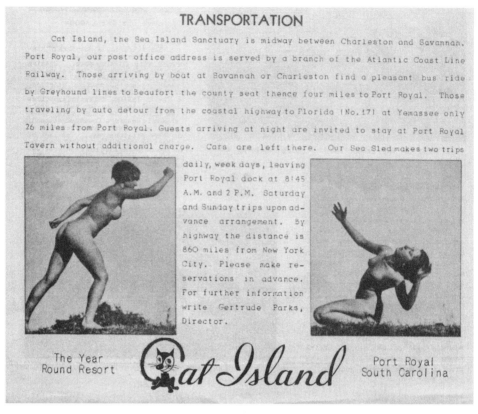

## TRANSPORTATION

Cat Island, the Sea Island Sanctuary is midway between Charleston and Savannah. Port Royal, our post office address is served by a branch of the Atlantic Coast Line Railway. Those arriving by boat at Savannah or Charleston find a pleasant bus ride by Greyhound lines to Beaufort the county seat thence four miles to Port Royal. Those traveling by auto detour from the coastal highway to Florida (No. 17) at Yemassee only 26 miles from Port Royal. Guests arriving at night are invited to stay at Port Royal Tavern without additional charge. Cars are left there. Our Sea Sled makes two trips daily, week days, leaving Port Royal dock at 8:45 A.M. and 2 P.M. Saturday and Sunday trips upon advance arrangement. By highway the distance is 860 miles from New York City. Please make reservations in advance. For further information write Gertrude Parks, Director.

The Year Round Resort   *Cat Island*   Port Royal South Carolina

Part of a brochure for the Sea Island Sanctuary, Cat Island. *Courtesy of the South Caroliniana Library, University of South Carolina, Columbia*

The little group is composed, so far, of the Englishman and his cousin, the German girl and a mother with her little girl. The German girl is expecting her brother and mother shortly. The little girl's grandmother will come soon too, and her father, who has a job in New York, will be down once in a while. There may be others, too, later, who will come either to live on the island or as boarders. There is a ten room house on the island nearly a hundred years old which will be repaired and used for paying guests who would like for a while the experiences of life on a sea island in South Carolina.

Along the little land leading from the boat landing to the "Big House" of the old days is a row of little cabins, most of them replacing the negro quarters of another day. One of these little houses is two storied with two rooms in each story. The rooms are quaintly shaped and its windows look far out across the water. Others are merely one-room cabins, sturdily built, and these will be occupied by family groups of the party or individuals. There is another house in the group, a modern bungalow, in which all of the party are living now until they can get settled.

### Reared on Farms

There is not a single one of the group who is not farm-minded. All of them with the exception of one woman have been reared or lived on a farm at some time and the one exception comes of a long line of farming people. Several of the group are experienced farmers. Already they are engaged in studying farming conditions in coastal South Carolina and preparing to adapt their own methods and needs to them.

Cat island, which contains 440 acres of fertile land, has always been considered one of the best farms in this section. Two hundred acres are under cultivation. The new owners plan to go slowly with their planting so as to learn as they go. They will live on their farm first of all, letting the idea of making money come later. Already they have shown their ingenuity and business-like methods by arranging with a Beaufort merchant to take over their surplus eggs and butter. This is to be the keynote of their farming methods. They are starting with one mule and as their venture grows, others will be added. There will be no negroes on the island, according to the present plans. Members of this group believe in doing their own work. However, they are sensible about it and if they find that they cannot do the work advantageously through the heat of the summer months, they plan to hire negro labor to help. There will be at least two men on the island and they realize that they will have their hands full. In addition to the farming proper, they plan to raise livestock.

**Women Work Too**

The women are not afraid of work, either. One of them has taken over the cow, of necessity, as the animal is a temperamental one and will allow no one else to milk her. These people get up at five thirty every morning and set to work and they keep at it until dark. But they don't consider it drudgery, because, to them, it is a dream come true.

Nearly everybody, it is said, dreams of going to New York and amounting to something. That seems to be the epitome of success. But these people explode that lovely balloon dream. They say there is nothing to it. In the mad scramble and hurry that is New York, they dreamed only of getting away to some quiet place where they could have peace and solitude.

They hit upon the coast of South Carolina quite by accident. One of the group had traveled through this section once en route to Florida and remarked that he had been very favorably impressed with this section. Then another happened to think that he once knew a physician in the navy who had been stationed at Parris island for a time and who had also been most enthusiastic about the coasts of South Carolina. So, acting upon impulse, five or six of them piled into an automobile and drove down to Beaufort. They had planned merely to rent or lease a farm and if they didn't like it, to go back home and call it a vacation. However, they were so pleased with Beaufort and the surrounding country that they bought Cat island and decided to make it their home.

One of the group has traveled in various parts of the world and says he has never seen a place he liked better. He is particularly charmed with the people he has met and all of them are as eager as children with a new toy. When they get tired working, they amuse themselves by exploration tramps over their island. They haven't nearly got over it yet and find new discoveries with each walk. They decide what they will plant here and there, then probably change it all over again before they get back. The other night, while walking under the stars, one of them exclaimed: "Just think, this time in New York, we would all be swinging onto a subway strap!"

### Regular Company

The group is organized into a company. It is a regular business arrangement with shares and the like and will be operated just like any corporation. However, they consider it much nicer than one which has its headquarters within four walls of an office.

Cat island is rich in historical and romantic interest. It is situated about three miles by water from Port Royal and is just across the river from Parris island. From the up-stairs windows of the big house on Cat island one can almost see into the very build-ings on Parris island, so close and friendly the marine training station seems just across the way. Cat island is supposed to be the location of the novel "A Son of the Carolinas" by Elisabeth Carpenter Satterthwait and indeed the sight of it would inspire anyone afflicted with the urge to put thoughts and feelings into words.

Upon this island, one loses touch with the outside world and misses nothing, if he or she is a lover of beauty and peace and the companionship of a chosen few. These people, isolated from news of the world for nearly a week, inquired only whether "Lindy had found his baby." Part of the world might have been destroyed, there might have been a war in progress—they were not interested.

The big house has a wide veranda and large spacious rooms whose walls tell many thrilling stories, if walls had tongues as well as ears. The building is in need of some repairs, but is still in splendid condition considering its age. There is an oleander-bordered pathway which leads down to the water's edge and many reminders of an old-fashioned garden.

Cat Island is beginning a new life, something that it probably never dreamed of before. First, the old plantation life with its "Big House" and slave quarters. Then the prosperous truck planter who grew rich and at last poor in the mad gamble of trucking. Now a group of eager, intelligent people who know what they want and go after it—wise people who have the courage to build up happiness and contentment for them-selves. ✄

This article was reprinted in the *Beaufort Gazette* on May 12, 1932.

The residents of Cat Island were a bit disingenuous in their shock at the rumor that they were "an alleged love cult, band of nudists, health fanatics and whatnot." They indeed were part of "the first nudist camp in America," according to an article by Lee Baxandall in *Nude and Natural,* the magazine of the Naturist Society. The island had been purchased in 1932 by Gertrude L. Parks for twelve thousand dollars. Parks was the wife of Gilbert Parks, advertising manager for a number of magazines published in New York by Bernarr Macfadden. Macfadden, according to his entry in the *Dictionary of American Biography,* was famed for promoting "exercise, fresh air, adequate rest, cleanliness, and an almost meatless diet, thoroughly chewed. He opposed alcohol, tobacco, coffee, and 'the baneful habit of overeating.'" Among Macfadden's interests was nudism, which Mr. and Mrs. Parks allowed at their Cat Island settlement named Sea Island Sanctuary.

A year later, in another *News and Courier* article, Mrs. Martin acknowledged that nudism was commonplace at Cat Island: "A secluded area of the island is especially set apart for sun bathing, where those who seek health through the sun's rays, or the perfect tan, may stroll freely in their birthday suits without fear of prying eyes and peeping Toms." After a 1934 article in the *State* newspaper featured photos of naked island residents, the settlement lost most of its privacy. The Ku Klux Klan grew interested. Gov. Ira C. Blackwood sent a law-enforcement group including Beaufort County sheriff J. E. McTeer to the island on two occasions, but the residents scared them off by racing to the boat landing without clothing and shouting "Aloha!" One of the constables cried, "Let's get the hell out of here!" and they fled. After that, McTeer showed no interest in bothering the residents, claiming, "There is such a thing as personal liberty in this country."

However, when the residents suggested to Mrs. Martin that they were back-to-the-land farmers, they were not inaccurate. Nudism was just one of their interests. They hoped to establish a self-sufficient farming community, and in 1933 they boasted in *Nudist* magazine that they had put up more than seven hundred quarts of fruits and vegetables. "From now on our only food purchases need be coffee, tea, sugar, and condiments." According to a brochure for Sea Island Sanctuary at the South Caroliniana Library, accommodations ranged from five dollars per month (campers or those building log cabins) to two dollars per day (furnished room and all meals). Twenty acres were set aside for sharecropping. In 1934 the residents expanded to offer market-fresh and canned vegetables. An eighteen-room house in Port Royal was purchased to serve as a car park, warehouse, and hotel.

Nonetheless the finances did not work out. On March 31, 1935, in a general article in the *News and Courier* about the beauty of Beaufort County, Mrs. Martin wrote that Cat Island was now "the proposed location for South Carolina's first self-help cooperative farming venture." The island was still owned by Mrs. Parks. Called Seacroft, this workers' education project was planned by Dr. William E. Zeuch, a left-wing professor who had earlier founded Commonwealth College (1923–40) in Arkansas. Seacroft released a bulletin on October 1, 1935, describing itself as "a non-factional, non-propaganda education community for workers." Unlike almost every other college in America, Seacroft would not be controlled by "political parties, religious bodies, business and industrial organizations, and persons of large wealth." Tuition cost forty dollars for the short fall semester and fifty dollars for the longer spring semester, and students were expected "to perform 15 hours of reasonably efficient work at community tasks each week." The first semester would begin October 1, 1936. There are no records of any actual classes. Mrs. Martin continued in that 1935 article: "The plantation house still stands and, until the last few years, the 'street' of slave days could also be seen."

Mr. and Mrs. Parks owned the island until the early 1970s, when they both died, and it passed to their daughter Priscilla Kaeser of Rockville, Maryland. Today the island is entirely developed with modern homes. Public nudity seems well contained.

# Chisolm Island

Once upon a time—and this story really has all the ingredients of a fairy tale, except that it is a true one—a New York employment agency sent a green young foreigner to a job on Chisolm Island, down on the coast of South Carolina. It was a day laborer's job on a large rice plantation. The young foreigner worked for a year and then, after a disagreement with the plantation foreman, he took a bateau and left.

But that was many years ago and time and momentous events, like sunshine and storm, have ripened to mellowness the green in the youth's character. It is a long story and a thrilling one and the end fairly takes one's breath away. For that youth has grown to be a world figure—Sir Thomas Lipton, of tea and good sportsmanship fame.

Chisolm Island has likewise passed through many stages—rice planting, sea island cotton, phosphate mining, trucking and, now, cattle raising and leisurely living. But it still basks in the reflected glow of that long-ago contact.

## Tropical in Appearance

The island is probably more nearly tropical in appearance than any of the other sea coast islands. The usual giant live oak with its streamers of gray moss is missing here, but instead the palmetto is plentiful. The Wimbee river curls about the island like a big, gray pussy lazying in the sun.

Sixty-five hundred fertile acres, with history written upon their face and infinite possibilities, stretch away. The rice which once grew here made its planters rich, likewise the cotton planters and, still later, truck. High piled earth offers mute testimony of the days when men disturbed the bowels of the earth for phosphate rock, which also brought wealth and many people and the whine of machinery to this island.

Now, all is still and peaceful here. Only the deep bellow of cattle or the grunt of hogs or the cry of a lamb disturbs the quiet, for the island has been given over almost entirely to the raising of cattle.

Original title: "Chisolm Island, Where as Youth Tea King and Sportsman Labored for Year, Becomes Property of Legare Sanders Native Carolinian Who Found Fame and Fortune in North." Publication date: July 19, 1931.

Chisolm island was formerly the home of Robert Chisolm, from which family it gets its name, although it is sometimes called Pacific because of the fact that the Pacific Guano company at one time owned it, the Chisolms having sold the island to the Pacific company in 1877.

## Thriving Mining Center

The Pacific company mined the island for about 25 years and the Charleston Mining company took it over and mined it until about 1913. During the time that the island was mined for phosphate rock, it was a thriving bustling place. There were many people, houses and buildings of various kinds, including a large store, and much evidence of prosperity.

During the ownership of the Chisolm family, an old plantation house stood on the island near the water and was known as Palmetto Hall. However, this building was destroyed by fire. At this time, there are said to have been many olive trees on the island and olives were raised and marketed to a large extent.

The island is now owned by Legare Sanders, a native of Beaufort county, who, twenty-five years ago, left to make his way in the world. When he was a young man, he was pay clerk in the United States navy and was stationed at Port Royal. About that time, an electric railway syndicate in Cincinnati, Ohio, needed a purchasing agent and Mr. Sanders was recommended by a friend for the position. He got it and went to Cincinnati, where he finally became president of the Cincinnati Car company, which was owned by the railway syndicate.

And, having attained his ambition, queer things began to happen to Mr. Sanders. For instance, his thoughts got to wandering far afield from electric railways and the like. They persisted in bringing home alluring pictures of the Carolina coast. Every once in a while they would even sneak in a dizzying whiff of brackish waters that gave him an alarmingly reckless feeling inside. Other times, they would intrigue him with the flash of the sun on a full, gray tide, and a glimpse of billowing sail. Or maybe it would be a silver arc the far-away music of a pack of baying hounds.

## He Comes Back Home

Anyway, it grew to be an insidious hunger that kept eating away his contentment and peace of mind. Picking out the hum of electric transcribed by a leaping fish, or cars among the myriad noises of the city, had somehow lost its kick. And looking out of the windows of his office brought nothing but the sight of tall buildings zig-zagging across the skyline and a din that had ceased to be musical and smells that had no pungency.

So, one day, Mr. Sanders just got right up out of his swivel chair and came back home.

That was three years ago and he has not been sorry. He bought Chisolm island and is having a grand time just being alive. His house is only a few feet from the river. He can look out of his windows and doors and see miles and miles of tidal waters and green islands. He can fish and hunt to his heart's content and fill his lungs with the tang of the coast. At night, in his unlocked house, he is lulled to sleep by the swish of the lapping river and the breeze that is its breath.

He is, in truth, king of all he surveys. Yet, in this island home, twenty-odd miles from the nearest town, there is no sense of loneliness. In a house beside him live his brother-in-law and sister, Mr. and Mrs. J. O'H. Whitsell and their family. There are often visitors and a radio brings the world to them.

Just across a little stream is Horse island, dotted thickly with palmetto trees, where Mr. Sanders raises sheep. He ships wool and lamb to northern markets and hopes to develop more extensively this phase. On Chisolm island, he is developing a herd of beef cattle, using the Hereford breed. Feed for the cattle is all grown on the island. Mr. Whitsell is associated with Mr. Sanders in his livestock and grain raising venture and he has been living on Chisolm Island for about twenty years, formerly being engaged in trucking. ✢

This article included no byline but reads like one of Mrs. Martin's.

Because the western half of Chisolm Island is known as Coosaw plantation, it is often confused with nearby Coosaw Island. Even Gov. Mark Sanford, who wrote his Furman senior college thesis on the plantation his family bought in 1965, has written that Chisolm Island has been known as Coosaw Island since 1797, when Alexander Robert Chisolm bought it from the Bull family.

A Civil War battle off the island sank a Union gunboat called the *George Washington*. Both sides tried to retrieve the two cannons that were aboard, but neither was successful. After World War II, Sheriff J. E. McTeer and a group of inmates from the Beaufort County Jail salvaged one of the cannons. It was later placed in front of Beaufort Arsenal.

During the phosphate years, the plantation house known as Palmetto Hall was rebuilt and called "Alligator Hall." Sanford claims that it was the site of a bar, dance hall, and "prostitution parlor." Phosphate continued to be mined until 1896, but it was curtailed dramatically after the hurricane of 1893 swept through. Four island workers were killed in the storm, most of the boats of the Coosaw Mining Company sank or were blown ashore, the wharves were destroyed, and the buildings were badly damaged. The company was dissolved in 1913.

In the early 1900s much of the island was sold to William and Michael Keyserling of Beaufort, who farmed there. They eventually sold it to the financier E. F. Hutton in 1917. Hutton owned about ten thousand acres in the lowcountry, according to Mrs. Martin's article on Laurel Spring, which was Mr. Hutton's main home in the area.

According to Governor Sanford,

Mr. Hutton gave Coosaw Plantation to a stock broker friend named Juan Ceballas in return for help in introducing his second wife into proper social circles. He also gave his long-time dog handler, Marshall Smith, 600 acres of other land. This tract, called the Smith Tract, has been added to Coosaw Plantation lands by its present owner, Dr. Marshall Sanford.

Juan Ceballas, one of Coosaw's most colorful owners, was a handsome, enter-
taining, hospitable man with no practical business sense. His parents owned the harbor concession in Havana to which all ships entering and leaving the harbor paid a
royalty. . . .

Ceballas . . . immediately launched into numerous projects at Coosaw. He built
a meat packing house and had cattle shipped in by rail. He had a little grist mill for
corn, in which he made grits. He harvested pecans and had pralines made, packaging
them in special wrappings marked Coosaw Plantation. With a water well digger he
dug wells searching for oil. He built the irrigation pond.

Another enthusiastic owner was Albert Love (1905–1971), a successful Atlanta publisher
who had been born in Walterboro with the name of Albert Bogeslov. Sanford wrote: "Love
wanted a showplace where he could raise thoroughbreds. He renovated Coosaw Hall, built
a manager's house and a new horse barn, a swimming pool, and rebuilt the dock, dredg-
ing an area to keep his 100-foot yacht protected." He also owned Airy Hall in Colleton
County. In 1965 he transferred Coosaw to Dr. Marshall Sanford, who ran the property as a
farm. "Thus Coosaw Plantation," wrote the future governor, "has come full circle, returning to its original use as a family farm."

Legare Sanders, whose story of leaving the world of business for Chisolm Island so cap-
tivated Mrs. Martin, owned his portion of the island for only a little more than a year after
her article appeared. He died in November 1932. Mr. James O'H. Whitsell, former manager
of a phosphate company, tried to revive the industry on the island until the 1920s, when
he gave up. Whitsell family descendants still own the property and continue to live there.

# Clarendon

Henry W. Corning, of Cleveland, Ohio, finds the coastal county of South Carolina so delightful that he spends several weeks of practically every month in the year at his hunting lodge on Broad river, near Grays Hill, Beaufort county. Sometimes he comes with his family or friends and sometimes alone. Just now, he is there alone with his servants. And he is having a grand time, he says, hunting and fishing and just lolling around.

It isn't at all hard to see why anybody would have a great time at the Corning place. Situated at the end of a smooth clay road, just beyond the tiny village of Grays Hill, it commands a magnificent view of the river. The home site is on a curve of the river and on either hand there is an uncluttered sweep of woods and waters. Standing at whichever spot on the wide, spacious grounds one chooses, he is conscious of a poignant sense of the splendor of nature and the unimportance of the petty affairs that harass man at his daily grind. Men of the world, after a few days of rest at this place, return to their work with renewed energies, the cobwebs blown from their minds and their souls, for, somehow, one sheds worries at the first glimpse of this nature-favored spot.

Riding over the leaf-carpeted, narrow winding roads that run through the shadowed forests of his three-thousand-acre estate, Mr. Corning was led to talk on the ever-popular subject of depression and unemployment and the good or evil of prohibition. And talk he did, forcefully and charmingly, out of his wide knowledge and experience but, somehow, under the spell of January sunshine slanting through brown woods, these things did not seem to matter particularly. They were not real. They were like the fire breathing dragons of fairy tales kept away from the enchanted forest by a kind godmother with a magic wand.

**Place Not Pretentious**

There is nothing ornate or pretentious about the Corning place. There are three simple one-story frame buildings. The main building, containing the living room, dining room and kitchen, is merely a remodeled and enlarged farm house, which was on the

Original title: "Henry W. Corning's Place. Cleveland Man Spends Part of Almost Every Month at House on Broad River, in Beaufort County." Publication date: January 24, 1932.

Clarendon facing the water, 1930s. *From Willis Irvin*, Selections from the Work of Willis Irvin: Architect, Augusta, Ga., *1937*

place when Mr. Corning bought it about five years ago. The large living room is comfortable, bright and cheery, but furnished with only the plainest and most substantial of furniture, a great home-made settee, piled with bright pillows, big easy chairs, tables and lights and many gay-jacketed books which climb high upon one wall. Tall windows frame arresting bits of woodland and water.

There are two cottages which are used exclusively for sleeping quarters. The furniture there is bright and cheerful and the rooms with their many windows command the maximum of light and air and scenery.

Mr. Corning has a small nursery on the place and has put out a number of azaleas which, at this time, are splashing the landscape with their burning beauty.

Included among Mr. Corning's holdings are some four or five old ante-bellum plantations, among which are Woodward and Laurel Bay, which have interesting histories. At Woodward may still be seen the old tabby ruins of a building and a wall which extends possibly as much as fifteen hundred feet in two directions. There is a magnificent avenue of oaks, not very large in dimension but believed to be very old, and many magnolia trees, both great and small.

A description in the Beaufort library of these old plantations, written by William Garrison Reed, of Dorchester, Mass., and enclosed with photographs of the two houses at Woodward and Laurel Bay as they appeared when he was in Beaufort during the years 1863–67, was sent the library several years ago. It describes the dwelling house at Woodward as having been built before the Revolution and as being very large and roomy. "Woodward," reads the description, "is opposite the place on the mainland where our forces landed for the battle of Honey Hill. The sailors from the gunboats came over and almost ruined the house, staying all night and burning the stairs, doors and whatever wood they could tear up. The windows were all broken out and even part of the roof torn off, the front steps taken away and finally the house was set on fire, but some of the people on the place saved it." It also tells of an oak at the back of the house which was the largest on any of the islands around and which covered more than a quarter of an acre. This plantation was owned by Robert Barnwell.

### A Story of Long Ago

Mr. Reed also sent a description and picture of the house and avenue of live oaks on William Barnwell's place at Laurel Bay, adjoining Woodward. The avenue, he wrote, was 85 feet wide and about 150 yards long and "is the handsomest show of trees down here. No person is supposed to have seen the sights on the island [Port Royal] unless he has been out to 'Barnwell's.'"

Mr. Corning cherishes a story told him of the old families who used to live here. The story goes that a daughter of one of the plantation owners fell in love with a son of a family who lived on a near-by island. The girl's father forbade the marriage, but, true to romance, the couple eloped, anyway. The irate father then forbade his daughter ever to return to his home and sent her clothes after her in a boat commanded by slaves. After a year, the young bride, heartsick for a reconciliation with her father, expressed to her husband a desire to go home for a visit. This, however, her husband emphatically refused to allow, telling her that if she left his house she could never return.

The girl, as determined as her husband, went anyway and was followed by her clothes from her husband's house. Twenty years later, the story goes, the husband was

Clarendon facing inland, circa 1932. *Photograph by Chlotilde Martin, courtesy of Chloe M. Pinckney*

walking with a close friend of both families on the streets of Charleston. He spied a very pretty girl sitting upon a doorstep and was so impressed with her that he passed by reluctantly. He remarked to his friend that he had been unusually taken with the girl and the friend informed the amazed father that the girl was his own daughter, whom he had never seen and of whose birth he was not aware.

But there is nothing left now to tell the tale of the stubborn pride and bitterness and travail of this husband and wife of long ago—nothing but deserted tabby walls and stillness broken only by the call of wild things to each other, that and the swish of the river upon a sandy beach, where, doubtless, on moonlit nights these lovers once strolled hand in hand. ✺

Warren H. Corning Sr. began his business career in Cleveland, Ohio, the city where John D. Rockefeller got his start in business about the same time. However, Corning's interests were in sewing machines and banking, not oil. The *National Cyclopedia of American Biography* describes him as "one of the most capable men of affairs in Ohio." He was a founder and president of the Standard Sewing Machine Company and a director with financial ties to three of Cleveland's major banks; one of these, Wick Banking and Trust Company, was controlled by his wife's family. Corning's son Henry (1869–1946) came into the business at Standard Sewing Machine after graduating from Harvard and eventually succeeded his father as president.

The Corning property on Broad River on Port Royal Island was acquired largely in 1927 and 1930. It comprised four major tracts—Laurel Bay, Woodward, Barnwell Island, and Tyler or Clarendon—some three thousand acres in all, to which the Cornings gave the name Clarendon. Although the subhead of Mrs. Martin's article refers to the plantation as the "Henry W. Corning Place," the deeds show that the lands were bought in the name of Warren H. Corning, Henry's son.

Laurel Bay was, at the time of the Civil War, the home of William Hazzard Wigg Barnwell, an Episcopal minister. With thirteen children of his own, in addition to his ecclesiastical flock, he had little time for cotton planting, so the family lived with a close economy.

Of the many Barnwells who lived at Laurel Bay, perhaps none had a more interesting life than Will Barnwell, a servant of Col. Robert Gibbes Barnwell (1761–1824), who accompanied his master in the Revolutionary War. For his faithful service, Will was given his freedom "but [was] left in charge of the children to be taken care of," wrote Mrs. E. B. Fuller after his death; "he lived a greater part of his life at Laurel Bay, and superintended the planting of the plantation." He died in Beaufort in 1850, a lamented friend; his age was given as eighty-five. Eight of Will Barnwell's letters to the Barnwell family (and Mrs. Fuller's letter) are in the South Carolina Historical Society archives. These are not the originals, and it is not known if Will had been taught to write or if his words were taken down by another hand.

Robert W. Barnwell (1801–1882), brother of Rev. William W. H. Barnwell, lived on neighboring Woodward's eight hundred acres. He was the most accomplished member of the Barnwell family in his generation. At Harvard he made a lasting friendship with Ralph Waldo Emerson. They differed on slavery and secession but never lost their respect for one another.

Barnwell's reasoned judgments and moderate political views brought him into government, first in the South Carolina legislature, next as a member of the U.S. Congress, and then in the U.S. Senate from 1850 until the election of President Abraham Lincoln, when he returned south. Robert Barnwell is remembered most particularly for his association with the University of South Carolina. Elected president when the school was still known as South Carolina College, he held office from 1835 until 1841, overseeing in that time the building of the library (the present South Caroliniana Library). After the war Barnwell was appointed professor of history and chairman of the faculty, until radical opposition forced his retirement. He returned to the school in 1877 as librarian, treasurer, and secretary in those difficult years after Reconstruction when the university barely functioned. It was said that "Barnwell was the university." Barnwell College on campus is named in his honor.

William Henry Trescot (1822–1898) of Barnwell Island was a lawyer and diplomat and the author of several books on diplomacy. His government services were on the federal level as assistant secretary of state in the administration of President James Buchanan and secretary of the American legation in London for President Millard Fillmore in 1852. After the war he represented the United States at various times in China, Mexico, Peru, and Chile.

The old Trescot house was moved from Barnwell Island to Beaufort in 1876 to a lot on Bay Street, where it remained for almost a century. Threatened with demolition in 1976, it was moved again, this time to Washington Street, and was handsomely restored.

The Cornings replaced the single-story buildings described in Mrs. Martin's 1932 article with Willis Irvin's handsome brick residence. It was built, she wrote in a 1935 article, on the site of the previous Grays Hill plantation house, a frame building that was moved elsewhere on the grounds. Irvin (1890–1950), of Augusta, Georgia, was trained at Georgia Tech, and his mastery of the "Southern Colonial" style, as his son called it, appealed to the new northern plantation owners, who wanted an elegant house among live oaks, wide lawns, and water views. The houses at Gregorie Neck, Bonnie Doone, Turkey Hill, Castle Hill, and Bray's Island were also Irvin's work.

On March 31, 1935, Mrs. Martin wrote in her "Lowcountry Gossip" column of this new house, which she said was completed

> at a reported cost of between $60,000 and $75,000. It looks as though it had sat beside the peaceful coastal river which curves in front of it for many years. Its new brick have been given a coat of whitewash, which lends it a mellow air of age and the thousands of blossoming flowers and shrubs surrounding it have actually taken years for the growing—but not in the spots where they now bloom. . . .
>
> The new building is of stately design, with a wing on either end, and contains eighteen rooms. Hundreds of azaleas and japonica bushes are in full bloom just now, making of the Corning estate a veritable fairyland.

Warren Corning sold Clarendon in 1944, two years before his father's death. Later owners were Julius A. White and his wife of New York, who bought it in 1947 and retained the place for almost twenty years. They sold it in 1966 to the Cox family of Atlanta, members of which still own it.

# Clay Hall, Nieuport

(also Green Point)

"Dis place ain't de same since Jedus done come and tuck Mr. Redmond up to Heaven to be wid He."

Becky Frazier, ancient black crone, stood in the door of her cabin at Nieuport Plantation on the Combahee river, where generations of her ancestors had stood before her, and tears glistened brightly in her eyes as she said the words of praise for G. L. Redmond, owner of several large plantations on this river, who died suddenly in Paris in May of this year.

"It was jest like slavery time when Mr. Redmond was livin'. He opened up he heart to us colored people. Come Christmas, he send for all we to come to Clay Hall and he gi'e us all present and ting and tell us he de big boss. Yes'um, us all lub Mr. Redmond and we too sorry Jedus had to carry him up to Heaven."

A bright kerchief around her head, her skirt tied at intervals around her body to keep it from trailing the ground, Becky did not know that she was among the last of the colorful pictures distinctive of the coastal country.

The cabin, in whose doorway she stood while the November sun glinted on her ebony face, is so old that Becky herself cannot remember when it wasn't there, although, she says, it was here when the "big gun shoot down on Hilton Head." Beyond that, Becky is hazy as to her own age.

As a matter of fact, there is nobody in the entire country who can remember when Becky's cabin and the three others that stand beside it in a row, all alike as are four peas in a pod, were not there. The cabins date back before the Revolutionary war and just how far beyond that there seems to be no reliable local authority.

The cabins are fashioned entirely of old English brick. They are patched here and there with tabby. Two of them are occupied by negro families and the other two are used as storage places for grain. All save one are in an excellent state of preservation and the

Original title: "Clay Hall, Redmond Mansion Lodge. Furnished with a World Collection, This Seventeen-Room House Overlooks the Lazy Combahee in Beaufort." Publication date: December 7, 1930.

fourth is intact with the exception of a few brick which appear to have been removed. Each cabin was originally one big room with a large fireplace, the brick being white-washed on the interior.

Becky's praise for Mr. Redmond was merely couched in different words from that of the others who were in his employ. He seemed to have been universally loved and respected by the people on both of his big plantations and his sudden passing at the age of 36 brought real sorrow to his people, although they had known him but briefly.

### Buys Two Plantations

When Mr. Redmond bought Nieuport and Clay Hall plantations in March of last year, it was the first time in Becky Frazier's lifetime, she says, that the plantation on which she lived had belonged to anyone save the Cheves family of Charleston.

At Clay Hall plantation, which is several miles up the road from Nieuport plantation, Mr. Redmond built a handsome hunting lodge which is said to have cost about $175,000.

The house, which is of New England Colonial type of architecture, is built of brick taken from two old rice mills which were found on the plantations. These are English brick and are very old, giving the place, although new, a time-worn appearance.

The house is entirely fire-proof, being built three walls deep. The brick from the old rice mills was used for the outer and inner walls, while the middle wall was made of new brick.

The lodge is of one-story construction, extending into long wings on either side. There are sturdy white columns on the porch in the center of the building and white blinds. The house is only about a year old, being barely completed when Mr. Redmond died. There are seventeen rooms in the house, all of them exquisitely furnished.

### Handsome Old Mantels

In order to secure the desired timbers for his gun room, Mr. Redmond purchased a house near Augusta, which was over a hundred years old, had it dismantled and the timbers moved to Clay Hall. There are handsome old mantels picked up here and there in his travels about the world. The house contains not a modern piece of furniture, all of it being rare old pieces bought in this country and in Europe. The rooms are plastered on the interior with the exception of the gun room, which is ceiled with yellow pine.

Clay Hall is situated at the end of a long country road, past a great gate and a vanguard of negro cabins. It nestles in the shadow of great moss-shrouded oaks and palmettos. It is surrounded, just now, with a carpet of emerald green and gleaming in the sun, just down a little slope, the lazy Combahee winds its way.

To the left is a cottage for the caretaker and at the side of that, the stables and dog kennels.

And there it sits, all new and lovely—and empty.

"And the trouble is," commented the young caretaker sadly, "Nobody seems to want it. Mr. Redmond loved it all so, I used to walk with him about the woods and fields and he never tired of it. Every now and then he would say: 'Ernest, I like it better every day.'"

Clay Hall, circa 1930s. *From John R. Todd and Francis M. Hutson,*
*Prince William's Parish and Plantations, 1935*

At Nieuport plantation there is a low, rambling white building which has just been freshly painted and re-roofed. It was used as a hospital during the yellow fever epidemic and it was Mr. Redmond's plan to preserve it as a memorial. It was undergoing repairs, at his orders, while he was in Paris in the spring and he cabled directions holding up further repairs for the time being.

At Nieuport, also, Mr. Redmond had just completed a handsome home for his superintendent, T. D. Ravenel. This house overlooks a little tidal creek along which, now, are reflected for miles the red and yellow glory of low-growing bushes and vines. The riot of color makes this part of the world look like a gypsy carnival.

The Redmond estate comprises more than four hundred acres of land, practically all of which is used as a hunting preserve.

At Nieuport and Clay Hall, the new has been delightfully blended with the old, the comforts of the one and the charm of the other uniting to create an atmosphere that is altogether charming.

One is saddened that the man who fashioned all this, not only for himself but for posterity, should have been privileged to enjoy it so briefly, but is cheered by the hope that the new hands into which it falls will be as kindly.

**Green Point Plantation**

Another pretty little estate on the Combahee, not far from Clay Hall plantation is Green Point plantation, owned by James H. Kidder. However, the place is listed on the tax books of Beaufort county under the name of the Bank of New York and Trust Company.

One is directed to Green Point plantation by a neat sign at the turn of the road. The attractive, small lodge is approached over a long, winding road and is situated at the end of it on a little rise of ground surrounded by grass and large oaks.

The lodge contains ten or twelve rooms and presents a homey look as though it would be ideal for a year-round place in which to live.

The tract contains 909 acres of land.

Mr. Kidder came to this section about ten years ago and has made many friends during his visits here. ✒

---

The history of Nieuport (or Newport, New Port, or Niewport, as the Middletons used several different spellings over the years) is more thoroughly recorded than that of any other plantation on the Combahee. Mr. Langdon Cheves III of Charleston, the last of the Middleton heirs to own the place, was a passionate keeper of records about property, including their related histories and expenses. These records are archived at the South Carolina Historical Society. Thanks to Mr. Cheves, we know a great deal about Nieuport in the period from 1873, when his grandfather took title to it, until the sale to Mr. Redmond in 1929. At the time of the sale the tract amounted to 3,670 acres.

The plantation had been in the Middleton family as far back as 1760, when it was one of the rice plantations of the Hon. Henry Middleton (1717–1784), president of the Continental Congress. It passed to his son Arthur (1742–1787), signer of the Declaration of Independence, and then to his grandson Gov. Henry Middleton (1770–1846). The value of Nieuport was one hundred thousand dollars in 1850, but the Civil War left it in ruinous condition. Its residence, mill, and barns were all destroyed in a series of raids that devastated many of the Combahee River plantations.

In November 1861 Union forces advancing up the Beaufort River from Port Royal Sound quickly occupied the town of Beaufort, routing the white citizens, who fled inland. By the spring of 1862 Port Royal Island and the adjacent Sea Islands were under the control of the Union army. St. Helena Sound and the mouth of the Combahee River lay to the northeast. Along the Combahee were some of the most valuable and productive rice plantations in the state, all of which were soon vulnerable to seizure or destruction as the war progressed. Planters were urged to remove their black workers to prevent them from going over to the enemy. Not all planters were willing to comply, as the profits from the crops continued to rise. Moreover the expense and particularly the logistics of resettling a large number of workers encouraged postponing a decision.

Thus in the spring of 1863 rice on the Combahee was flourishing in defiance of the Yankees ten miles away in Beaufort. It could hardly have been imagined that a black woman, recently come to the area, was intent on leading to freedom the enslaved members of her own race then working the rice plantations.

Harriet Tubman was in her early forties at the time. She had been born in slavery on a Maryland plantation, and the date of her birth was not recorded. If any single occurrence in that unjust system turned her away from resigned servitude, it was witnessing the sale "to the South" of two of her sisters. Tubman slipped away from her owner in 1849 and was thereafter a fugitive.

When she came to Beaufort on a Union ship in 1862, she had already accomplished a number of bold rescues in the North, taking her charges into free states or to Canada. Gov. John Andrew of Massachusetts, who knew of Tubman's success as a conductor on the Underground Railroad, where she was known as "Moses," asked her to join a group of northern volunteers going to Hilton Head to assist the large number of freedmen settling on the island. Though Mrs. Tubman was unable to read or write, she possessed a remarkable sense of human possibilities and a clever turn of mind that carried her through the most challenging adversities. She served as a nurse at the freedmen's hospital at Port Royal, making many contacts among the newly freed slaves, from whom she learned the lay of the land.

The black workers on the Combahee were aware of the Yankees at Beaufort from the heavy gunfire to the south and the numerous rumors circulating on the plantations. Three Union gunboats headed up the river on June 2, 1863, with a crew of more than three hundred soldiers and a lone woman, and when they came to shore at the ferry landing at Nieuport plantation, a crowd of anxious fugitives was waiting to come aboard.

A record of this day of liberation and destruction comes from the letters of two young Confederate soldiers, sons of Combahee planters, writing to their families on the day after the raid. "The last raid has been perfectly terrible," reported William Mason Smith. "Uncle Lowndes [of Oakland] has lost nearly 300 negroes. . . . Mr. Kirkland [Rose Hill] and Mrs. Nichols [Long Brow] everyone except a little boy and a dying woman, their dwelling, mills and everything else . . . and Mr. Wm. C. Heyward [Cypress], 200, his dwelling, mill & out building. . . . The destruction is terrible. . . . The marauders were entirely negroes, led by white chiefs."

Walter Blake of Bonny Hall gave a similar account: "The Yankees came up to Combahee Ferry yesterday morning with two gun boats & broke up the pontoon bridge, burning all of the houses up to that point & carrying off all the negroes. . . . They carried away all the negroes from New Port and from Uncle William C. Heyward & burnt the dwelling houses. . . . The Yankees found out that this country was undefended & came to destroy the crops & carry off the negroes. I suppose they must have got nearly 300." An official count indicates that 750 people were freed.

Near the end of her life, Mrs. Tubman said, "My train was always on time and I never lost a passenger." The Combahee raid was her greatest single success as a conductor. The new bridge on Highway 17 crossing the Combahee at the old ferry landing on Nieuport has been named in her honor.

After the war Mr. Henry A. Middleton (1793–1887) held a fifty-thousand-dollar mortgage on Nieuport, and as the debt could not be paid, he accepted the plantation even though its value was now only a fraction of that amount. It was at Nieuport in May 1876 that the rice-field workers first went out on strike. Four months of battles followed, some of them violent, between the plantation owners and the laborers. In August the strike spread to Clay Hall, among many other plantations.

At Henry Middleton's death in 1887, the property went to his six daughters. The heirs requested partition, and four of the daughters, Harriott and Alice Middleton, Isabella Cheves, and Annie M. Hunter, bid to keep the property in the family, adding to it Blandford, Clay Hall (the old Heyward place), Dawson's, Elliott's, and part of Green Point in 1892.

Langdon Cheves III and his brother Henry supervised the successful planting of rice under the active management of Mr. W. F. Colcock, known in his day as "The Lion of Combahee" for his exceptional skill as a rice planter. He served the Middleton-Cheves family for thirty-four years before retiring in 1913. Rice planting was gradually phased out, the last crop harvested in 1923.

According to Mr. Geraldwyn L. Redmond's obituary in the *New York Times*, he was a resident of Long Island and had served in World War I with the U.S. Flying Corps. Through his mother he was a member of one of New York's oldest families, directly descended from Robert Livingston, who had settled in the seventeenth century on the Hudson River on what became known as the "Manor of Livingston." (Livingston "was known as the first Lord of the Manor.") After Mr. Redmond's death, his wife, who favored Aiken as a winter home, put the plantation on the market.

The buyer was Percy K. Hudson, a member of the New York Stock Exchange. He was active in the exchange until 1921, then intermittently so until 1936. Through his gold-mining interests in South Africa he arranged a safari in the Serengeti Game Reserve in Kenya and returned home with forty-four animal heads for his private collection. He later presented this collection to the Beaufort Museum. Unfortunately the skins were found to have been treated with arsenic by the taxidermist and were disposed of.

In 1942 Hudson, who had once operated a coffee plantation in Guatemala, established a home there. Two years later he became a citizen of that country. In 1945 he sold Nieuport plantation to the Carolina Laurentian Company, of which Eugene du Pont was president. Nonetheless, Hudson maintained ties with the lowcountry. When the *New York Times* reported his death in 1962, it claimed, "He died in Clay Hall, Yemassee, S.C." He was buried in Savannah's Bonaventure Cemetery. The Du Pont family still owns Nieuport and has established the Nemours Wildlife Foundation to manage their ninety-eight hundred acres of land and sustain the wildlife there.

The T. D. Ravenel whom Mrs. Martin mentions is Theodore D. Ravenel, formerly a principal owner of Laurel Spring plantation across the Combahee from Nieuport. (For more on Ravenel, see Mrs. Martin's article on Laurel Spring.)

The Kidder family money came from a successful coal and tar business in New York, where James Kidder was born in 1869. The family was also associated with the founding of the New York Stock Exchange. Mr. Kidder attended Harvard, after which he seems to have led an independent life, given over principally to hunting large game. Expeditions took him to South America, Mexico, Europe, and the Middle East. In the 1890s he spent several years in Alaska, where he shot the largest Kodiak bear on record. He had it mounted and later exhibited at the Smithsonian Institution. On another trip he discovered a bear that had never before been identified; it was given the name "Kidder" bear in his honor. He hunted with his friend Theodore Roosevelt and knew the western writer Zane Grey. In Beaufort his pal and "local financial administrator" was Sheriff J. E. McTeer.

Mr. Kidder bought Green Point in 1922. He filled his house with a collection of medieval arms and weapons, his own rifles and shotguns of the finest craftsmanship, and antique furniture and valuable books. In about 1929 he purchased Cow-Pen's Point on Edisto Island, about a mile from Edingsville Beach. Green Point was sold in 1946, and Mr. Kidder bought a house in Beaufort. A few years later, because of declining health, he moved to Charleston to be near his daughter. He died there in 1956. The property is now part of the Du Ponts' Nemours plantation.

# *Coffin Point*

One of the very first men from the north to become sufficiently interested in the coastal section of South Carolina as to cause him to want to make his home here was the late Senator J. Donald Cameron, of Pennsylvania.

This was more than 30 years ago and although the senator has been dead for about 17 years, the proof of his love for his island home in Beaufort county remains in the provisions of his will. Throughout all the years since his death, the handsome Cameron estate at the end of St. Helena Island has been maintained and properly cared for.

Senator Cameron became interested in this section through his friend, the late Admiral Beardsley, who himself left a beautiful home in the town of Beaufort, which is still one of the show places.

Senator Cameron was at that time chairman of the naval committee and the present Cameron home was then being used as a club by a number of naval officers from Parris island, among them being Admiral Beardsley.

Senator Cameron purchased this house after the club was disbanded, and used to spend about four months of each year there. He usually came down in a boat, bringing a number of his friends.

## House 150 Years Old

The house, which is said to be more than 150 years old, formerly belonged to Thomas Aston Coffin and was one of the big plantation homes of the low country prior to the Confederate war. The Coffins left their home about the time of the war and never returned. However, the place is still known as Coffin's Point.

The house has been added to and enlarged but there has been little actual change in the original building. The Coffin home was narrower, being only one room deep. What is now the front of the house was at that time the back and is said to be very little different in appearance. However, considerable change has been made at the back of the

Original title: "The Cameron Estate on St. Helena. Pennsylvania Senator, Pioneer Purchaser, of Coastal Plantations for Winter Residence, Chose Barrier Island Site Deserted by Coffin Family in Sixties." Publication date: December 14, 1930.

Two views of Coffin Point. *Top: 2008, photograph courtesy of Robert B. Cuthbert; bottom: 2007, photograph courtesy of Lisa Hayes*

house, used then as the front because it faced the water and boats were used to reach the place.

The house is three stories high. It is peculiarly arranged on the interior, arched doors and small bay windows featuring the two front rooms. The walls are papered in quaint designs. The paneling is hand-carved and the mouldings lovely. The graceful, curving staircase, although painters of recent years made a mistake and painted it white, is in reality a fine piece of mahogany.

### House Up Avenue

The front porch is reached by wide, winding stairs on either side and the upstairs front porch gives upon a view that is breathtakingly lovely at this time of the year when the island trees are shot with red and yellow and purplish smears in the distance. The house is approached after a long rough ride across the entire island, through great wooden gates, and up a long wide avenue of trees, with fields on either side.

From the upstairs porch, the long avenue is soon lost in the trees, only the tops of them finally visible, looking in the fall like so many gaily colored balls that blur into each other.

At the back of the house is a wide open porch on the first floor and upstairs a sun porch encased in glass. From this porch one can see over the tops of the giant oak trees that lead down to a high bluff, from which the river drops sheerly, and far down St. Helena sound.

To one side is Hunting Island with its lighthouse. Almost directly in front is a blot upon the water which is Egg Island. This island is government property and is kept in reserve solely for the use of birds. In spring the island is said to be so thick with eggs that a step cannot be made without crushing them. Caretakers at the Cameron place say that sometimes there are so many birds on the island that they look like smoke coming out of the water when they rise. No one is allowed to molest these birds and their eggs.

### Butterflies in Spring

The Cameron place is plentiful with gorgeous butterflies, too, in the spring, and is often visited by collectors of birds and butterflies.

At the back of the house, with great limbs almost brushing the walls, is an immense live oak with a spread of 95 feet. The grounds, during the first Mrs. Cameron's lifetime, were said to have been exquisitely lovely. Even now, in the spring, it is worth seeing for the thousands of narcissus and lily bulbs, which were planted long ago in a wide circle surrounding the entire place, come to life and fill the air with fragrance. A walk of oyster shell, made years ago, is still faintly visible and outlines the beds of flowers.

Several years ago the handsome furniture in the Cameron house was sold at auction and since then the many rooms have been empty. Each year workmen come, do what repairs are needed and go away again. The big house and the other buildings on the place have just been given a fresh coat of paint, the colonial yellow, which was the color that Senator Cameron always chose, with trimmings of white.

Even though the two upper stories are empty, there is to be found interest aplenty in the basement, which, in itself, is large enough to house a good-sized family.

### Mammoth Ice Box

The basement is enclosed at the back by a thick, high tabby wall, approached by a cool, latticed porch. Entering the door, one finds to the right probably the largest ice box he has ever seen. It was evidently made on the plantation and would fill a room of modern proportions.

In the great kitchen is an ancient plantation stove, dark red with the rust of years, but still intact. It takes up one entire side of the room and seems to have been built into the wall. The stove has two fire boxes with a large oven on either side. There is a piece of wood, partly burned, sticking out of the top of the stove.

Out in the hall of the basement is a large furnace, which was evidently used to heat the entire house. There is also to be seen the old laundry room with its stationary tubs and tall linen closet.

At the front of the basement is a little room, which would be strange appearing to this Volstead generation. It is the old wine cellar. There is a hospitable looking outer room and a smaller inner sanctum with many shelves and cupboards and a trusty stout door in which swings a rusty, useless lock.

Walking down the wide path at the back of the house, one comes to an old-fashioned picturesque stile. Up one side and down the other and there is the beach at the foot of a little cliff.

The ceaseless beating through the years of the water against this cliff has driven the land farther and farther back upon itself. Now, however, many logs have been placed as a protection against the pounding waves.

On this long stretch of beach, the scenery changes three times. At one end is a clump of palmettos and such luxuriant growth that it is like a scene in some tropical country. Another part is like a miniature desert and the third is just an ordinary beach.

### 800 Pecan Trees

The place is cared for by C. S. Steinmeyer, who lives with his family in an attractive house close to the big one. Mr. Steinmeyer farms 260 acres of the land and takes care of the 800 pecan trees on the place. Mrs. Steinmeyer is interested in turkeys and hopes by next year to have a regular turkey farm.

This is all of the place that is visible to the eyes of a visitor, but there is something else quite hidden except from those who know. There are two charming little cottages so tucked away into the deep woods by the water that, once there, the world seems to drop away and one loses sight of time and space.

These cottages, also painted a colonial yellow, were built by Senator Cameron for use by different members of his family. One of them has a porch entirely around the house. Entrance is made into a quaint living room with a red brick fireplace at one end, equipped with a tea kettle crane. There are two small rooms off from this and up the narrowest, most picture-book stairs are two wee rooms, one of them fashioned exactly like a ship's cabin. There are windows that swing outward and, perched upon a window sill, one looks down through the tree tops into the gray waters of St. Helena Sound. There is not a sound here, save the call of a bird in the distance and the faint whisper of tree to tree.  ✄

Coffin Point (the current spelling) has one of the richest histories of all the plantations Mrs. Martin wrote about—or, indeed, of all plantations in the lowcountry. An intriguing cast of characters has peopled the property over two centuries.

When twenty-seven-year-old Ebenezer Coffin of Boston arrived in Charleston in the early 1790s, he intended to establish a mercantile career. His future was to change, however, when he married Mary Mathews, the daughter of Benjamin Mathews of St. John Colleton, a prosperous planter. Mathews settled his 1,120-acre Point plantation on St. Helena Island and sixty-three black workers on his daughter in trust for her children. Coffin set about building on the property, and by 1802 or soon thereafter the residence was ready for occupancy. He proved himself a successful businessman and planter, and on his death in 1818 he left a substantial estate to his and Mary's six children, to be held in equal undivided shares.

Coffin's son Thomas Aston Coffin, twenty-three at the time, assumed management of the estate for the heirs. An astute planter, by a careful selection of seed he was able to maintain the highest-quality crops. He earned a reputation as the most successful planter on St. Helena. A Harvard education, an extensive library that impressed a Union officer looking through the abandoned house at Coffin Point in 1862, a Charleston house, and a summer place at Newport, Rhode Island, suggest that the family was more cosmopolitan than many of their neighbors.

Over the years Coffin increased the family holdings with the purchase of two additional plantations: Cherry Hill, of 255 acres; and the 200-acre McTureous property. For himself he bought William Grayson's Frogmore plantation of 2,139 acres, with 170 black workers.

In early November 1861 word quickly spread on the island that the Union fleet was advancing from Port Royal Sound and the Confederate defenders were retreating. The planters on the islands and the citizens of Beaufort gathered a few clothes and other immediate necessities for their families and fled to the mainland; most never returned. Cmdr. Samuel Francis du Pont of the Union fleet reported, "every white inhabitant has left the island." When Edward L. Pierce, a Treasury Department agent, went to Coffin Point in 1862, he found 260 black workers on the plantation but not a single white person.

Thomas Coffin died in Charleston in 1863, leaving a wife and three children. In his will he claimed only thirty-five black workers as his own. Listed are a large number of securities, bonds, notes, and the house at Newport, but all the St. Helena lands had been confiscated.

With the capture of Port Royal, federal authorities found themselves guardians of ten thousand freedmen. The Treasury Department under Salmon Chase took over jurisdiction of the abandoned plantations and the welfare of the freedmen. Land superintendents and missionaries from the North came down to "train the contraband for civilization" in what became known as the "Port Royal Experiment." They were mostly idealistic young men and women, college graduates dedicated to helping the freedmen adjust to their new independence. The men were charged with supervising the planting of cotton on the confiscated plantations, hoping to demonstrate the superiority of wage labor over the old forced-labor system. The missionaries, most of them women, were to teach reading, arithmetic, writing, housekeeping, health, and religion. In compliance with the Federal Direct Tax Act of 1862, the land abandoned by the planters, on which taxes had not been paid, was to be sold.

Despite the good intentions of many people, the Port Royal Experiment was deemed unsuccessful. The effort was marked by mutual antagonisms, misunderstandings between freedmen and their benefactors, and mistreatment and lack of sympathy for the freedmen by the military, which was impatient for results. Edith M. Dabbs, in *Sea Island Diary: A History of St. Helena Island,* wrote: "Most workers felt that in spite of all their efforts, the humanitarian experiment was a failure."

Edward Philbrick, a thirty-four-year-old Boston engineer and architect, came south in 1862 with the first group of superintendents and missionaries. At Coffin Point he was in charge of the government's experiment in cotton planting with free wage laborers. When the plan was terminated and the land put up for sale, Philbrick—earnest in his desire to help the freedmen become self-supporting citizens and fearing that the plantations would be bought at auction by speculators to the exclusion of the freedmen—arranged, with the support of a group of northern men, to buy eleven of the properties, including Coffin Point. He assigned the freedmen as much acreage as they could reasonably plant in cotton, paying them for their labor and the cotton he sold.

However, Philbrick was no more successful than the government had been. By 1865, "with many vexations and losses," he decided to sell the land, some to white men from the North and many small tracts to African Americans. Philbrick returned to Boston in the fall of 1865. He is credited with giving the black residents of St. Helena a "headstart in citizenship," and his dedication to helping them cannot be doubted. Detractors later charged, however, that he sold the land for several times more than he paid for it, making a large profit for himself. A cursory look at land records in Beaufort County shows at least 136 properties on St. Helena in Philbrick's name sold in the decades after the war.

In 1889 a local newspaper reporter interviewed Pennsylvania senator J. Donald Cameron (1833–1918), who had been in the Beaufort area. He was prospecting for land for, as he put it, sporting purposes—hunting and fishing—to relieve the pressures of business and political responsibilities. By the fall of 1891 Cameron had found what he was looking for; he bought a one-third interest in Coffin Point, 298 acres, later securing an additional 634 acres.

Cameron was a significant national figure. His father, Simon Cameron (1779–1899), a powerful man in Pennsylvania politics, served as secretary of war in President Lincoln's cabinet, in the U.S. Senate, and briefly as minister to Russia. He also organized and controlled a Pennsylvania bank and the Northern Central Railroad. After graduating from Princeton in 1852, young Cameron took charge of a number of his father's business interests, becoming president of the bank and the railroad, allowing his father more time to advance himself politically.

When in 1876 a vacancy occurred in President Grant's cabinet, Simon Cameron used his influence to have his son appointed secretary of war. His service, however, was brief, as President Hayes, elected the next year, objected to the Camerons' political methods and refused to reappoint the son. His father, in a crafty move, resigned his own seat in the Senate and pressured the state legislature to appoint his son to fill out the term. An observer noted that "a more striking example of entrenched political power could hardly be found." Don Cameron served twenty years in the Senate, until 1897, including, as Mrs. Martin notes, several years as chairman of the Committee on Naval Affairs. Both father and son were shrewd, ambitious, powerful men, but unlike his father, Don Cameron was never blemished by corruption.

There was always great excitement at Coffin Point when Senator Cameron came south for the winter. As his great yacht entered St. Helena Sound, the vessel's whistle started blowing, alerting all the plantation residents of his arrival. They were at the dock to welcome him, and to receive the silver coins he liked to pass out in a gesture of munificence as he stepped ashore. He was remembered for high-stakes poker games and high-style entertainment; Broadway showgirls are mentioned. Beaufort sheriff J. E. McTeer, writing of Cameron in this respect, placed him in the company of Arthur Barnwell of Pleasant Point and William Copp at Spring Island.

Coffin Point remained in the Cameron family for many years, though it was rarely occupied. The Cameron family held on to the property until 1952, when the trustees of the estate sold the 932 acres to Sheriff McTeer.

McTeer had served as sheriff of Beaufort County since 1926, when at age twenty-three he was appointed to fill the unexpired term of his father. He was the youngest man in the country to hold that office and served for thirty-seven years. McTeer described that period in *High Sheriff of the Low Country,* one of the four books he wrote about this part of South Carolina. He possessed the natural talent of a raconteur, and his slim volume is still to be found on booksellers' shelves. Speaking of him in the introduction to the book, Judge W. L. Rhodes said that McTeer had "an almost legendary stature in Beaufort County . . . tall, ruggedly handsome, McTeer personified 'The Law' in Beaufort County."

All but overshadowing the sheriff's career in law enforcement has been his calling as "Dr. Root." His interest in the subject of witchcraft and voodoo came of his association with the Gullah people of the lowcountry, where there were both believers and practitioners. McTeer's outwitting of Dr. Buzzard (a black man by the name of Stepheney Robinson), "the most authentic and powerful of all Beaufort witch doctors," helped him gain knowledge of some of Dr. Buzzard's most potent black magic. However, McTeer never practiced the dark side of the occult and said emphatically that he never harmed an innocent person. He had witnessed the disabling and sometimes mortal effects of black magic on those susceptible to its power, and he used his "white magic," as he called it, to remove hexes and spells, relieving the frightful anxiety of the sufferers. His knowledge was taken seriously, and his advice was often sought by medical professionals.

By the time McTeer bought Coffin Point, the days of cotton planting were in the past, but the land was suitable for livestock: cattle, pigs, and chickens. He improved the property with three spring-fed lakes. A few years later McTeer began laying out residential lots at Coffin Point. Hurricane Gracie in 1959 caused extensive damage to most residences on

St. Helena, including Coffin Point. Mrs. Martin wrote in her "Lowcountry Gossip" column in 1961 that after the storm the McTeers had moved into the old overseer's house while they decided whether—and later how—the house could be restored. Eventually two rooms that had collapsed when a beam broke were removed. After the sheriff retired in 1963, real estate became his new career.

The old Coffin house was sold in 1969 to George and Priscilla Johnson McMillan, both noted authors. He wrote *The Making of an Assassin: The Life of James Earl Ray* (1976); she translated of the letters of Svetlana Alliluyeva, daughter of Josef Stalin (1967), and wrote *Marina and Lee* (1977), about the marriage of Kennedy assassin Lee Harvey Oswald and his Russian-born wife. Once the center of a 1,120-acre plantation, the house sat on a lot of less than four acres. Under the care of the McMillans (including McMillan's later wife, Cecily, also an author), the house has been maintained, and it has remained much the same for more than 150 years. The view from the porch across the water is as outstanding as Mrs. Martin reported in 1930.

Sheriff McTeer died in 1979. The death notice in the newspaper said that he had succumbed to pneumonia, emphysema, and the complications of old age (he was seventy-six). However, the rumor spread through Beaufort that the high sheriff had gotten on the bad side of a powerful witch doctor from the Caribbean, who had come to the area not long before McTeer began to fail, and that a little black magic may have been involved in his demise.

Like most journalists, Mrs. Martin and her newspaper's typesetters occasionally battled. Paragraphs or sentences of this article were chopped off, and apparently Mrs. Martin did not have a chance to edit them. The editors of this volume have silently corrected all those incomplete sentences when they were able. The last sentence of this article, however, presents more difficulties. In the newspaper it read, "Outside, the friendly path coaxes into the world for a little way and then, as though losing interest in its own mission. . . . " More black magic?

# *Cotton Hall*

Harry Payne Bingham of New York, with Mrs. Bingham, have been paying a short visit to their magnificent newly completed home at Cotton Hall plantation.

It was the first time that Mr. Bingham had seen his place completed and as he visited over his property, now on horse back, now afoot, he seemed as enthusiastic as a boy.

The house was so brand new that the interior decorator was still there, the contractors had not gone and the landscape gardeners had barely begun their work on the grounds which at the time were so muddy from recent heavy rains that they had been unable to make any headway.

Cotton Hall plantation is located near the vicinity of the ruins of the Old Sheldon church and is about twenty-four miles from Beaufort. It comprises around 1,300 acres of land and was owned, until it was sold to Mr. Bingham about the first of the year, by Henry Rast.

At one time the property was owned by George Martin and the new house is erected upon the site of the home of George C. Heyward, which was destroyed by Sherman's troops during the Confederate war.

### House of 26 Rooms

The Bingham home, which was built by Clarke & Clarke, of Savannah, is of New England Colonial type of architecture. It is painted white and has twenty-six rooms and nine baths. The main part of the building is two stories and it spreads out into long, low wings on either side. The front is fashioned of brick, painted so as to simulate age. There is a little rail balcony, reminding of Romeo and Juliet, at the front, two sturdy white columns and a shiny brass knocker. The heavy wooden shutters are painted green and there are two great chimneys at either end of the main part of the house.

From the back of the house, which, however, will be used as the front by the Binghams, it is said, there is to be had an excellent view of the old rice fields.

Original title: "20-acre Lawn to Surround Bingham House in Beaufort. New Yorker Builds 26-Room Mansion at Cotton Hall Plantation on Site of George C. Heyward Home Destroyed by Sherman." Publication date: December 2, 1930.

Cotton Hall. *Photograph by Ned Brown, courtesy of Barton and Barton*

Inside, the house is happily furnished. The halls and stairs are papered, the arresting green designs upon a white background being reminiscent of early American life.

The furniture is of maple, mahogany and other dark woods and shows, also, here and there, the atmosphere of early America. The dining and living rooms have great windows giving upon the old rice fields. The living room is bright and cheerful throughout and the dining room is accentuated with blue. There is another smaller living room, also facing the rice fields, which is particularly delightful. This room, ceiled with polished knotty pine, is designed especially for use on dark and dreary days. Its windows are draped with a heavy opalescent material which is like a flaming sunset. The lamps, here and there, are like spots of glowing embers, lighting the somber walls.

### Bright Colors Prevail

The bedrooms are entrancingly gay. From one a splash of yellow leaps out like the sunshine. In another there is a flash of vivid blue like that in the deepness of a still lake. In each adjoining bath, bright colors blend and weave their charm.

The furnishing of the entire interior of the house was designed and executed by Schuyler L. Parsons and Marguerite S. Valk, interior decorators at 78 Church street, Charleston. These decorators had in view continuously while at their work the idea of securing the maximum of taste at the minimum of cost. They boast proudly that the dainty curtains for this room cost only this much and the rich bedcovers for another room cost only that much.

Outside are dog kennels which well might be the envy of the other dogs of the country-side.

The house is situated back from the grove of great old live oaks rather than among the trees as so many houses of this section are placed. It is said that Mr. Bingham preferred to look at the trees from a little distance instead of having them crowded close about him.

The Bingham home is approached after leaving the public highway over a new clay road and the white house gleaming through the trees presents a most pleasing picture to the visitor approaching Cotton Hall.

Twenty acres surrounding the house will be planted in lawn grass, which will extend to the very edge of the ancient rice fields. Camellia japonicas and azaleas will be featured in the garden.

It is rumored that Mr. Bingham has spent in the neighborhood of $200,000 on his property at Cotton Hall and will enjoy it mostly for hunting purposes. He is expected to return some time the early part of December, for another visit. ✣

The land now known as Cotton Hall had been the property of the McPherson family as early as 1784. Daniel Heyward (1810–1888) bought it in 1832. He is described in his kinsman James Heyward's book on the family as a man with "a high order of mentality . . . good education enriched with much good literature and polished with culture of fine arts" and with plenty of "common sense and executed ability." Such is attested to by the fact that after the ruin of the Civil War he was quickly able to adjust to the new system of labor and within a few years had recovered much of his lost fortune.

Heyward conveyed Cotton Hall to his daughter Anne, wife of Charles F. Hanckel, in 1882. She sold the 997-acre property to George G. Martin and Charles C. J. Hutson the year after her father's death. When Henry Rast bought the plantation in 1917, he added to it the 372-acre Laurium, originally part of the McPherson property.

In 1930 John K. Hollins of New York, the son of Harry B. Hollins and active in real estate in Beaufort and Jasper counties, bought Cotton Hall and Laurium. The two properties at that time measured 1,797 acres. (The Hollinses eventually acquired some fifty parcels, as recorded in the Beaufort County Register of Mesne Conveyance.) John Hollins sold Cotton Hall and Laurium the same year to Harry Payne Bingham of New York.

Bingham (1888–1955), whose first cousin Payne Whitney had owned land on the Combahee River since 1923, was a nephew of Col. Oliver Payne, one of John D. Rockefeller's early partners in Standard Oil, which put him in good standing both socially and in business. Bingham's father, William Bingham, headed the family hardware manufacturing company in Cleveland. Harry Payne Bingham graduated from Harvard in 1912, served in World War I, and eventually settled in New York. He was successful as a banker and became well enough established to have been named a trustee of several major institutions, including the Metropolitan Museum, the American Museum of Natural History, and the New York Zoological Society.

Outside business, Bingham's great interest was marine biology. He sailed the waters of southern Florida, the Caribbean, and California gathering three thousand specimens, which he donated to Yale in 1930. He also funded the Bingham Oceanographic Foundation. "Philanthropist, Sportsman, Art Patron" was the way the *New York Times* summed up his accomplishments in 1955. In April 1946 Bingham sold Cotton Hall, Laurium, and 6,777 additional acres of land in Hampton County to L. J. Williams.

Williams held onto Cotton Hall and Laurium for only two years before he sold the property to Harold W. Allen, who in turn passed them on to Atlanta and Savannah businessman Robert Edward Turner II in 1959. Turner had made a fortune with his Atlanta billboard-oriented advertising agency, but after he committed suicide in 1963 at his nearby Bindon plantation home, his twenty-four year-old son, Robert Edward Turner III, known as Ted, took over the family business. Ted Turner sold Cotton Hall to the Rural Land Company, Inc., of Greenville, South Carolina. In 1970 he merged his father's old billboard company with Rice Broadcasting, and began a long involvement in television that eventually led to the development of a media empire, including the CNN news network, which made Turner one of the most successful businessmen in the country. Part of his wealth was invested in land, most notably more than two million acres in the West. In 1978 he purchased Hope plantation in Colleton County, returning to the South Carolina coast that his father had loved. His holdings in South Carolina have been estimated at more than ten thousand acres.

# Cuthbert Point

(Pleasant Point)

Though he travel far and climb to high places, a low countryman, in his heart, remains ever faithful to the lowlands. The roar of mighty cities can never quite drown in his ears the swish of water along a beach. The smell of marsh grass creeps in unguarded moments through the mingled perfumes and stench of crowded places. Mirage like a long, clean sweep of sea and sky can blot out in a twinkling the confusion of tall, zigzagging buildings.

Years of eating hunger for the place of one's nativity cause the thoughts more and more to turn homeward and, at last, the steps with them.

This is the thing that has happened to Arthur Barnwell.

Born in Charleston, but closely welded by family connection to the Beaufort country, he heard the call of ambition as a youth. Ambition is a sorceress, inflaming her subjects with desire. She is a will-o'-the-wisp that they follow exultantly, hunters all, until wearied of the chase, they turn yearningly home.

## Builds Beaufort Playhouse

Arthur Barnwell was a wary hunter. He refused to be outwitted by the lying jade. He had fun, is still having it, but having got what he thought he wanted, he finds there still an unsatisfied hunger in his heart.

The New York stock exchange, fascinating though it may be, has not the power to possess a man of Arthur Barnwell's caliber. The call of gray, winding waters and undulating marshes is low but persistent. It beats a tattoo against the brain and wins, finally, over the strident voice of ambition.

But there was something else that tugged at the heart of Arthur Barnwell, a need more vital than that for the romance of the coast. This need was the feel of the saltwater on

Original title: "Arthur Barnwell Spends Wall Street Gold on Coastal Playhouse. Builds Beaufort County Retreat. Invests More than $150,000 in Home and Swimming Pool. Returns to Native Land. Huge White House Contains Only Three Rooms and Kitchenette." Publication date: January 11, 1931.

his body. Doubtless, for years in the sweltering heat of New York's summers, he was wont to conjure up for himself the cool gray-greenness of the tidal water. So the gold that this son of the coast piled up so gleefully in the stock market, he is bringing back home with equal delight, spending it lavishly like a happy boy.

The toy that he is making for himself just now is a marvelous saltwater swimming pool. It is surrounded by hundreds of acres of land on a point far removed from places and people. Just a few feet beyond, down a little cliff, the gray water hugs the land caressingly and winds reluctantly to sea.

And it is to this country, through the tapestry of whose background history has woven his name right sturdily and romance has dyed it vividly, that Arthur Barnwell has come to re-root himself in native soil.

The spot which he selected, whether from sentimental reasons or otherwise, is closely connected through marriage with the history of his family.

**On Yacht Route**

Cuthbert's Point may be reached either by water or land. Standing on the point and looking across at Beaufort Shores, or Pigeon Point as it is familiarly known, the distance seems only a stone's throw, but it is in reality about a mile and a half away. Trim yachts steam along this stream between the lines of marsh grass and anchor at the smart new landing that juts far out over the water. But around the bend there is another landing, now rotting and tumbled down, relic of another day, as is the ancient house that one comes upon at the end of a little grass grown path.

To reach the point by land, one crosses the new bridge that connects Beaufort with Lady's Island and, turning a little way up the highway, bumps uncertainly for eight or nine miles along a white sandy road through a wilderness of moss shrouded trees. Here and there a tiny cabin with wide-eyed piccaninnies peeping slyly round the corners, long stretches of marsh and solitude, shaky little bridges, wooded curves, flashes of water and then the gleam of white that is the beautiful swimming pool through the thick trees.

From the front, the huge white building, now in the process of completion, looks like a summer hotel with its wide porches facing the south. An inquiry of one of the workmen as to the number of rooms brought the astounding reply: "Three rooms and a kitchenette."

**Great Living Room**

The workmen grinned at the amazed expression on the inquirer's face, but he stuck to his story. And a trip inside proved him a truthful man, for the building really consists of only three rooms and a kitchenette—but what a three room affair!

The great living room which one enters first is immense, paneled and beamed with native pecky cypress. Just off of this great room is the kitchenette—so-called. Upstairs are two huge bedrooms and off of each a dressing room and bath, tiled in yellow and white. At the back of the building is the pride and treasure of Mr. Barnwell's heart—his saltwater swimming pool. The pool measures 20 by 60 feet, is eight and a half feet deep and holds 57,000 gallons of water, which has been chemically treated and clarified so

Cuthbert Point. *Photograph courtesy of the South Carolina Department of Archives and History*

that it will more than meet the strictest health requirements. The water may also be heated in cold weather. The pool is tiled in blue and white, roofed with glass and illumined with colored lights from below. In each wing of the building is a dressing room with showers.

The building is fashioned of native cypress, double balcony effect and painted a dazzling white. The style of architecture is termed by the architect, C. R. Macdonald of the J. E. Sirrine company of Greenville, which concern is building the house, as coastal colonial, in keeping with the old homes of the coast. The living room faces three ways and the whole is steam heated. It is understood that the building will be completed about the middle of December.

### Preserve Old Trees

Mr. Barnwell proves his love and appreciation of coastal treasures in the effort he has made to preserve the trees at Cuthbert's Point.

A hoary oak to the left of the new building has been the mutual joy of generations of negroes and opossums at the point. It was hollow throughout its great height. The opossums treasured it because it furnished an ideal hiding place from hungry negroes and the point's darkies delighted in it for the same reason, for they could the better get at the opossum family.

Once, the tree caught fire. It was like a roaring furnace and its hollowness made of it a veritable smoke stack. Harold E. Scheper owned the place then and he and his family and the negroes on the point were badly frightened. They fought the fire nearly all night with water dipped from the river and at last put it out.

Mr. Barnwell had the tree treated, the dead wood cut out and the various cavities cemented. Now it stands much patched and scarred, but proudly for all that and supplies a balance for the oak on the opposite side of the great building.

Cuthbert's Point is without doubt rich in history, but that history is so covered with dust of the years that there is none to tell it. Although the original Cuthbert home stands there intact and is now a boarding house for the workmen on the Barnwell home, very little is known about it save that it has been there for nearly on to 200 years. Some estimate its age as more than 200, although the more conservative say it is not quite so old and put it as somewhere between 150 and 200 years.

### House of Cypress

The most that can be learned around here about this old place is that it was a grant of land from the king of England to the first Cuthbert who came to this country. The house is made of cypress and built high off the ground. It is surrounded by great oaks, moss draped. However, old residents say these trees are not very old nor nearly so beautiful as those which were destroyed at this point during the '93 storm.

The Cuthberts are said to have been border people, living between Scotland and England, and ardent Royalists. There is a story handed down, authentic or otherwise, of how one of the Cuthberts used to stand upon his porch and play his fiddle, while the squirrels in the surrounding trees sat upon their respective limbs to listen.

The point has changed hands many times. When Harold Scheper lived there, a young enthusiast, he planted 700 fig trees which he planned to develop commercially, and also a dairy. However, the trees were not successful and he later gave them to Gen. Eli K. Cole, now dead, of Parris island, who gave one to each quarter and they are still living and bearing fruit on Parris island.

Mr. Barnwell is said to be spending between $150,000 and $200,000 in his winter retreat at Cuthbert's Point. Whether he plans to preserve or tear down the original Cuthbert house is not known.

In addition to the 520 acres which he owns at this place, Mr. Barnwell has also bought the Walter Richardson home in Beaufort, a handsome place, improved and furnished it elaborately.

### Reforesting Experiment

Probably his most constructive and interesting investment in this section, however, is a reforesting experiment which he is conducting upon nine thousand acres of land near Yemassee, in Colleton county. On this land he is allowing the trees to propagate themselves by the simple method of giving nature free reign and affording her protection after she has done her duty. He has four or five families living in the woods whose duty it is to prevent fires and keep hogs from rooting up the young trees. Left alone, hogs will enter woods about the first of February and root up young trees until they completely destroy a young forest. With this simple care, the trees on Mr. Barnwell's land are growing so thick and fast that it will soon be necessary to thin them out in order that they may attain a natural growth.

Besides the properties around Beaufort, Mr. Barnwell several months ago bought No. 1 East Bay in Charleston.

Although he worked hard and had lots of fun within the tall confines of Wall street, Arthur Barnwell is bringing his gate receipts home to enjoy and share them in coastal Carolina. ✣

Beaufort author Gerhard Spieler has suggested that James Hazzard Cuthbert, son of Dr. James Cuthbert, gave the plantation its name and probably built the old house, which was located to the right of Mr. Barnwell's large clubhouse, in the late eighteenth century. That house still stands and is privately owned.

Edward Philbrick, a Union officer, made this observation in 1862: "[I] rode on to Cuthbert's Point to sleep with Joe Reed and Mr. Hull. I found them delightfully situated in a small house on Beaufort River surrounded by a Superb grove of live Oak, clear of brush and nicely kept. It is the finest situation that I have found in the State, but the greater part of the plantations on Lady's Island are miserably poor."

Arthur Barnwell was handsome, rich, and an outstanding athlete. His wish to play professional baseball, one of his passions, was overruled by his father, who instead took him into the family business in New York. Through his firm, Arthur Barnwell and Company, he took a seat on the New York Stock Exchange in 1907. His success on the exchange was such that he was able to retire from business in 1933, at age fifty-five. Mr. Barnwell bought Cuthbert Point (the usual spelling) in 1928 and soon began construction of the house that Mrs. Martin describes.

For years the Beaufort community was titillated by tales of Arthur Barnwell's many lady friends. His wife, from whom he was long separated, was said to be living in France. Young Beaufort lads of the 1930s and 1940s reported on the sunbathing pavilion built on the edge of the bluff, where Arthur and any number of young women were said to take the sun. Rumors spread of New York showgirls cavorting in Cuthbert Point's saltwater pool. It is no surprise that he dropped the Cuthbert name in favor of "Pleasant Point."

Mr. Barnwell died in 1955. The property has been developed as the semiprivate Country Club of Beaufort at Pleasant Point.

# Dataw Island

People who do things are always interest centering. A woman who does things is regarded with more than casual interest by an avid public.

For three years the people of Beaufort have watched the doings of Miss Kate Gleason with curiosity. If there were no other reason except that one of the world's multimillionaires had come to live among them, that fact would be sufficient to hold their interest. But Miss Gleason does things, so many of them as to make one gasp at their scope. This woman, who has the leisure and means to fashion life to her will, is probably one of the busiest women in the whole country, and her interests are so wide and varied that she surely suffers the minimum of boredom.

Miss Gleason is by inclination and profession a builder, a creator of beauty. Yet she keeps her unquenchable desire for beauty under perfect control. She has a practical mind, developed through long years of necessity, and the thrill that she gets is not solely from building beauty, but in building it so as to get the richest possible returns at the smallest investment. Simply making beauty would be easy for her and, therefore, tiresome. It is coming up against knotty problems that adds zest to the game for her, and keeps her mentally supple and spiritually vital.

Miss Gleason was at her building in California when the town of Beaufort, South Carolina, was first brought to her attention through a girl in her employ, Miss Elizabeth Sanders, granddaughter of Mrs. H. L. Waterhouse, of this place.

### Builds at Beaufort

Miss Sanders proved herself such an ardent booster of Beaufort that she "sold" the idea of the town to Miss Gleason, who came down for one day and was impressed with the place as being one which her mother might possibly enjoy as a winter home. The fact that Beaufort was nearer their home in Rochester, N.Y., than California was a deciding factor in this decision.

Original title: "Miss Kate Gleason. Woman Multi-millionaire Builder Interested in South Carolina Sea Island Development Buys Entire Beaufort Island." Publication date: November 30, 1930.

Kate Gleason standing in the ruins of the old Sams House chimney on Dataw Island. *Photograph courtesy of the Historic Beaufort Foundation*

Miss Gleason returned a month later with her mother and spent four days here, purchasing a piece of property on the water front. Here she has since built the Gold Eagle Tavern, old-world in atmosphere, but withal as modern a hostelry as can be found anywhere. The original house, which was the old home of the de Saussure family, and said to be close to 200 years old, Miss Gleason has repaired and is now occupying part of it, which is connected with the Gold Eagle Tavern by a pergola. While having repairs made, Miss Gleason discovered that the frame of this old house, which is still good, was put together with wooden pegs. The attic of the old house, Miss Gleason has fashioned into a charming sitting room for her own use. The windows, which surround three sides of the huge room, give a magnificent view of the river, marshes and wooded islands along the coast. The gay curtains and upholstery of glazed chintz make this room colorful and delightful on even the dreariest days.

Gold Eagle Tavern. *Photograph by Chlotilde Martin, courtesy of Chloe M. Pinckney*

Miss Gleason is erecting a loggia, which, in her estimation, commands a view which equals that from the famous loggia in Florence, Italy. Miss Gleason is also fond of birds, and at the back of this loggia is having a bird house and cage built so that her feathered friends may find food and shelter from the weather.

### Restores Buildings

Miss Gleason has taken a great deal of pleasure in "rescuing," as she phrases it, a number of other old Beaufort homes, which had fallen upon hard days.

In each instance, she has accomplished her plans with as little expense as possible, keeping always in mind her desire for the maximum of beauty at the minimum of cost. Some of these homes she has made into small apartments, which she lets reasonably, thus enabling people of moderate means to live in comfortable and pleasant surroundings at little cost.

In all of her building and remodeling, Miss Gleason makes a point of utilizing native products wherever possible. She has used native pecky cypress in ceiling and paneling all of her rooms. This, after being polished, in Miss Gleason's opinion, is much more desirable and about half as expensive as plastering. This wood is distinctive of the coast and should be popularized, she believes.

But her completed work in the town of Beaufort is dwarfed by Miss Gleason's plans for future development, some of which are already under way. While her appearance and that of others like her in Beaufort when it was basking in the glory of its sea island cotton could not only have been undesirable but resented, Miss Gleason says she believes that the time has come when Beaufort and other coastal towns like it must learn to commercialize its climate and natural beauties. To do this, she thinks it will be necessary to furnish attractions in order to invite outsiders into this section.

## Plans Yacht Club

To this end, she is planning the building of a large saltwater swimming pool and yacht club house just across the bridge on Lady's island. The yacht club house is to be an inducement to tempt yachts passing in the inland waterway to stop at Beaufort. She also hopes to get a number of Beaufort businessmen interested in providing boats so that visitors here will find it convenient and easy for fishing and boating along the lovely tidal waters.

She has interested her sister, Miss Eleanor Gleason, in the possibilities for riding in Beaufort. Miss Eleanor Gleason visited Beaufort recently, and was so pleased with the many winding bridle paths scattered all over the various islands that she plans to return during the winter season and provide a stable of horses so that other visitors here may enjoy riding, too.

Another project which this tireless woman has begun is the purchase of between two and three thousand acres of land on Lady's Island, which she plans to develop into home sites of five acres each, and will sell to families of moderate means who desire them.

Miss Gleason boasts that, with one exception, she has never made an investment which was not profitable, and these undertakings here have, as a matter of course, brought her monetary returns. Still, they have been undertaken more or less in a philanthropic state of mind.

## Buys Entire Island

But the joy of her heart is her island. She has bought an entire island of her own, and it is so remote that she is having to build a causeway across two islands to reach it. The island is Dawtaw, the home of the Sams family from 1690 until the War Between the States. The island is nine miles long and a mile wide. Upon it still remain the ruins of the old Sams home, and it is Miss Gleason's plan to reproduce this home as nearly as possible like the original home.

Some of the tombs where lies the dust of members of the Sams family are still in good condition, although they date back to 1740. There are also the ruins of the old church where this family worshipped. It was the custom of each generation to send its most ecclesiastically minded member to Oxford for an education in divinity, so that he could conduct the services in the church. In addition to the Sams family, there were a thousand slaves on Dawtaw island.

In order to reach this island, Miss Gleason has already completed the causeway from St. Helena to Polawana island, and will soon build one from Polawana to Dawtaw. It is of more than casual interest that the causeway is being built by Reeves Sams, the present head of the Sams family in this section, who, by his bridge, is connecting the properties of his mother's father with that of his father's father.

Although Miss Gleason will repair the ruins of the old church so that they will be in a state of preservation, she does not plan to restore the building.

### Owns $28,000 Yacht

Miss Gleason is the owner of a handsome $28,000 yacht, Ellen of the Isles, which she bought for $1,000. This yacht is a testimonial to her business sagacity, and she delights in telling of how the boat came into her possession. The yacht had been a rum-runner between Jacksonville and Cuba, and had had hard luck. It was captured and sold at auction, later traded for a Florida lot and finally came into the hands of Miss Gleason. She had been interested in buying a yacht and, learning that there was to be a sale, she spent 87 cents for a month's subscription to the Jacksonville Times-Union, for the purpose of reading the advertisements. Through this medium she learned about Ellen of the Isles, but still doubtful, told the owner that she would give him a thousand dollars for the boat if he brought it safely to Beaufort. It was later, while having some engine repairs made, she learned from the original builders that the original purchase price was $28,000.

Miss Gleason has had a varied and exceptionally interesting career. She did not inherit her money, but made it all herself. Her father was head of a little machine shop and she grew up with it, helping to build it along with her father and brothers. When she was scarcely out of her teens she began work for her father and later became secretary, treasurer and sales manager of the concern that grew and grew until it became the now famous Gleason Works of Rochester, N.Y. Her sales ability made her widely known and took her not only all over this country but to European nations as well. It was after her father invented the Gleason gear planer that the factory ceased making machine tools and began to grow with determination. The concern made money hand over fist, and in 1916 Miss Gleason resigned from her position there, although she still retained her financial interest, and became a joyous rover over earth.

Postcard view of Gold Eagle Tavern. *Courtesy of the South Carolina Historical Society*

However, during her roving she has stopped at intervals here and there to do a hard stretch of work, and when she has moved on there was always plenty of evidence of her having been there.

### Managed Eight Factories

In East Rochester, N.Y., she built and managed for a time eight factories. She was the first woman ever to be elected president of a national bank in this country, holding this position with the National bank in Rochester for three years. She also designed and constructed more than 100 homes in Rochester, built a golf course, a clubhouse and an apartment house there. She spent a great deal of time in the study of the architecture of small houses and built a number of them in California.

Her building activities have not been confined to this country, for in France she bought two war-torn castles and reconstructed them. There she also opened as an A.E.F. memorial a library and moving picture theater for the people of Septmont. She spends three months of each year at Septmont. In the spring and summer she is at her home, Clones, Rochester, and spends her winters in Beaufort.

In 1914, Miss Gleason received the honor of being unanimously elected the first woman member of the American Society of Mechanical Engineers. She was also the first woman to be appointed receiver by a bankruptcy court. She was made manager of this concern, a machine shop which was in such bad shape that it was supposed to be worth about ten cents on the dollar. The stock was turned over as worthless and the debts were $140,000. She took charge January 1, 1914, and by August 1, 1915, the debts had been paid in full, the stock turned over to the stockholders and the plant was a going concern, which by 1917 had made a million dollars.

Miss Gleason is sensible about publicity. She admits candidly she has learned long since that people who do things cannot escape a certain amount of publicity. Her chief objection to it, she says, is that it floods her mail with so many requests from people who want everything from automobiles on up. Although she has never married, publicity has brought her more than 200 proposals of marriage.

The latest request that has been made of her is for money with which to deflect the Labrador current so as to warm the coast of New England, regardless of the annoyance to the people of Spain and the other countries it might affect.

Miss Gleason is approachable and charming in manner. She has the faculty of putting a stranger immediately at ease. Although her hair is snow white and she is not a young woman any longer, there is a vitality and sheer force about her which have their roots and draw their nourishment from some rich source of eternal youth deep within her, which has nothing to do with years. ✒

Though the spelling of the island's name is now "Dataw," historical records include eleven different variations, including "Datha." The island was supposedly named for the legendary Indian king Datha.

Kate Gleason died of pneumonia on January 9, 1933, in Rochester. A *Charleston News and Courier* article datelined Beaufort, and probably written by Mrs. Martin, included:

Colony Gardens on Lady's Island. *Photograph by Chlotilde Martin, courtesy of Chloe M. Pinckney*

Miss Gleason's most elaborate Beaufort development to date was well under way at the time of her death. On Lady's Island, where she owned between 2,000 and 3,000 acres of land, a project which she named Colony Gardens is now being consummated. It centers around a house to contain twenty connected apartments, a swimming pool, a golf course and numerous little homesteads scattered over the estate. Eight of the apartments have been completed or will be within the near future. They are being constructed around the swimming pool. The golf course has also been finished.

The little homesteads are to each include a house and three acres of land.

Miss Gleason is also known to have done a great deal of relief work here, most of it secretly to all save a few friends. She did not contribute heavily to organized charity in this section, but found many ways to help those in need. A suffragist, she credited her mother's friend Susan B. Anthony for many valuable suggestions that helped her succeed.

Mrs. Martin had more than a passing knowledge of Colony Gardens, for, as her daughter, Chloe M. Pinckney, has explained, her mother helped Miss Gleason rent units there when Miss Gleason was not in Beaufort. For several summers Mrs. Martin took both of her children there, staying in a Colony Gardens apartment for a month. Though Colony Gardens Road remains, the apartment complex has been torn down.

Today, Miss Gleason is most known in Beaufort for having given the land on which Memorial Hospital was built. The park behind the hospital is named for her and her portrait hangs in the hospital. The Rochester Institute of Technology's College of Engineering also bears her name.

In a romantic article about Beaufort County published on March 31, 1935, in the *Charleston News and Courier,* Mrs. Martin wrote again about Kate Gleason and Dataw: "[A] short while before her death [Miss Gleason] had artist's plans drawn of the old Sams home, which she had planned to reproduce as a home for herself. The romantic island with its tabby ruins of the Sams' home and family chapel appealed strongly to her imagination. At her death, she willed this island to Miss Elizabeth Sanders, of New Jersey."

In 1936 Elizabeth Sanders married Richard Rowland of Buffalo, New York, and the Rowland family held on to Dataw for almost fifty years—hunting and fishing there and occasionally leasing some of the land for timbering and tomato farming. (Dr. Lawrence Rowland, a son of Elizabeth and Richard Rowland and today the leading historian of Beaufort, points out that the island supported about three hundred enslaved workers, rather than the "thousands" that Mrs. Martin mentions. The earliest tomb on the island records a death date of 1798, not 1740. The entire island measures about four miles across, not nine.) In 1983 the Rowland family sold Dataw to Alcoa. It has since been developed into a major residential community. Alcoa and later a group of residents who worked under the name of the Dataw Island Historic Foundation have overseen the preservation of older buildings on the island and the collection of records and artifacts. Of particular interest have been the buildings of the Sams family.

In the 1780s William Sams, grandson of the Indian fighter Col. John "Tuscarora Jack" Barnwell, purchased the island. He planted Sea Island cotton and in 1786 built a tabby plantation house. His sons Berners Barnwell Sams and Lewis Reeve Sams divided the island, Berners occupying the "old house" and Lewis building a new one on the island's north shore. A family chapel was constructed in 1833.

The Sams brothers died in the 1850s within a year of each other, so they were spared the sight of the island occupied by Union troops and sold for nonpayment of taxes. Among the Sams buildings that remained were the old house, which Berners had expanded but which burned about 1880; a good-sized kitchen house; a blade house (for storing cornstalks or "blades" for fodder); the dairy; the stable; slave houses; and the chapel. Almost all traces of roof construction have disappeared, but the remaining ruins have been stabilized, along with the cemetery. Lewis's house on the shore of the Morgan River is thought to have been destroyed by the great hurricane of 1893.

In 1927 much of Dataw was owned by the heirs of Samuel G. Stoney, who sold their acreage to Miss Gleason. With an eye toward real estate development, she built seawalls but died before she could achieve her goal.

Henry W. de Saussure (1763–1839), appointed director of the mint by President George Washington, was responsible for the first United States gold coins. When Kate Gleason built her tavern or inn adjacent to de Saussure's old house, she chose the name Gold Eagle to commemorate that early coin. The tavern opened in the spring of 1930 with about forty rooms and attracted from the first a prominent clientele. It was first managed and then owned by L. E. Wilder, son of Dr. Francis Wilder of Hilton Head. L. E. Wilder's daughter, Mrs. A. E. Samuel, sold the Gold Eagle in 1965, a few years before it was taken down.

# *Foot Point*

Of all northern men and women who have come to Coastal South Carolina to buy land and build hunting lodges and winter homes, there is perhaps none who has so frankly deserted the land of his birth to throw in his lot with the land of his adoption as has Harry Cram, young scion of a wealthy New York family.

Young Cram is the son of Sergeant Cram, now retired, who was for many years one of the Tammany Hall leaders. He is also the nephew of Governor Pinchot, of Pennsylvania.

Harry Cram lives in reality almost "at the end of nowhere."

By the time a visitor, who, by chance, had not heard of Harry Cram, had reached the end of the little rutty road that seems to stretch interminably before it comes at last to Foot Point, about ten or twelve miles from Bluffton, he would have become thoroughly convinced that any man who deliberately chose to bury himself alive in this far corner of the globe must be either crazy or deadly dull, pale and anemic.

What a jolt such a visitor would get!

### "Wild Young Millionaire"

However, there are very few who come to this part of the country and remain for long without hearing about Harry Cram and his escapades. Generally, he is supposed to be a "wild young millionaire" who "ran through a million dollars in no time at all so that his father packed him off down here and told him he couldn't have but three thousand dollars a month pin money." He is also supposed to be reckless in his forty-foot speed boat and to give "wild parties and that sort of thing."

There are others who say he has tried everything else and that this is novelty to him for the time being. And there is a little old lady at Bluffton who used to board him and she adores him.

Original title: "Harry Cram Lives at End of Road. Young Scion of Wealthy New York Family Dwells Ten Miles below Bluffton in Little White Cottage with Three Servants to Take Care of Him." Publication date: August 2, 1931.

Harry Cram showing off a blue goose at Foot Point, 1953. *Photograph courtesy of Peter Cram*

Whatever it is that they have heard about him, the fact is that everybody in this section has heard of Harry Cram.

In reality, he is as harmless as a young puppy and just as friendly and as curious about the world. Everything that comes within his range of vision is something to chew on and everybody is a possible friend.

Harry Cram is still in his twenties. He is stalwart and tall and fair and as rosy as a cherub. He accepts everybody with his quick infectious smile that is like the wagging of a puppy's tail.

He lives in a little white cottage with three servants to take care of him. He raises turkeys and has a lot of dogs that, unleashed, almost match him in energy. There are twenty-five hundred acres of land in his tract and he says he is thinking of turning seriously to farming.

Two miles down from his house is a point of land, which forms a high bluff overlooking the Colleton river. Here, young Cram plans to build himself a "real house" just as soon as he "can get hold of some money."

At this point is said to be the deepest water this side of Norfolk and Harry Cram is very proud of this possession and one can see that he is mulling over its possibilities in his mind.

## He Loathes Cities

At this point, amid a wild thicket of trees and underbrush, there is an orange tree which he says was about the first planted in this entire country.

Somebody inquired of him: "What struck you to dig in way off here?"

Young Cram laughed: "I just missed three weeks being born at Hilton Head and I've never forgiven my mother that."

The fact is that his father has been coming to South Carolina on hunting trips since before his son was born. He owned all of this land at Foot Point, but never built a home because Mrs. Cram did not like the isolation. However, he continued to come and used to bring young Harry who grew to love the coast so much that now he has decided to make it his permanent home. He says he loathes cities and is content here.

Asked where he went to school, young Cram replied: "I am uneducated. I can't even spell. Now, my brother, Johnnie, who also has a place down here, is the student. He is at Princeton now."

Young Cram was just recently married and has brought his bride to Foot Point. Mrs. Cram was the former Edith Kingdon Drexel, daughter of Mr. and Mrs. Anthony J. Drexel, Jr., of New York. They were married May 5 of this year at St. Bartholomew church. Mrs. Cram, who is young and widely traveled, is apparently contented and happy in her new home. ✍

Foot Point fronts the Colleton River and, like its neighbors Belfair and Rose Hill, was part of Sir John Colleton's Okeetee or Devil's Elbow Barony. Judge Henry A. M. Smith, in his account of the barony, tells us that Foot Point is on deep water, "up to the very wharves." In the nineteenth century it was regarded as an ideal site for "a great commercial city." The idea never materialized, although in 1969 officials of the German petrochemical company BASF announced their intention to construct a chemical plant there at Victoria Bluff. The attractions were the excellent deep-water harbor and the lack of a low, interfering bridge. They had the support of the state development board and other business promoters, but the widespread opposition of environmentalists, fishermen, and Hilton Head residents. The company dropped its plans.

Until the beginning of the American Revolution the barony was still largely in the possession of the Colletons. Just prior to the war, they sold some six thousand acres of the original twelve thousand. The land was particularly suitable for indigo, and later in the antebellum period the finest quality of Sea Island cotton flourished in the sandy loam. By 1828 the Colleton heirs had disposed of all their holdings. This Colleton area was "distinguished botanically," says Judge Smith, for the number of plant species that made it their northernmost boundary. Two eminent early South Carolina botanists, Stephen Elliott and Dr. James Mellichamp, did many of their field surveys and studies on Colleton Neck.

A photograph of Harry Cram in old age shows the willful determination that he no doubt possessed his entire life. It is no surprise that when the youth was offered a hunting trip to Hilton Head or to the forty-thousand-acre estate called Dunbeath in Scotland (which his father leased), or a fishing trip to Florida, young Harry put schooling out of his head. Then came duck shooting on Long Island and polo and, of course, partying. With three generations of accumulated wealth in his background—his father and grandfather were lawyers, and a great-grandfather was a prosperous merchant—Harry was fixed for money.

The family was an old one, having settled in Exeter, New Hampshire, in 1640. His father, John Sergeant Cram, occupied a position in New York City government for many years

Harry Cram in 1988. *Photograph courtesy of Peter Cram*

as president of the dock board. His crony was Tammany leader Charles F. Murphy; some sources say that Cram was Murphy's "social mentor." So powerful was Murphy in New York politics that, when he died in April 1924, the *New York Times* reported, "City business will be virtually at a standstill during the funeral." John Sergeant Cram claimed never to have used his friendship with Murphy for personal advantage, and no scandal ensnared him. Harry's mother, Edith Clare Bryce Cram, made headlines after World War I when she became a pacifist and campaigned extensively throughout the country.

When Mrs. Martin interviewed Harry in 1931, he had a new wife, as well as youth, independence, and wealth. However, this good life did not last, for his wife died suddenly in New York in 1934. In time Harry remarried, this time unsuccessfully, and then twice more after that.

Local residents love to tell Harry Cram stories, and in 1982 an article in the *Atlanta Weekly* magazine recounted many of them: "Stories of Harry Cram shooting the telephones when they irritated him—the centers of the dialing discs made fine targets. Stories of Harry Cram shooting the jam jars when his wife failed to bring home Cross & Blackwell. Stories of Harry Cram parties when all of Bluffton was invited over for shooting, hunting and drinking. Sometimes the festivities lasted all week."

One of the most popular accounts concerns Mr. Cram's horse ride from Foot Point to Savannah and into the lobby of the Desoto Hotel. "We removed the shoes before we rode into the ballroom," he claimed with a straight face, "so I don't think it caused any harm." Another popular tale recalls his confrontation in 1976 with two marines who had swum in wet suits to his home on Potato Island (which he called Devil's Elbow Island). The marines "broke in and held his son Peter at knife point, marching him down a hall toward his father's room. Cram came out from behind the door, his son managed to get out of his line of fire and Cram shot the two Marines with his .38-caliber pistol. He killed them both instantly with shots between the eyes." Cram was cleared of all charges.

A few years later he and his fourth wife returned to Foot Point, to a new house not far from the cottage where Mrs. Martin had met him in 1931. The 1982 article claimed that he had stopped drinking six years before, though family members noted that he occasionally forgot his pledge of abstinence. Mr. Cram died in 1997 at the age of ninety. His son Hank now lives at Foot Point.

Mrs. Martin repeated some of the stories she heard without confirming them with Harry Cram. Or maybe he confirmed good anecdotes even when they were not accurate. His son Peter wrote to us about her article: "Harry wasn't really fixed for money. He relied on raising cattle until after his mother died. I would be suspect of him going through a million dollars or having three thousand a month. The parties I can believe. As for education, my father had tutors because they traveled a lot. He told me that he attended The Lawrenceville School at some point. The L'ville records show that he got a diploma but show no other records for him. I found no photos or mention of him in their annual."

# Fort Fremont

It is a far cry from a lubricant business located in the midst of the hum and bustle of New York to a Spanish villa upon the top of an old fort off the coast of South Carolina. Yet, that is the dream of Frederick J. Barnes, who is retiring from active connection with the New York and New Jersey Lubricant company, to seek peace and rest amid the beautiful scenery and ideal climatic conditions of coastal South Carolina.

This dream of Mr. Barnes, who has with him his brother, A. C. Barnes, is shortly to be realized, and the work of clearing and temporary building has already begun.

During the Spanish American war Fort Fremont was built on a protected site across the water from Parris island. It was formerly reached by boats plying between Beaufort and Savannah and may also be reached from Beaufort by land, being about 16 miles away at the very end of St. Helena island.

**Guns Carried to France**

The fort was maintained by the United States government as a fort until 1912, when it was disbanded. However, a small garrison was kept there until only a few years ago. The guns were dismantled during the World war and carried to France, among them being some ten-inch disappearing guns.

Since it has been abandoned, Fort Fremont, once teeming with life, shining and efficient and paraded by soldiery, has fallen into decay.

Government houses have been removed one by one. The place has run wild with plant life and there remains only the old fort, great and grim and gray, the square, red hospital building, the observatory and a tank.

These remaining buildings show the marks of years of neglect. What pillage and vandalism have failed to accomplish, creeping vines and bushes have brought about, covering their damage, hypocritically, with caressing fingers.

The great brick hospital building that once gleamed from constant scrubbing and polishing has been for years the playground of rats and other varmints. Its many

Original title: "Builds on Top Beaufort Fort. Frederick J. Barnes Plans Spanish Villa to Cap Fort Fremont Whose Guns Were Dismantled and Carried to France for World War." Publication date: December 21, 1930.

The old hospital at Fort Fremont. *Photograph courtesy of the South Carolina Department of Archives and History*

windows that once caught and held the sun's rays like so many sparkling diamonds have for a long time gazed sightlessly across the waters. Doors have hung awry, floors have sagged and the once trim building, whose walls have listened to many moans of pain, stares disconsolately down upon the water, which alone is just the same, beating upon a beach which has acquired a shaggy, ill-kempt look through remembering the tread of joyous feet along its white hardness.

### Seems Part of Hillside

The long, squat fort, sullen and forbidding in its hidden place, seems almost to rise a part of the hillside, so perfectly does it fit into nature's background.

For years, bats and crawling things have been its sole inhabitants and its great steel doors have hung open purposely. Dank, evil smelling dungeons down narrow winding stairs reverberate hollowly to the sound of footstep or voice. Here and there a bright lizard flashes around a corner, the only bits of color and life in this dismal place.

The marrow chills in one's bones at a thudding sound along a dim corridor. Suppose one of the immense doors should clang shut and one be imprisoned in this lonely place!

For miles there is not a sign of human habitation. Just this collection of huddling buildings overlooking wide, gray waters which beat continuously against the lonely beach.

Where, now, are the sun-browned, uniformed men whose white teeth were wont to gleam and whose eyes to shine beneath their jaunty caps? Where the gay ladies whose colorful frocks made bright splashes as they flitted in and out among the primly laid walks about the fort?

### Build Bungalow First

But now that the Barnes brothers have come with romance in their hearts, there is sure to be brightness again. None but one who had beauty in his soul would have come to this far-off, lonely spot to make a home.

They have built a little brown wren of a bungalow about halfway between the fort and the hospital building, which they are occupying until they complete their plans for permanent building.

Upon investigation, they found that the hospital building contained such good materials that they feel it would be a great pity to tear it down. It is large and commodious and commands a splendid view of the water, situated, as it is, right on the beach.

However, the idea of the Spanish villa upon the top of the old fort itself is dear to the heart of Frederick Barnes and it is more than a possibility that this plan will win out and some other disposition made of the hospital building.

Mr. Barnes' purchase around the fort comprises between 170 and 180 acres of land. He plans to use this only in connection with his home.

Fort Fremont is reached from Beaufort over a seemingly interminable little road that winds in and out through thick woods, with here and there a negro cabin to break the loneliness.

### Debris Being Cleared

However, even these cease some distance from the fort. The way is marked at intervals by signs that read: "To Land's End" and it is in reality that. Just when one gets to the point that he is reasonably sure the road has no ending, the woods give way suddenly upon a wide emptiness.

At first, straggling bushes and stunted trees obstruct the view and then, all at once, the land does end upon a sweep of curling waters and winding, white beach.

Already, the fort presents a shorn and shaven appearance, in sharp contrast with its rough, neglected look of only a few months ago. Negroes are kept daily at the job of cutting bushes and removing debris and disorder. Their songs, coming intermittently from the natural amphitheater, out of which the fort rises, make a happy sound in the stillness.

The past is past and perhaps it is always wiser to close the door gently but firmly upon it, keeping one's face to the faint ray of light which sifts through the opening that is the future.

The Fort Fremont of the future, topped with its Spanish villa overlooking the sea, its rolling swards of well-kept green, its cleared, gleaming beach, is a picture which the mind delights in contemplating, eager for its completion. ✦

Mrs. Martin's original article included references to both "Fort Fremont" and "Fort Freemont." The spelling has been standardized to "Fremont." The fort was named for Gen. John C. Frémont, western explorer and presidential candidate, who was born in Savannah.

The fort has virtually no history as a military installation. It was built in 1899 to protect Beaufort from Spanish attack, but construction was not completed until the Spanish-American War was over. As early as 1906 the War Department considered closing the fort, and it was decommissioned in 1911. The federal government advertised the 170-acre Fort Fremont property for sale in 1930, placing a value of $3,500 on the land and two buildings.

Frederick H. Barnes of Long Island, New York, bought the fort in 1931 for $12,200, more than its advertised price just a year before. There is no evidence that Barnes ever constructed the Spanish villa that Mrs. Martin claims he wanted to build. He made his home there until 1946, when he sold the fort to a group of local businessmen for development as a summer resort. In 1951 Mr. and Mrs. Schumeir made a hunting and fishing lodge out of the old hospital. In the 1970s the old fort was the property of Beaufort's G. G. Dowling and his wife. The Beaufort County Parks and Leisure Department has now purchased nine acres of the fort, including the concrete gun emplacements, and is developing the land as a park with nature trails, a swimming beach, and an interpretation center.

# Hilton Head Island

(Part 1)

Roy A. Rainey, New York coal exporter, has owned a large estate on Hilton Head island, Beaufort county, for about twenty years. This place, which comprises twelve thousand acres, or about three-fourths of the entire island, was formerly owned by J. P. Clyde of the Clyde Steamship line.

While not elaborate, the Rainey home is attractive and comfortable, a low white frame building of single-story construction with about twelve rooms. The house was built by Mr. Clyde and has been used by the Raineys as their own home during their visits to South Carolina each winter.

Mr. Rainey himself comes but rarely, but Mrs. Rainey is an enthusiastic hunter and a frequent visitor to the island. During Thanksgiving she and her son and daughter-in-law, Mr. and Mrs. Roy A. Rainey, were down on Hilton Head. When the Raineys come down, they usually charter the Beaufort-Savannah boat line to meet them and bring them to their home here.

Paul Rainey, who is now dead, brother of Roy A. Rainey, Sr., was a well-known hunter of big game and hunted lions with trained dogs in Africa. These dogs were trained by Superintendent Shelley of Good Hope camp, Jasper county, who has written a book on this subject.

The young Raineys, who are good friends of young Harry Cram, of New York, who owns a tract of land at Foot Point, are a lively, friendly pair. Mr. Rainey sprained his ankle at the horse races held in Bluffton on Thanksgiving day and was laid up in bed at Harry Cram's home. Unable to walk but so brim full of energy that he was unable to lie still for long at a time, he exercised himself and amused his friends by crawling around wherever he wanted to go.

Original title: "Hilton Head Island Estates. Rainey and Hurley Holdings Comprise Seventeen Thousand Acres of This Ideal Bird and Game Preserve in Beaufort County." Publication date: January 12, 1931.

### Hurley Estate

On Hilton Head, also, occupying about an eighth of the island is the estate of the late W. L. Hurley, of Camden, N.J. In this estate there are 2,732 acres with an additional 2,079 acres which have been leased for hunting purposes. This estate is about three miles from the Rainey home.

The handsome hunting lodge of the Hurley estate is located on Broad Creek Bluff, about two miles back from the ocean. This lodge was remodeled in 1921 from an old hunting lodge and is now commodious and comfortable, as well as very good to look at. It served as a home as well as a lodge.

The building is situated in the midst of a lawn of four or five acres, bordered by palmetto trees. Palmettos have also been set at regular intervals along Broad creek and on each side of the lane which leads from the lodge to the main road, thus creating a most picturesque and beautiful effect.

The Hurley home, it is understood, is for sale to settle the estate.

### Life on Hilton Head

Hilton Head island is on the Atlantic ocean, between Port Royal and Calibogue sounds, and may be reached by boat from Savannah or Beaufort. On the island there is one of the finest beaches on this coast. It stretches eighteen or twenty miles long and is so hard that automobiles are raced and planes landed with perfect safety.

Mail is delivered on the island and taken away three times a week. There is a government lighthouse on the island and the government maintains a telephone here, so that those living on the island are enabled to make telephone or telegraphic communication with the outside world.

Hilton Head island is said to have one of the most wonderful bird preserves in this entire country and great hunts are enjoyed here. The island is a natural game preserve, the scrub oaks and palmetto trees offering shelter for deer, which are to be found in great numbers. The fields furnish feeding ground for quail, which are also numerous. Snipe, marsh hen and "gator" shooting are enjoyed too.

A dam has been built to retain the fresh water and wild rice has been planted to provide a refuge for the many ducks and geese which pass over this island. Flocks of wild doves feed in the open fields and offer good hunting also. Another sport enjoyed at Hilton Head is hunting wild pigs, which exist in great numbers in the densest portions of the island, feeding upon acorns, palmetto berries, herbs and roots. These pigs, properly roasted, make eating fit for lords.

Good fishing is enjoyed in the waters about the island. "Spot tail bass" may be caught from the docks on the island in the spring and fall or may be speared with the aid of a torch at night on the flats close by. Sheepshead is also plentiful in the waters about Hilton Head island. Oysters are available here in profusion.

Before the Confederate war this island was made up of several large old plantations, which flourished during the days of long staple cotton. However, they were deserted when Sherman marched to the sea, as were nearly all of the coastal plantations, and their owners never returned.

There remain of this former day only a few blackened fireplaces and chimneys of the old slave quarters. These, and the old graveyard where lies the dust of those who had life and happiness on the far-away island. In this cemetery is the tomb of the Baynard family, fashioned of red stone with doors of polished marble.

At the northern end of the island are still to be seen the breastworks which were thrown up to resist invasion by way of Port Royal Sound during the war.  ❧

William P. Clyde, president of the Clyde Steamship Lines and son of its founder, was one of the earliest northern sportsmen to acquire large acreage in the South Carolina low-country as a hunting preserve. Clyde had served in the Union army on Hilton Head and was so impressed with the tropical environment that he determined to return one day. He began to satisfy this intention in 1889, when he started buying property on the island. He bought Honey Horn plantation and additional tracts, eventually totaling nine thousand acres, all for about a dollar or two an acre.

The house at Honey Horn was built by William Graham just prior to the Civil War and was the only plantation residence on the island still habitable at the time of Clyde's purchases. The title "Honey Horn," some have suggested, was a mutation of "Hanahan," the name of an early owner of the property. The name sometimes locally was pronounced "Hanny-han."

Clyde kept the plantation until 1919, four years before his death in New York. There were at the time an estimated one thousand to fifteen hundred black persons living on the island and about a dozen white families. The only access to the island was by boat.

Honey Horn. *Photograph courtesy of the Bluffton Historical Preservation Society*

The nine-thousand-acre tract was bought by Roy Rainey of New York for ten thousand dollars. Rainey was a son of W. J. Rainey, known as the "Coke King" long before the word referred to a carbonated drink. The new owner favored expensive whiskey, high-stakes gambling, and a sport the island had not known before: live pigeon shooting, in the order of trapshooting but with live birds. As Mrs. Martin writes, Rainey's son became fast friends with Harry Cram at Foot Point, both enjoying the carefree life of the young wealthy. However, for the Raineys that life came to an end with the 1929 stock market crash. Their troubles continued even after they sold their Hilton Head land. Roy Jr., just thirty-two years old, died in Savannah following an abdominal operation in 1938.

William Hurley bought the eight-hundred-acre Otter Hole or Otterburn plantation on Broad Creek from Dr. Francis E. Wilder (1837–1924), originally of Massachusetts, who came south in 1865 to plant cotton and stayed the rest of his life. He was active in the local Republican Party and was a member of the South Carolina Constitutional Convention of 1868. He also served as a Beaufort County commissioner and a school commissioner. Some of his descendants continued to live in Beaufort, managing and eventually owning the popular Gold Eagle Tavern.

Additional purchases by Hurley brought his estate to twenty-seven hundred acres. The Hurleys lived in the same high style as their neighbors, with a yacht on Broad Creek and an automobile brought over to Hilton Head for land transportation. His 1928 obituary in the *New York Times* reported that "for nearly 20 years he has spent most every winter at his home on Hilton Head Island." He died there after an illness of nine weeks.

Soon after Mrs. Martin published this article, most of Hilton Head was sold. A year later she returned to the island for an article entitled "Hilton Head Island Estates Merged."

# Hilton Head Island

(Part 2)

Landon K. Thorne and Alfred L. Loomis, of New York, have recently purchased the Roy A. Rainey and W. L. Hurley estates on Hilton Head island and have become joint owners of these lands, comprising about 15,000 acres. Mr. and Mrs. Thorne and Mr. and Mrs. Loomis arrived at Hilton Head in January and will spend a time at the former Rainey cottage.

The Hurley estate consisted of about 2,000 acres and a two story, green shingled hunting lodge directly overlooking Broad creek. The late owner died at his hunting lodge several years ago. The other estate, comprising about 13,000 acres, was purchased by Mr. Rainey of W. J. Rainey, Inc., of New York, from W. P. Clyde of the steamship line, in 1918. Mr. Clyde had owned the lands for a number of years and until his possession they were still in the hands of local plantation owners. The old pre-war plantations were combined to make the two large estates and now the one estate on the island. There are twenty thousand acres in the island. Of the five thousand not in this large northern holding, there is a tract of about 1,800 acres owned by what is known as the North Carolina club, another tract of about 900 acres owned by Miss Harriet Gonzales, of near Adams Run, and the remainder of the land, between two and three thousand acres, is owned in small plots by the negroes of the island, about six hundred in number.

### "Steamer Day" There Yet

There are between fifty and sixty white people living on Hilton Head and Jenkins islands together, the two being connected by a causeway and considered almost as the same island, because of the fact that the only post office, Hilton Head, is actually located on Jenkins island. This island, although very small, containing only about 250 acres, is the point of embarkation for both islands. Here it is that the steamer *Cliveden*, of the Beaufort-Savannah line, stops on its trips three times a week, both going and

Original title: "Hilton Head Island Estates Merged. Brothers-in-law of New York Purchase Rainey and Hurley Holdings of 15,000 Acres in Beaufort County." Publication date: February 7, 1932.

coming, being the only means of communication with the outside world, except the telephone which the government has built to the lighthouse on the island and the radio. These last, although there is only one telephone besides that at the lighthouse, this being in the home of J. E. Lawrence, superintendent for Mr. Thorne and Mr. Loomis, keep the island from being so isolated, and several of the island residents possess radios which bring the world to them at the touch of a switch. This does not keep "steamer day," as the island people term it, from being the high light of the week, however. The radio is great, of course, and the telephone is there in cases of life or death or other important matters, but nothing takes the thrill out of "steamer day" and they all gather to greet the plodding, friendly, old steamer which brings them letters and packages and papers at least two days old.

Mr. Lawrence might be termed "dictator" of the island, although he instantly dis- claims such a stern-sounding title. But in reality he manages everything. In his position of superintendent of the large holdings of Mr. Thorne and Mr. Loomis, who are, by the way, brothers-in-law, he employs about fifteen of the family heads on the island at steady jobs, while others are given more or less steady employment as day workers. Thus, he naturally falls into the position of "head man." He looks after school matters, attends to the roads when they get too bad, and other affairs. He is also the island police force, although his duties in this capacity seem to be more or less light. Likewise, he is the official entertainer and when strangers come to the island, as they sometimes have occa- sion to do, he takes them in, perforce, else they would be obliged to spend the night under the stars.

### The Negroes Leaving

Mr. Lawrence came to Hilton Head in 1892 to work in one of the stores on the island, which at that time, he says, did an annual business of from $25,000 to $30,000. He re- mained for a few years, then left, but lured back by the charm of the island, he returned in 1903 to accept the position as superintendent of Mr. Clyde's estate. He has remained ever since, working for Mr. Rainey and now for Mr. Thorne and Mr. Loomis. At that time Mr. Lawrence says there were about three thousand negroes on Hilton Head and Jenkins islands, but they have left in increasing numbers each year until only a handful of them remain. They farm very little, their small patches of land for the most part lay- ing in waste.

The chief occupation of those not employed at the oyster factory on Jenkins island, which has been practically closed down this season, or on the large northern holdings, is said to be bootlegging. A recent raid by the sheriff of Beaufort county, however, tem- porarily paralyzed this business.

Hilton Head island was a strategic point during the Confederate war and was head- quarters for the federal forces. Old negroes throughout this section have since dated time from when "gun shoot on Hilton Head."

During this time there was so much activity on Hilton Head island that it is said The Savannah Morning News carried more advertisements from business concerns on Hilton Head than from any other place within its territory. There are said to have been streets there paved with brick at that time. The father of one of the present residents of the island reports having at one time read an article which told of Jefferson Davis' being brought to the island and put aboard a ship.

**The Graveyard**

But all traces of paved streets or business concerns or any sort of bustle or hurry have been as completely wiped off this island as though they never existed. All evidence, too, of an earlier, more leisurely living and prosperity—that of the old plantation life—has also been obliterated at least to the casual roving eye. But there is one spot on the island, logically enough, behind a whitewashed, neat negro church, where, hidden among tangled vines and bushes and great trees, one searching carefully may find a link to guide him back to that stately past. This is an old graveyard, centered by a tall, brown stone vault whose heavy doors hang open and the skeletons of whose rotted coffins lie exposed to a curious world. At the top of the vault is the inscription: "Wm. E. Baynard—Integrity and uprightness." There is no date. The vault is a handsome affair with room for many coffins. Two of the coffins are form fitting and made of metal. These, however, have rusted and fallen to pieces at the bottom. Other coffins have been desecrated, the tops pried open and the skeletons left exposed. Several of the tiniest coffins, which are also open, contain only a gruesome dust. The outer doors of the vault are massive affairs made of two thicknesses of heavy wood. The inner doors are of marble, one of which is broken and the other of which is covered in every available space with names of visitors—"fools' names like their faces—."

It is said that the vault, which had been sealed, was burst open by Yankee soldiers who believed it contained valuables. In the cemetery outside are a number of tottering stones, the inscriptions upon many of them being intelligible. Dates upon those that can be read show that in every instance those who were buried beneath died at early ages. There was scarcely one who had reached the age of fifty years. Family names on the stones were as follows: Irvine, Flinn, Webb, Davant, Wagner, Roberts, Kirk and Baldwin. The earliest death, decipherable on the stones, was that of Lydia Davant in 1795.

**Old Families Gone**

There is not a descendant of any old family now living on the island and there is only one house left standing which was there at the time of the war. This is the house formerly used by the Rainey family and now occupied by Mr. Thorne and Mr. Loomis when they come down. This house was not quite completed when the war broke out and for some reason was left standing when the Yankees left the island. It belonged to the Hanahan family and Mr. Lawrence says the first cook he had when he came to Hilton Head had been a slave in the Hanahan family. This house is just a low, rambling cottage, attractive and comfortable, but not elaborate. Its furnishings are simple and charming, just as the Raineys left it. The house is situated in a large grove of cedar trees and the Lawrence home, a smaller white cottage, is close by, both of them occupying wide spacious grounds enclosed by a fence. Just across the road are the barns, dog kennels and cottages occupied by several of the employees of the estate.

The Hurley home is farther down on the island, more isolated, and facing the water. While the Rainey home was furnished as a home, the Hurley place is more on the order of a hunting lodge. It is built on the interior after the fashion of the English hunting lodge, with a balcony enclosing the second story, which is made into bedrooms. The entrance is into a huge hall, at the end of which is a great open fireplace. A caretaker occupies the cottage near this lodge, but the lodge itself is not used by Mr. Thorne and Mr. Loomis, both of whose families prefer to stay together in the more centrally located cottage.

### Duck Ponds Built

One of the developments by the new owners is the building of 400 acres of duckponds, which are now in process. This has been a big undertaking and the work of pumping from the driven wells has been constant since June because of the continued drought. About three thousand or more ducks have been turned loose into the ponds as a nucleus for breeding. It is expected that this pond will eventually furnish the best duck shooting anywhere in this section. Other game are plentiful on this island, deer and quail particularly. There are also wild hogs, which were once domesticated.

Hilton Head island, in some sections, is so tropical appearing that it does not require much imagination to believe one's self in the tropics. From many sections of the island the roar of the ocean can be heard distinctly. Hilton Head boasts one of the very finest natural beaches along the Atlantic coast. There are sixteen miles of as hard, white beach as can be found anywhere. At low tide a car can be driven here with perfect safety for miles. This beach is used as a landing field for planes at times.

There is a powerful lighthouse on the island with both an inland and outer light. The outer light throws its beams for twenty miles.

Hilton Head, which is located about midway between Beaufort and Savannah, has an interesting spot, concerning which the inhabitants know very little. This is a landing known as Spanish wells. There are the remains of old springs here, which it is said Spaniards used to visit during the earliest settlement of this coast.

### No License Plates

Probably the great surprise that a stranger gets when he steps from the gangplank of the steamer at Jenkins Island is the number of smart looking automobiles parked here and there. It seems a little absurd that here on a lonely island, one should be immediately greeted by this reminder of sophistication. But after one learns the distance these people travel, he does not wonder. But he cannot but be startled to be riding along one of the serpentine, sandy, lonely island roads and have the driver suddenly blow his automobile horn while rounding some turn. While it does not seem so queer to be riding in a car, another automobile is somehow the last object one expects to meet. One bane of modern existence these people escape is the buying of automobile license tags. Nobody keeps up their roads, therefore they escape the tax. Mr. Lawrence buys tags for his cars, although he never puts them on.

Except for the wide spaces, the stillness and the absence of people, one who likes solitude would not feel too cut off in the Lawrence household. There are the radio, books and many magazines to bring amusement, the telephone for emergency and comfort, automobiles and horses for rides over the island, waters full of fish and sea food and forests full of game for sport and food.

Landon K. Thorne is the son of Edwin Thorne who recently bought Tomotley plantation in Beaufort county and whose wife died shortly after the purchase. ✺

Brothers-in-law Landon Thorne (1888–1964) and Alfred Loomis (1887–1975) bought the Rainey and Hurley estates in 1931, giving them control of about eleven thousand acres. Throughout the 1930s they continued to purchase land on Hilton Head. They bought anything available, and at the end of the decade they owned some twenty thousand acres and 80 percent of the island. They made their home at Honey Horn, adding a drawing room and additional bedrooms.

Hilton Head was just one of many investments the men shared. In 1920 they bought out the shareholders of Bonbright, the utilities financing company, which at the time was facing bankruptcy. They soon made it a major force, creating utility holding companies for the electric power industry. Between 1924 and 1929, Bonbright supplied $1.6 billion for rural electrification, then rapidly spreading across America. Their most successful business venture was with Commonwealth and Southern Corporation and United Corporation, both in 1929. However, in that same year, Loomis and Thorne were wise enough to understand how dangerously overvalued the stock market was becoming, and they decided to liquidate their holdings in favor of long-term treasury bonds and cash. When the stock market crashed, they were safe.

Though Loomis and Thorne had contrasting personalities, "they were as close as two men could be, professionally and personally," wrote Jennet Conant in *Tuxedo Park: A Wall Street Tycoon and the Secret Palace of Science That Changed the Course of World War II*. Loomis had a mathematical, analytical, mind; he had no interest in social approval or amassing wealth. He valued scientific knowledge, not possessions. Thorne was different, observed Bart Loomis, Alfred's grandson: "He liked to own things . . . art, antiques, horses, . . . yachts, railroads, you name it, he bought it. . . . Talk about big money, [he] was big money." The gardens that Umberto Innocenti designed for Thorne's Long Island estate, said to be among his finest works, suited Thorne's sense of style perfectly.

To relieve the stress of business, Thorne favored active sports: swimming, sailing, fishing in summer, and hunting in winter. In 1930 Thorne and Loomis were two of the three members of the Whirlwind Syndicate, which built the J-class yacht *Whirlwind* and sailed it in the America's Cup trials, losing to Harold Vanderbilt's *Enterprise*. Thorne was helmsman on the *Whirlwind*.

However, Loomis was increasingly turning to other interests. In 1926 he bought Tower House in Tuxedo Park, New York, and converted it into a private laboratory for experimental work on high-frequency sound waves and chronography. By 1933 Loomis had told Thorne that he was through with business, intending to turn his attention to science full time. His ample financial resources and influence in the banking industry made it possible for him to support his own experimental work in physics and that of other scientists. He helped develop the electroencephalograph for recording electric impulses in the brain and worked on the microscopic centrifuge, an aid in the study of cell structure. During World War II, as head of the radar division of the United States Office of Scientific Research, Loomis helped perfect the Loran Electronic Navigational System. He worked with microwave radio and nuclear fission. Loomis had enormous conceptual powers and imaginative energy, and he could work out the designs for mechanical apparatuses; analytical work he left to others.

He received many honors for his achievements, including honorary doctorates from the University of California and Wesleyan University. When Yale University awarded him an honorary master's degree in 1933, he was referred to as "the twentieth century Benjamin Franklin." The United States government presented him its Medal of Merit, and for service in England during the war he received the King's Medal.

During World War II, Thorne and Loomis came south less frequently, and by the late 1940s their property was known to be on the market. In 1945 Loomis abandoned an ailing wife for the young wife of a close associate, alienating members of his family and fracturing the intimacy of the Honey Horn household. Nonetheless, "although they went their separate ways," according to Loomis's son Henry, "their partnership lasted until the end of their lives . . . they never really stopped working together."

Fred C. Hack, a young Georgia lumberman on an inspection trip to Hilton Head, learned that the south end of the island was for sale. Seeing the potential for timber harvesting, he returned with Gen. Joseph B. Fraser and C. C. Stebbins. In March 1950 the three men bought the eighty-four-hundred-acre tract for $450,000, and they formed the Hilton Head Company in May 1951. Hack, Stebbins, and O. T. McIntosh, under the name of Honey Horn Plantation, acquired the remaining eleven thousand acres from Thorne and Loomis for $600,000.

In 1953 the island was still so undeveloped that Samuel Hopkins Adams wrote, "Hilton Head is perhaps the wildest and most beautiful island of the archipelago. On its ocean side stretch . . . miles of flawless beach." However, Hilton Head soon began to lose its isolation, with timbering, the laying out of new roads, and the first limited residential construction. The same year as Adams's visit, the state began operating a nine-car ferry service between Buckingham Landing and the island. Three years later the James F. Byrnes Crossing was in place, and in the same year General Fraser's son Charles had his Sea Pines Plantation under way. The resort community that Fraser envisioned was the creation of the finest land planner in the country, Hideo Sasaki, chairman of Harvard's landscape architecture department. His approach to the land was deeply thoughtful and respectful. From Fraser and Sasaki's beginnings, Hilton Head Island has grown into one of the most notable resort communities in the United States, though few of the developers have followed Sasaki's vision.

# Lady's Island

It is not every woman—nor man, either, for that matter—who can develop into an artist at the age of sixty-six. And doubtless, the number of either sex who, at that age, can row a boat four miles across a tidal river and practically build a house, would be just as few.

But there lives on Lady's island, in Beaufort county, a woman who has accomplished all three of these feats. A retired teacher, she did not know that she possessed any artistic talent, although she was instructed in art, until four years ago. She might never have known it had she owned a kodak or had there been a photographer in her vicinity. Indeed, she might never have known that she was an artist had she not first helped to build her house. And her rowing ability developed through necessity, also, because she built her house on an island, exit from which was possible only by means of water and a long, country island road, at the end of which was a bridge—and she had no automobile.

When Miss Emma Wines finished her house, she was very proud of it, as well she might be, for she helped to build it with her own hands. A carpenter did the outside work and set the house in shape, but Miss Wines herself ceiled her living rooms, hung her doors, built her book cases and shelves and did various other interior work to finish her house.

**Negroes Pose for Her**

Then, when it was finished, she wrote glowing accounts of her house to her family in Springfield, Ill., and they were anxious to have a picture of the place. But Miss Wines had no kodak and she knew nobody who had one, so one day, she sat herself on a little stool in front of her house and began to make a drawing of it for her family. They were so well pleased with it and so surprised at her talent that they encouraged her to continue drawing. So, she has.

Original title: "Rows Boat Once Each Week 4 Miles, to Town and Back. Miss Emma Wines, Graduate of Bryn Mawr, Became Attached to Coast When on Faculty of Fermata at Aiken." Publication date: November 25, 1934.

**Above:** Emma Wines's house on Lady's Island. *Photograph courtesy of Priscilla Merrick Coleman*

Silhouette of census taker and farmer by Emma Wines. *From Eva L. Verdier,* "When Gun Shoot": Some Experiences While Taking the Census among the Low Country Negroes of South Carolina, *1932*

Miss Wines says she cannot carry objects in her mind. She has to have them before her, in order to make a drawing. She has found a happy medium to express her artistic talent through the Gullah negroes, who are her nearest neighbors. They help her about the place, run errands for her and lend themselves wonderingly, but patiently, in posings for her pictures, which take the form for the most part of silhouettes done with pen and ink.

Miss Wines says she is not very fast with her sketching and sometimes her objects grow weary, but they see it through scrutinizing the finished reproductions of themselves with mixed emotions. Miss Wines' work first came into notice when she illustrated a little booklet, "When Gun Shoot," published a year or so ago by Miss Eva Verdier, of Beaufort. These little silhouettes greatly added to the attractiveness of the booklet and created considerable interest.

### Wanted—Way to Keep Hog Still

Just now Miss Wines is at work on a number of small black and white drawings which she will sell for Christmas gifts through a local gift shop. She sketches the outlines of her object, then fills it in with ink at her leisure. In sketching a hog the other day, she says she had a merry time. The hog wouldn't stand still, so the negro woman who owned it gave the animal an ear of corn. However, the corn had the opposite from the desired effect upon the hog. Instead of standing still, as Miss Wines had hoped, it began to walk around and around in a circle while eating the corn. So Miss Wines was reduced to the extremity of walking around and around after the hog, while she sketched. Anybody who passed, she said, must have wondered which was the crazier, she or the hog.

Miss Wines' house is of peculiar construction, consisting of three completed rooms and a screened in front porch. Her living room is beamed and ceiled in natural colored pine, with stairs leading to her bedroom, a large room directly over the living room and kitchen, which is back of the living room. This summer she decided to add a pantry and bath, but the carpenter who was doing the work for her quit and left the rooms partially exposed to the elements. She had the open places walled up, hung a door to shut it off from her kitchen and uses her pantry, even though it still lacks a good bit toward completion.

When she is not carpentering, Miss Wines is working somewhere on her grounds, which she is beautifying with decorative shrubbery, fruit trees and grapevines. But, just now, all labor is at a standstill, while she draws, for she has determined to finish a certain number of pictures for Christmas sales.

### Town 2 Miles by River

Miss Wines' house is located on Woodlawn creek, which empties into Beaufort river. It is two miles from Beaufort by water and six miles by land. Her nearest white neighbor is Colony Gardens, a mile distant. She rows to Beaufort once a week to get supplies. She has an oil burning refrigerator now which keeps food cool, but she used to bring her ice across the river in a row boat. She had to have the ice broken into pieces small enough for her to carry from the boat and up the long dock to her house. On the days when she goes to Beaufort, rowing the two miles there and the two back, she considers that she has had a full day.

Miss Wines has been coming to Beaufort for twelve years to spend her vacations. It was while she was teaching at Fermata, the school at Aiken founded by Mrs. Josef Hoffman, wife of the famous musician, that she decided to buy a place on the coast where she could spend the month vacation she had at Christmas and her long summer vacations. She chose Beaufort and bought a place first on the waterfront between Beaufort and Port Royal. She later sold this place at a profit, had her house torn down and moved to Lady's Island, where she has bought five acres of land.

Miss Wines was born in Springfield, Ill., and was graduated from Bryn Mawr. She taught school for twenty years in various sections of the country, her subjects being French, English, Latin and mathematics. She tells an amusing story of the first time she taught Latin. She had had only the required high school Latin, but was called to take a position as instructor of Latin at Virginia college. She had to study very hard night and day in order to teach this subject and keep one step ahead of her pupils. Once, she ran up against something puzzling and went to the office to inquire who the head of the Latin department was.

The registrar stared at her in astonishment. "Why, you are!"

Miss Wines says she was much nonplussed. Finally, she managed a wry grin. "Well," she replied, "I'm glad at least that my pupils haven't discovered that—I didn't know that!"

Miss Wines is the daughter of Frederick H. Wines, who was for thirty years secretary of the Board of Charities and Corrections of the State of Illinois, and the author of the book, "Punishment and Reformation." Her grandfather, Enoch Wines, founded the National Prison Congress.

Miss Wines must have inherited their interests, for her one diversion, aside from a good game of bridge, is the reading of detective and murder stories. She reads these there until late at night, all alone in her house with no one closer than half a mile or farther. But she is not in the least afraid. The negroes on the island are all native island negroes and she considers them her friends. It would never occur to her to be afraid of them.

So, at the age of sixty-six, she goes on being happy and contented living alone in her secluded place among the woods, puttering in her yard, building her house, drawing pictures and rowing her boat once a week to Beaufort for supplies. ✄

In addition to her home, Emma Wines owned land on St. Helena Island, which she sold in several parcels between 1939 and 1950. In 1953 she sold to Prentice D. Ashe her ten-acre homesite on Lady's Island and her one-third interest in another lot on the island. She died soon after that, in 1954, just three weeks shy of her eighty-sixth birthday, and was buried in St. Helena's churchyard. A very private individual, Miss Wines lived in Beaufort for thirty-five years but today is scarcely remembered. Her artwork too is generally unknown.

One of the few who remember her is Mrs. Charles Webb of Beaufort. When Mrs. Webb was a young girl, she lived in Stanton, Virginia, across the street from Miss Wines, who then taught at Manch College. She occasionally visited her neighbor for tea parties, at which the older woman wore lace. Mrs. Webb says that when Miss Wines moved to Beaufort, she changed her style dramatically, wearing sneakers through which her toes poked and living as a "recluse." Nonetheless Beaufort residents helped her out, carrying her groceries down to her rowboat after her shopping trips.

The house still stands, though it has been expanded greatly by subsequent owners and is now part of the Partridge Woods subdivision. The present owners can point to elements of Miss Wines's original structure. One of the present owners of the house is an artist and teacher and seemed pleased to learn that Miss Wines had the same interests.

Lady's Island today is perhaps the most intensely developed suburb of Beaufort. It is hard to imagine a sixty-six-year-old rowing to her own hand-built home there.

In 1940 Mrs. Martin researched the earliest spellings of the island's name and determined that it is properly known as "Lady's" Island. Ever after she railed against individuals and especially government agencies that misspelled it, as, in fact, she had often done.

# Orange Grove

(also Fripp [Seaside])

Several of the large pre-war plantations on St. Helena island have been purchased in recent years by northern sportsmen who have made various developments and come down for several months each year to enjoy hunting and fishing.

One of these is Henry L. Bowles, former United States congressman from Massachusetts and inventor of the arm chairs so much used in restaurants in the north.

Mr. Bowles' place is known as Orange Grove plantation, which contains about one thousand acres. There was once a real orange grove on this plantation and Mrs. C. H. Evans, whose husband has charge of the place, and who, with her family, lives in the pretty new home recently built there, is a native of this section and says she can remember seeing the orange grove when she was a child.

In addition to Orange Grove plantation, Mr. Bowles has acquired hunting leases on about a thousand or fifteen hundred acres on St. Helena.

The story is told of Mr. Bowles that while working as a boy in a shop in Vermont and taking his lunches out in restaurants, he conceived the idea of the arm chair for lunch rooms. He placed his idea to a chair manufacturing concern in Pittsburgh and this company began the manufacture of his chair, which met with immediate success.

**On Johnson River**

Mr. Bowles, whose home is in Springfield, Mass., has been out of Congress for about a year. He is about 60 years old and comes to his St. Helena island plantation every year.

His new home at Orange Grove, completed about two years ago, is most attractive, containing nice rooms. It is of New England type of architecture, painted white. There is a long living room across the entire house, facing the west.

Original title: "Northern Sportsmen Acquire St. Helena Island Property. Henry L. Bowles, Former Massachusetts Congressman, and Dr. A. W. Elting, New York Surgeon, Control Five Thousand Acres." Publication date: December 15, 1930.

Orange Grove in 2008. *Photograph courtesy of Robert B. Cuthbert*

The Johnson river, a tidal stream, flows just a few feet away from the windows of this room and at the back, beneath protecting trees, is an old plantation grave yard. The oldest grave there is that of Peter Perry, who died in 1814.

The living room has walls of pecky cypress and is furnished with old Colonial furniture. A particularly interesting piece is an old desk which was made by Mr. Evans's great, great, grandfather.

There is a furnace, also a power plant and every convenience that could be desired on this plantation, which is located about ten miles from Beaufort.

An old brick plantation home, which had been owned by the Fripp family before the Civil war, was torn down to make way for this new building.

### Owns Fripp Lands

Another interesting personage from the north who comes down for the hunting season each year and owns three old plantations on St. Helena island is Dr. A. W. Elting, noted New York surgeon.

One of Dr. Elting's plantations is the Edgar Fripp place, which is located several miles down on the road from Mr. Bowles' place. This tract contains one thousand acres and the old Fripp family home is situated here.

The house, which is in an excellent state of preservation and is well cared for by Dr. Elting, is said to be about 45 years old. It is a large, two-storied building, set high off the ground and facing the Trunkard river. Although the house is very large, it contains only six rooms and two large halls. There are also big porches, front and back. The rooms are very large and the two front downstairs ones have tall, hand-painted pictures above the mantels. The stairs are graceful and curving and the railing is of mahogany. Midway of the stairs, there is a picturesque fan shaped window. The house is occupied by the caretaker of the place.

Sixty-five acres of the plantation land are given over to pecans and there are 1,200 trees which are just beginning to bear. Ten or fifteen acres are planted to seed for birds and the remainder is used solely for hunting.

### Pine Island and the Pope Place

Dr. Elting makes his home when he is on St. Helena at his Pine island home. The house on this island was built in 1901 by Thomas Lee and sold to Dr. Elting in 1918. The timber, brick, mantels and some of the other materials in the house were taken from the old Jenkins' home on St. Helena island and moved to Pine island by boat.

Mr. Lee gave $75 for the timber and $75 for the brick. The old mantels are hand carved and are considered to be the handsomest on the entire island. The staircase is solid mahogany.

The old Jenkins' home had been damaged by the 1893 storm so badly that it had gone to pieces and parts of it were being gradually taken down and sold to pay taxes. It was at one time one of the show pieces of the island.

Mr. Lee did not attempt to duplicate this house at Pine island, but built a simple eight room house with seven open fireplaces.

Pine island cannot be reached except by wagon or horse-drawn vehicle during full moon tide, as the water overflows the causeways at that time. The island is reached by a long ride across St. Helena, through a narrow road heavily carpeted with pine needles. There is a garage for cars just this side of the causeway.

Dr. Elting also owns the old Pope place on St. Helena. This tract of 235 acres contains no house. He has a total of 2,930 acres. All of his places are looked after by R. F. Ford, who lives at Frogmore on St. Helena.

Dr. Elting is a great hunter. He recently was on a hunting expedition in Africa. A number of Beaufort people had the opportunity of seeing moving pictures of this hunt when Dr. Elting was at Pine island last winter.

Solomon R. Guggenheim of copper fame owns 500 acres of land on Lady's island, known as the Lady's Island Hunting club. In addition to this, he has leased about one thousand acres for hunting purposes. Mr. Guggenheim has made no developments upon his property yet, although it is understood that he intends to build at some future date. ✤

Early owners of Orange Grove were the Chapman, Perry, and Evans families. John Evans, who held the 473-acre plantation in 1775, was among the wealthiest men in Beaufort District and the largest indigo planter on St. Helena. (Indigo was the area's principal crop before the introduction of Sea Island cotton.) Three hundred fifty acres of the original plantation were sold to Edgar Fripp of Seaside in 1845 by then-owner Thomas Fuller. At the time of the Civil War, Orange Grove, abandoned by its owner, was confiscated by federal authorities and included in the Port Royal Experiment.

Orange Grove during the ownership of John Snow,
circa 1940–65. *Photograph courtesy of Margot H. Rowland*

Massachusetts congressman Henry L. Bowles bought sixty-one acres of Orange Grove in 1921. Born in Vermont in 1866, Bowles, as a young man of eighteen, went west to Iowa and California. He was at one time or another a farmer, rancher, and lumberjack. By 1898 Bowles was establishing himself in the food-service business in Massachusetts, eventually building a successful chain of restaurants, and, of course, overseeing the design of the chair that so interested Mrs. Martin. His interest in Massachusetts politics brought him to the attention of the Republican Party. When a vacancy occurred in the state's congressional delegation in 1924, he was elected to the seat, and he remained in office until 1929, after which he returned to private business.

Bowles added to his Orange Grove holdings in 1928, when he purchased another sixty-one acres in small parcels. That year he tore down the original house and built the present one as a "hunting cottage." According to a pamphlet about the house prepared by the present owners, remaining from the earlier era "are the mantel which is now in the living room of the 1928 house; the tabby ruins of the original plantation kitchen building; and the Fripp family graveyard, surrounded by a tabby wall. Ann Perry Fripp (1799–1830), along with her daughter and one other family member, are buried in the graveyard under the oak trees to the north of the house."

Mr. Bowles died in 1932, and in 1936 his heirs sold the six-hundred-acre plantation to L. H. Carter of Ridgeland, South Carolina. Orange Grove became the property of John B. Snow of New Jersey in 1943. Snow, a Wall Street broker who also worked with his family's brake-shoe company, made his home at Orange Grove until 1963, when the Trask family, under the name Orange Grove Corporation, took title to the property. They have owned it ever since.

In 1972 Mr. and Mrs. John M. Trask Jr. rebuilt the Bowles house, making major interior changes to accommodate their family and opening up the back of the house with glass to take advantage of the natural views. In addition they added the east wing to the house, built a walled-in garden, installed landscaping designed by Robert E. Marvin, and planted an avenue of live oak trees. The architectural design of the front of the house remains essentially unchanged from Congressman Bowles's day.

The old house at Seaside, or Fripp, dates from about 1810. It is located about two and one-half miles southeast of Orange Grove and backs up on the broad marsh behind Fripp Island. The Fripps were established planters on St. Helena beginning in 1725 and were known as the largest landowners on the island.

"Proud Edgar," as Fripp was called, was a successful cotton planter. He was careful in the selection of his seed, which yielded a crop of the highest quality and made him a rich man, particularly in the decade before the Civil War, when cotton prices were high. Fripp

Seaside. *Photograph courtesy of the South Caroliniana Library, University of South Carolina*

had an Egyptian-style vault built for himself in the Episcopal churchyard on St. Helena. He also had the funds to construct in 1856 one of the largest houses in Beaufort, known today as Tidalholm. However, Fripp was a difficult man. Called a "Colossal egoist" by those who knew him, he liked to flaunt his money among those of lesser means. He had the traits of a petty tyrant and employed them on those unfortunate enough to be subject to his controls. We are told that he whipped any black man he met who did not immediately remove his hat as a sign of respect. More disturbing is the account given in Edith M. Dabbs's *Sea Island Diary* of an incident that happened in 1855 on Fripp's plantation.

Fripp's overseer, a man named Harvey, caught a hungry black man stealing a watermelon from the garden. Knowing his employer's thinking in such affairs, Harvey had the man confined in a shed until high tide. Then four men carried the fellow to the river and repeatedly "ducked" him until he was exhausted. They then stretched him over a log, and the overseer beat him until he was bloody, in which state he was thrown into a cart and dumped on the public road. He was dead the next morning. Harvey was arrested and taken to jail in Beaufort. He would have been hanged had not Fripp paid a fine for his release. However, Harvey never returned to the plantation.

Fripp died in 1860. He was not in his marble vault long before Union troops occupied Beaufort. Thinking valuables might be concealed inside, they broke it open.

As Edgar Fripp was childless, he left Seaside to his relative Edgar W. Fripp, a minor at the time of the war. Edgar in 1872 reclaimed the 732-acre plantation. He lived there until it was sold to Dr. Elting in 1920, saying at the time of the sale that he had lived at Seaside "almost 42 years since my youth."

Dr. Arthur Elting, a surgeon of Albany, New York, acquired more than 150 parcels of land on St. Helena between 1920 and 1948. The most significant of these were the 732-acre Seaside plantation and Pine and Hunting islands, the last of which he conveyed to Beaufort County for use as a park. Many of the smaller tracts were owned by the descendants of freedmen. (Mrs. Martin wrote again of Dr. Elting a year later, describing his Pine Island property.) Dr. Elting sold the 777-acre Seaside in 1946 to Willard Graham, who held the property until 1959 before selling to Margaret E. Sanford of Fort Lauderdale, Florida, the mother of future South Carolina governor Mark Sanford. When the Sanfords bought Coosaw plantation on Chisolm Island in 1965, Seaside was conveyed to William C. Anderson.

Though Mrs. Martin gives little attention to Solomon Guggenheim, he was one of the major industrialists of his era and an important figure in the South Carolina lowcountry. He owned, in addition to land on Lady's Island, the twelve-thousand-acre Elgerbar plantation in Colleton County and a grand house in Charleston at 9 East Battery. An important art collector, he allowed the Gibbes Art Gallery in Charleston to show his extensive collection of abstract art in 1936 and 1938, the first such shows in the country. Later he would use this collection as the base for his Guggenheim Museum of Art in New York City.

# Palmetto Bluff

Until a few years ago, Palmetto Bluff, the palatial winter home of the late R. T. Wilson, Wall street banker, was one of the show places of the low country of South Carolina. However, disaster and time have combined to lay heavy hands upon its beauty and, although it is well kept, there is evident to a close observer that subtle sadness which settles upon any spot which knows no longer the touch of the hand which created and loved it.

Palmetto Bluff, located between Hardeeville and Bluffton in Beaufort county, is correctly named, for it is a high bluff, overlooking the May river, and so thickly dotted with palmetto trees in some sections as to resemble a tropical country. This strip of land is a peninsula between the May and New rivers.

The estate is hidden away at the very end of a long road which zig-zags through heavily timbered woods. The property is entered a short distance off the road through

The Wilson house at Palmetto Bluff. *Photograph courtesy of the Palmetto Bluff Conservancy*

Original title: "Palmetto Bluff in Lower Beaufort. Curving Oyster Shell Driveways and Boxed Walks Take Up 14 Acres of the 25,000-acre Estate That Overlooks May River." Publication date: December 28, 1930.

high gates, which a tiny boy, doubtless the son of the gatekeeper, scrambles up to open. Undirected, a visitor would lose himself in the maze of winding roads that lead here and there through the estate. At last, the main road branches off to the left into a white shelled road which leads to another pair of gates that open upon a garden. This garden strikes an amazingly incongruous note, there at the end of that veritable wilderness. It is as though in the midst of a meadow rank with wild grasses, one had suddenly come upon hot house flowers growing in orderly rows.

There are fourteen or more acres of boxed walks and curving driveways, which glisten whitely. These walks and drives are made of crushed oyster shell and gleaming here and there among the trees and shrubbery are picturesque little white stucco cottages built for the various employees of the Wilson estate.

There are small cedars and beautiful shrubbery bordering the driveways and walks about the estate. At the upper end, immediately overlooking the river, are the ruins of the magnificent Wilson home, which was destroyed by fire four or five years ago.

### Only Columns Left

There is nothing left now of this beautiful home save several broken and crumbling white columns and a great pile of blackened mortar and brick. But the shelled walk which leads away to the river bluff is as fresh and green as ever and in the bright sunshine the birds call to each other as blithely as in the olden days.

The Wilsons made this their winter home and their two daughters were born there.

Across a little wooden bridge, just beyond a wilderness of palmetto trees, is a large, low white house, also facing the river. This house was built by W. K. Vanderbilt, brother-in-law of Mrs. Wilson, and occupied by the Vanderbilts during the winter months. The house is in excellent condition and is used by the present owner, George W. Varn, of the Varn Turpentine and Cattle company, of Valdosta, Ga., and his family when they visit Palmetto Bluff on hunting trips or on business.

The photograph of the Vanderbilt house at Palmetto Bluff that accompanied the original *Charleston News and Courier* article, with the caption "Palmetto Bluff clubhouse which was the former Vanderbilt home." *Photograph courtesy of the Charleston County Public Library*

This concern bought the place from Mr. Wilson several years ago for its timber and turpentine. The company does a big turpentine business and there are, now, piled about the grounds of the Vanderbilt home about seven hundred barrels of rosin. Mr. Varn sells his turpentine and rosin in Savannah. He is a big, hearty, genial fellow and radiates hospitality. There are about sixty-five people in his employ at Palmetto Bluff.

This estate comprises around 25,000 acres of land, including marsh, and is a splendid hunting preserve. On Thanksgiving Day Mr. Varn gave a hunt and five fine bucks were killed.

## Of Many Plantations

Palmetto Bluff is made up of a number of old, ante-bellum plantations. Among these are Halsey, Moreland, Pettigrew, Theus, Big House, No. Eight plantation, Baynard, Refieum, Box, Mt. Plier, Chinkapin Hill and the Gen. Thomas F. Crayton plantations.

These plantations were accumulated by J. H. Estill, founder of The Savannah Morning News. Mr. Estill built the main part of what was the Wilson home and later sold it to Mr. Wilson, who elaborated on the house and made it into the handsome structure it was. This home was built on what was the old Halsey plantation.

In the center of the hundreds of barrels of rosin near the Vanderbilt home there is, almost hidden from view by the barrels, a square stone wall. Inside this are three tombs. One of them, a low flat stone that covers the entire grave, is without inscription of any kind, and there was found no one about the place who could give any information concerning it. One of the other tombs is in memory of Dr. Samuel Fairchild, who died in 1826 at the age of 62 years. There is a third tomb, which is dedicated on one side to the memory of Samuel Breck Parkman and four of his children, all of whom perished on the steamship Pulaski by the explosion of her boiler while at sea on the night of June 14, 1838, on their passage from Savannah to Baltimore. Mr. Parkman was born in Boston in May, 1787. On the other side of the monument is an inscription to his wife in effect, as follows: "The stone above marks the spot where are deposited the remains of Theresa Halsey, wife of Samuel Breck Parkman, and two of her children. . . . "

The story told by some of the people at Palmetto Bluff is that these bodies washed ashore near there and were brought to Palmetto Bluff and buried. However, information to be obtained here of this tragedy of nearly a hundred years ago and its connection with Palmetto Bluff is vague and meager.

Mr. Wilson, former owner of the place, died a few months ago and one of his daughters, Louise, who was born at Palmetto Bluff, and who is now Mrs. L. S. Turnure, owns an estate down below Palmetto Bluff about nine miles from Bluffton. Mrs. Turnure's home, a newly built one-story frame house of simple yet artistic construction, is situated in a thick grove of trees overlooking the Colleton river. It is reached by a torturous road through heavily timbered lands. There is a glass-enclosed sun porch from which a splendid view can be had of the river.

This estate was originally two plantations, Oak Forest and Trimblestone, and was owned by Joseph Huger of Savannah, who sold it to Mrs. Turnure. ❧

Samuel Breck Parkman's children who died in the explosion of the *Pulaski* were Authexa, Carolina, Theresa, and Whitney. The ship was destroyed off the coast of North Carolina, so no bodies could have washed ashore in southern South Carolina. For more on that disaster, see the entry for Pimlico in Berkeley County.

Mrs. Martin does not describe in detail "the ruins of the magnificent Wilson home, which was destroyed by fire four or five years ago," and it is almost forgotten today. However, it was one of the largest private homes ever built in South Carolina: a three-story, forty-room, neoclassical mansion fronted by four massive columns that rose to the roofline. Built in 1915 by Richard Wilson Jr., it burned to the ground in March 1926. After that, according to an extensive study prepared by Brockington and Associates in 2004, "Wilson lost interest in Palmetto Bluff, sold out, and returned to New York, where he died three years later."

Wilson was the son of Richard Wilson Sr., a Confederate veteran who became a New York railroad and banking tycoon and who is thought to have been worth forty million dollars at his death. About 1902 he purchased the Beaufort County property from John Holbrook Estill and also bought additional land on the May River. The Brockington report identifies fifteen nineteenth-century plantations that made up Palmetto Bluff, the name given the property by the senior Wilson.

Before the Wilsons became involved, acreage that would become a part of Palmetto Bluff was purchased by timber interests in the late nineteenth century. Wilson Sr., his son Richard Wilson Jr., and his son-in-law Cornelius Vanderbilt Jr. continued this industry and many others. A 1968 report explains: "Something of a principality, the estate had 8,000 acres under cultivation, growing cotton as well as produce. There was an electrical plant, water towers, refrigeration house, laundry, a school for employees' children . . . even a post office. And a doctor to look after them all."

After the fire and their sale of Palmetto Bluff, the Wilsons continued to make news in the lowcountry. The younger Wilson's daughter, an avid horseback rider, was featured in the *Charleston News and Courier* in a February 25, 1932, article titled "Woman Plantation Owner Weds Sentenced Foreman": "Mrs. Louisa S. Turnure, daughter of a Wall street banker and owner of two Beaufort county plantations, was married here today to Wendell Simmons, 25, her foreman, who is under sentence to serve twenty-two months in the federal penitentiary at Atlanta for violation of the prohibition law. Simmons was convicted at Charleston last October 24 along with others arrested in the largest raid ever made in Jasper county."

A glowing article about Mrs. Simmons ran in the *News and Courier* in 1935. (It is unclear if Mr. Simmons had been released from the federal pen yet.) She had bought a Beaufort County plantation, was raising three hundred head of cattle there, and was maintaining a stable of twenty horses, including several "thoroughbreds brought from her father's racing stable at Saratoga." Her neighbors included W. Moseley Swain of Belfair, Col. W. M. Copp of Spring Island, Harry Cram of Foot Point, and her younger sister, Miss Marion Wilson, who owned the adjoining Hog Bluff Plantation. The author claimed that Mrs. Simmons had "set a precedent" for other northern plantation owners by settling down in the area rather than just visiting her land for hunting trips.

The Varn family and their Valdosta company owned the property until 1937, when more than eighteen thousand acres of Palmetto Bluff land were bought by Union Bag and Paper Company. After mergers the company name was changed to the Union-Camp Corporation and then to International Paper Company. It was the largest landowner in southern Beaufort County with a total of fifty-six thousand acres. At the end of the twentieth century, much of the land was used for an extensive residential community that bears the name Palmetto Bluff.

# Pine Island

If there should be one searching the world over for a spot which affords perfect peace and quiet, he would find his search ended when he reached Pine island, off St. Helena. This small island with its hundred wooded acres is such a still, quiet place that its peace wraps one around like a warm blanket. Visitors here leave their troubles one by one along the causeway over which the island is approached, so that once they are across, they feel strangely free and light-hearted.

So secluded from the world is Pine island, it cannot be reached except when the tide is low unless one travel by wagon or horse-drawn vehicle, as the water overflows the causeway when the tide is high.

The long drive to the causeway is through thick pine woods and the narrow curving road is heavily carpeted with fragrant pine needles. The long causeway is extremely narrow and the gray tidal creek laps it close on either side.

Pine island itself is high and dry and densely wooded. There are only the caretaker's cottage and, farther on, the hunting lodge of Dr. A. W. Elting, of Albany, N.Y., who owns the island.

The lodge, brown and two-storied, seems to have been slipped with effective unobtrusiveness into the brown and green woods which surround it.

The interior of the house is plain and substantial with an air of simple beauty and dignity. The living room has a large bay window, all of glass, which affords a sweeping view of the woods and water beyond. The furniture is mostly hand-made, built simply and durably. There are book shelves in the living room, filled with books whose gay jackets add gaiety to the room. Across the hall is the dining room, where a great deal of the game killed is cooked in the large fireplace. The kitchen itself is a separate room in the yard. Bedrooms are at the back and upstairs.

This hunting lodge was built from timbers which were taken from the old Jenkins' plantation home on St. Helena. In its day, before the Confederate war, this house was

Original title: "Beaufort Island Hunting Lodge. Pine Island, Beaufort County, Offers Seclusion and Sport. Hunting Lodge There Owned by Dr. A. W. Elting, of Albany, N.Y., Was Constructed of Timbers from Famous Coastal House." Publication date: December 20, 1931.

one of the handsomest in these parts, but after the war, it was left to fall to pieces. For a time, taxes on the place were said to have been raised by selling various parts of the interior from time to time. Thomas Lee, a Northerner who bought and sold much property on St. Helena island, purchased the timbers in this old house finally for the sum of $75. He also bought the brick, the handsome hand-carved mantels and the solid mahogany staircase, all of which he removed by boat to Pine island and built into this hunting lodge, which he later sold to Dr. Elting. The house has eight rooms and seven large open fireplaces, each of which has its huge bed of ashes. These ashes are not allowed to be moved and once hot, they keep the rooms warm and comfortable.

An interesting feature of this Pine island place is its grounds. These have been left in their natural state, rising and curving as they will. Walks and drives are bordered by a natural hedge of casina, laurel, and so on, which are kept trimmed to the desired height. There is also a natural lawn, the natural undergrowth being kept closely clipped. All of this is evergreen and the whole presents a cool and lovely view.

Dr. Elting, who is an enthusiastic hunter, is a frequent visitor to his home at Pine island during the winter season and often has guests who come down to hunt and rest. In addition to Pine island, he also owns other large holdings on St. Helena island.

Dr. Elting was on a hunting expedition to Africa a year or so ago and there is to be seen at the lodge an interesting book of this expedition which includes a photograph of Dr. Elting.

Dr. Elting, among other positions, was at one time a member of the staff at Johns Hopkins, was surgeon-in-chief of the Albany hospital, child's hospital at Albany, professor of surgery at the Albany Medical College.

R. F. Ford, of St. Helena Island, is general superintendent for Dr. Elting's properties on St. Helena. ✀

Thomas Lee (1858–1936) of Westport, New York, came to the Beaufort area in 1896. Two years later he was constructing his shingled hunting lodge on Pine Island, his winter home for more than twenty years. By nature Lee was an outdoorsman: naturalist, craftsman, hunter, and fisherman. He graduated from Harvard in 1879, briefly studied law, gave it up to enter a Boston investment firm, but was unsatisfied in that field too. (Money inherited from his father permitted a relaxed attitude about business.) Still restless, in 1884 Lee applied for and was accepted as a volunteer naturalist with the Smithsonian Institution in Washington, D.C. For the next few years he accompanied museum scientists on many exotic ocean voyages, collecting and cataloging specimens of animal and plant life.

With his later move to Pine Island, Lee was a neighbor of the Penn Center, the school established in 1862 to assist the freedmen on St. Helena. Lee took an interest in the work of the school and served for a period as an adviser on agricultural matters. Lee shared Pine Island with Dr. Arthur Elting from 1919 to 1926, selling his interest to Elting in that final year and moving across St. Helena Sound to Raccoon Island near Edisto.

Today Lee is remembered most for having designed a chair for sitting outdoors at his hilly New York home; while he called it a "Westport," it is now widely known as an "Adirondack" chair. He placed some of them on Pine Island and found that they worked just fine in the flat lowcountry.

Pine Island main house and guest cotttage in 2008. *Photographs courtesy of Robert B. Cuthbert*

Dr. Elting, a distinguished surgeon, was a graduate of Yale and the Johns Hopkins Medical School. He was an officer in a number of medical organizations, including the American Surgical Association, of which he was president. During different periods he taught surgery at Albany Medical College and served on the staff of Johns Hopkins Hospital.

He was also an avid quail hunter, with a hunger for quail-hunting land. In addition to his approximately three thousand acres on St. Helena, making him the second-largest property owner on the island, he leased the hunting rights to another seven thousand acres. In *The Gullah Mailman,* Pierre McGowan estimates that Dr. Elting controlled more than three hundred coveys of birds and never shot a covey twice in a hunting season. When he purchased Pine Island from Thomas Lee, he also acquired six hundred acres on the northern part of Hunting Island. In 1936 he and co-owner James M. Cameron transferred their Hunting Island property to Beaufort County for use as a park. Today Hunting Island is the most popular park in the state's system. It features five miles of beach, campgrounds, and a number of buildings constructed by the Civilian Conservation Corps during the 1930s.

Arthur Elting died in 1948 at the age of seventy-five, leaving his wife a life interest in all his Albany and Beaufort properties. After personal bequests, his residual estate was to go to Phillips Academy in Exeter, New Hampshire. A school trustee sold Pine Island, plus the nearby St. Helenaville and Cherry Hill plantations, in 1949 to Theodore Ayer Randolph of Upperville, Virginia, for ten thousand dollars. Less than two years later all of the lands were transferred to Dr. Robert D. Johnson and his wife, Frances, of Syracuse, New York, who held on to them until after Hurricane Gracie in 1959.

The Johnsons were renting out the property at the time and came down after the storm to check on the damage. Lowcountry timberman Harry Hanna of Estill, South Carolina, who already owned much property in the area, was then removing some of Pine Island's fallen trees. When Dr. Johnson said that he thought he should sell the land before another hurricane came through, Hanna agreed to buy it. In 1960 he did so, with his brother Leslie. Along with the property, the Hannas received a boat, a Jeep, and all the household furniture, including two of the earliest examples of Lee's Adirondack chair. Members of the Hanna family still own the land (and the chairs) and use it as a vacation spot. The houses described in Mrs. Martin's articles remain essentially as they looked during her visit. Harry Hanna now owns more than sixty properties in the area—a large number but, as county officials have pointed out to him, considerably fewer than Dr. Elting.

Joe Hanna and Harry Hanna sitting in the original Adirondack chairs at Pine Island. *Photograph by Robert B. Cuthbert*

# Polawana Island

Forty acres of island near here has just been sold to Dr. George G. Davis, of Chicago, head surgeon of the United States Steel corporation. The property formerly belonged to Sam Brown and I. J. Brisbane, both negroes, who have lived on the island all of their lives. On tracing the titles Dr. Davis found that the property was first sold to the fore-bearers of these two by the direct tax commission of the United States just after the Civil war.

The island, Pollowanna, on which this property stands, is one of the most beautiful of the smaller sea islands in this section. It lies just north of the village of Frogmore, on St. Helena island and south of Dataw island. Jenkins creek runs to the north of Pollowanna.

Tropical in its beauty, Pollowanna abounds in quail and wild duck. Besides the shooting, Dr. Davis, a lover of the water and water sports, is very much interested in fishing and sailing. He is a member of the Yacht club of Chicago and owns a thirty-foot sailing craft which he expects to bring to Beaufort.

Dr. Davis stated that the island property was purchased with the sole idea of making a playground and recreational spot of it. He will spend several of the winter months on it every year, developing it and enhancing its natural beauty.

Dr. Davis is one of the foremost surgeons in the country. He is a graduate of the University of Chicago and a native Chicagoan. During the World war he served in France as a surgeon and has served the United States government in the Philippines as a surgeon.

As a great sportsman and lover of nature, Dr. Davis has traveled extensively and declares that this section of South Carolina cannot be rivaled anywhere in the world in beauty.

Dr. Davis was interested in Beaufort through Miss Kate Gleason, of Rochester, New York, who has a large number of properties in the neighborhood of Beaufort as well as owning property in the city of Beaufort, where she has her winter home. ✺

Original title: "Chicagoan Buys Beaufort Land." Publication date: March 15, 1929.

This short article carried no byline, but it reads like one of Mrs. Martin's.

The collection of letters and diary of Laura M. Towne, the Pennsylvania woman who ran the Penn Center on St. Helena for several decades, includes this account about Polawana (there are still several different spellings commonly used) from November 1862: "Tina, of Palawana, was telling us today how her master's family were sitting down to dinner in their far off lovely island, when the news came that everybody was flying. They sprang up, left the silver on the table, the dinner untasted, packed a few clothes for the children, and were gone, never to come back."

According to the Agricultural Census of 1860 and Sams Family Papers at the South Carolina Historical Society, Lewis Reeve Sams M.D. (1810–1888) owned Polawana Island at the beginning of the war "though he lived in St. Helena village on the Seaside Road near Coffin Point."

While Sam Brown and I. J. Brisbane had once owned land on the island, as Mrs. Martin writes, Dr. Davis did not buy the property from them or their descendants. In January 1929 Kate Gleason purchased the property, and she sold it to Dr. Davis for just $120 two months later. (This article was actually published two weeks before the sale was completed.) He allowed Miss Gleason to access her lands at Dataw Island through Polawana. In January 1931, less than two years after this article appeared, Dr. Davis sold Polawana back to his friend Miss Gleason.

The property has gone through several hands. Brothers-in-law Jim Rentz and Marvin Godley owned most of it from the 1950s until the 1980s, and it is now heavily developed. It still allows access to Dataw.

# *Retreat*

Seven miles from the town of Beaufort, in the direction of the Parris island causeway, across a plowed field and through a thick wood, is to be found the oldest house on Port Royal island—the Retreat.

This house is so old that nobody seems to know just how old it really is. It was there when the woods of this section were still full of Red Men and the people who lived in it climbed to their beds at night by a ladder and then drew the ladder up with them for protection from the Indians.

True, the house is rapidly falling in decay, but it could be put into livable condition again without too much expense, so excellent is the material with which it is built. In fact, it was occupied until only a little while ago.

The house is made of tabby, which is still in a perfect state of repair. Only the wood-work is rotting. It is a gabled building with shutters of heavy wood and a little crooked, winding stair which has been added since the house was built. The fireplaces are of old English brick and the window through which the ladder was wont to be pulled, has since been bricked up.

The house was built by a Frenchman a long time before the Revolutionary war. The history of the Frenchman, who went by the name of Lagay, is shrouded in mystery.

## Alone with Slaves

One day he appeared in Beaufort, purchased the land and set to work on his house. He made no explanations to anyone, living alone with only negro slaves to look after him. He never spoke to anyone save on business and although there were people in Beaufort who offered him friendliness, he froze them out and they finally let him alone.

He had a tragic ending. Two of his slaves murdered him in a boat one night. One escaped, but the other was captured and quartered and his head stuck up on a pole at a spot on what was then the main highway. It remained there for two generations and this

Original title: "French Hermit Built Oldest House on Port Royal Island. Believed a Political Exile, He Came to Beaufort, Sought No Acquaintances and Was Murdered by Two Negro Slaves." Publication date: November 30, 1930.

Retreat. *Photograph courtesy of the South Carolina Department of Archives and History*

place, which is now a point of marsh near Beaufort, is to this day known as "Nigger Head." However, there are few now living who have heard and none who remember how the place got its name.

It was said that the Frenchman was cruel to his negroes and it is supposed that was the reason he was murdered. The Frenchman was killed about the year 1776 and died without a will. His house was searched, but not a single scrap of paper could be found to throw a light upon his identity.

It was generally believed that he was of the French nobility and a political exile from his country. That he was a gentleman was obvious to those who came in contact, brief though it was, with him. But aside from that, the Frenchman came to Beaufort, lived and went his tragic way without in any way revealing himself. Whatever his secret, it was buried in the grave with him.

**Gives Purchase Away**

The property, which then became escheated, was sold at auction and bought by Stephen Bull. It is said that on his way back from the sale, Stephen Bull began to regret his purchase and to wonder what he would do with it since he already had so much property. While pondering upon the matter, he met John Barnwell and asked him if he did not want the Retreat.

In this way, the Barnwells came into possession of this house and it is still in the hands of descendants of John Barnwell.

The Retreat has one of the loveliest locations imaginable. Coming suddenly out of the thick wood into a little clearing, there it is, gleaming whitely through the trees. It faces Battery Creek, the little tidal stream being only a few feet from the steps of the old house.

Aside from the addition of the staircase and the screened front porch, the Retreat is as it always was in the essentials. The heavy old shutters, there is no glass to the windows even yet, were once painted red and the tabby walls were kept always spotless with white wash.

Inside, there are deep window seats and immense, wide fireplaces which, at intervals, have been bricked up and then re-opened again. The thick doors are paneled on the interior and the great mantels and wainscoting are hand carved. Some of the wainscoting is missing, apparently torn off. It was probably sold by some hard-up tenant as has been the case in so many of the old houses along the coast.

The Retreat was damaged by the earthquake of 1886, some of the tabby being jarred away. This was patched with brick and whitewashed.

It is said that neither John Barnwell nor his son, who was also John, ever allowed to be cut the great hickories and oaks which hid the Retreat from the world. Nor did they allow these woods to be hunted.

### Miss Emily Walker

On this visit to the Retreat, the writer was accompanied by the oldest living descendant of John Barnwell. She is Miss Emily Walker, 85 years young, for Miss Emily does indeed possess a mind and spirit, the resilience of which would put mere youth to shame.

She had not seen the place for a long while and when the woods broke and gave upon the clearing with its well-remembered spot, her blue eyes widened and shone.

She ran from room to room like a happy child. She touched lovingly one of the deeply recessed window ledges. "I used to sit in this very window and read my Bible. I read it five times through in this same window."

She stood at the foot of the little crooked stairs and looked up with one eager hand upon the railing. But the stairs were rickety and there was a rotting hole at the top. She was jerked back by an alarmed kinsman.

Miss Emily hesitated for only a moment. Then she laughed with scorn and scampered up as agilely as a little gray kitten. Laughing gleefully, she eluded her pursuers and scoffed to the only one brave, or foolish, enough to follow her: "'Fraid cats."

She stood in the doorway of one of the two upstairs rooms, a soft smile curving her mouth. "This was my mother's nursery and here," she stooped to open the door of a queer little closet at one side of the fireplace, "my sister, Ann, and I played at dolls—eighty, eighty-one, eighty-two years ago."

Downstairs, Miss Emily stood pensively looking out upon the water. Then she turned. "I'll tell you a story. During the Revolutionary war an English gunboat anchored out there and some officers came up here hunting John Barnwell, who was away fighting with the Colonists. Food must have been low. There was a pot of peas cooking here." Miss Emily walked over to the mantel and placed her hand upon it. "His son, John, was then a little boy and he was anxious about those peas. He stood before them, his hands behind his back, and defied the English officers to touch them."

As the party drove away, leaving the Retreat to its memories, Miss Emily turned in her seat, ejaculating sorrowfully: "Oh, Ann has been cut down!"

Then she caught sight of the puzzled faces of her listeners and laughed. "Do you see that great, tall pine yonder? Well, once there were two small pines close together. One was named Emily for me and the other Ann for my sister. But only Emily is left."

She laughed again. But there was a misty gleam in the eyes which the gallant little old lady turned swiftly away. ⚶

Mrs. Martin's guide, Miss Emily Barnwell Walker, lived until March 23, 1933, dying at the age of eighty-seven. She was the daughter of Rev. Edward T. Walker and Ann Bull Barnwell Walker. The book *The Walkers of South Carolina,* in the Beaufort County Public Library, describes her as "Beaufort's reference library."

In that volume Miss Walker tells the story that in November 1861, when Beaufort townspeople learned that U.S. troops were about to attack Port Royal, her mother sent their servant "Daddy Jimmy" to Retreat to pick up the family's longboat. By lamplight Emily, her cousin Sarah Stuart and her two infants, and her father were rowed by six servants up the Beaufort River and across the Coosaw River. When they reached the mainland in the morning, they could hear guns booming in the distance.

Mrs. Martin reported the story of the murder of the "French hermit" no doubt as it was told to her, but the truth seems to have been different. According to the first volume of *The History of Beaufort County,* by Lawrence S. Rowland, Alexander Moore, and George C. Rogers, the murdered man was Charles Purry, elder son of the founder of Purrysburg, who was Swiss, not French: "In 1754, Charles Purry was poisoned by one of his trusted household slaves. It was the most famous slave murder case in colonial Beaufort and sent shudders through the lowcountry planter community. The slave perpetrator was tried, executed, and gibbeted on Bay Street in 1754." The authors of that volume explain that it was John DelaGaye who owned Retreat until 1769, when he retired to France.

When Mrs. Martin wrote this article, Retreat had not yet been purchased by a northerner, but that happened less than a decade later. In November 1939 James H. and Meredith N. Sturdevant of Syracuse, New York, bought one hundred acres of land and the home at Retreat for $10,500 from Nathaniel B. Barnwell, executor for Heyward S. Walker. A 1975 magazine article claimed that "the house and grounds had fallen into almost total ruin" when the Sturdevants purchased them. However, they soon restored the property and sold it to Bronson Lamb, who made many renovations. Later Antonio Ponvert of Oyster Bay, New York, a retired Cuban sugar plantation owner, owned the property for several years before selling it to a Beaufort builder and his wife, Mr. and Mrs. B. G. Pinckney. Today, Retreat is a residential community known as Pinckney Retreat.

# Rose Hill

"Kirk's Folly," the queer, mysterious old house not far from Bluffton, has probably been visited by thousands of people in the course of its years, people drawn by its curious appearances and intriguing history.

And one passing it would naturally pause to stare. For nothing like it exists in this part of the country. Many-gabled and imposing, it sits upon its quiet Hill, entirely surrounded by great live oaks which lead down to the road. At first glance, it has the effect of a grand cathedral or church and one considers in bewilderment what such a building can mean in this out-of-the-way place until it slowly dawns upon him that it is a house and not a church.

"Kirk's Folly" was built by Dr. John Kirk before the Confederate war. The war stopped the work and the house has never been finished on the interior. Supposedly of French architecture, the house was designed and built by a European. It is fashioned upon palatial lines and of magnificent proportions. The great doors and windows resemble those of a large cathedral and not of a house at all. There are fourteen rooms and many queer corners and steps that go up and down in unexpected places. The bedrooms on the second story all open upon a balcony formed by the stairway.

It is this stairway and the immense and splendid dome which cause one to stop stock still upon entering the tremendous hall, which, by the opening of sliding doors into a room on either side, can throw the entire front of the house into one floor. The stairway, fashioned of hand-carved solid mahogany, curves up three sides of the house. The dome was never completed and its dark, unfinished aspect lends an atmosphere of gloom to the great hall. The exquisite stained glass, imported to this country for the purpose, was placed in position, however, before the work on the house had to stop. In later years this glass fell to the floor, an alarming distance for glass to fall, but it was only slightly damaged. It was packed away and never replaced in the dome. The interior walls are unfinished, but the woodwork is exquisitely beautiful.

The name "Kirk's Folly" is obvious in its meaning—for the building of such a house was locally considered as nothing short of folly.

Original title: "Lowcountry Gossip." Publication date: November 13, 1932.

Rose Hill. *Historic American Buildings Survey, photograph # SC, 7-BLUFF. V. 1-4*

The back of the house is occupied by a white tenant family, but the beautiful old rooms of the remainder of the house are echoingly empty. At one time it is said a number of families of negroes occupied the old place.

The Episcopal church at Bluffton was designed by the same European architect as designed "Kirk's Folly" and there is to be seen a similarity in the styles of the two buildings.

Rose Hill was not designed by the same architect as was the Episcopal Church of the Cross in Bluffton, as that structure was the creation of Edward B. White of Charleston.

The Rose Hill property, eighteen hundred acres in all, was given to Dr. and Mrs. John Kirk as a wedding present by her father, John B. Kirk (the couple were cousins), owner of Callawassie Island. In addition, Kirk gave the couple a European honeymoon that was reputed to have cost twenty thousand dollars.

"Kirk's Folly" was a favorite plantation of Mrs. Martin, and she wrote about it often. On February 26, 1939, she dedicated her "Lowcountry Gossip" column to it because plans were then in process to have the building completed and used as a hunting lodge for the Rose Hill Plantation Club. The club was organized, she writes, by John E. Clements, Harry Moore of Washington, D.C., J. B. Walker, Mattie Simmons, and York Wilson of Bluffton. In that 1939 piece she claimed that the house had been built in 1850. She wrote:

> Since the plan was very elaborate and every piece of wood which went into it hand hewn by slaves, the building was long and tedious. The interior had not been completed when the War Between the States was declared. Sherman's army came, burning as they passed, but as the match was about to be struck to Rose Hill the officer in charge announced that he could not burn so beautiful a house and it was the only one spared in this section.
>
> For a long time a succession of tenant farmers has occupied Kirk's Folly, living huddled together in a few rooms while the rest of the great empty house seemed to crouch all around them like some sinister terror. They tell tales of strange noises, of sounds like footsteps creeping through the halls and up the stairs at night.

On January 23, 1938, Mrs. Martin wrote in her column that Emily Kirk Moore, daughter of the original owners, John and Caroline Kirk, was a botanist who wrote many articles on southern plants. One article on sugar cane resulted in a request from the British gardener of the emperor of Japan for a sample, which was sent from Rose Hill. So, Mrs. Martin claims, "the sugar cane industry in Japan had its inspiration from the writings of a young Bluffton woman." The property was noted for its plants. Among them were a soapberry tree from Central America and tanya, related to elephant ear, apparently brought from Africa, which was planted to hold the rice field banks.

Rose Hill stayed in southern hands for more than a decade after Mrs. Martin wrote this article. Mr. and Mrs. Joseph O. Pinckney sold the house and 562 acres of land to James M. and Florence B. Sturgeon in April 1946. Though the house suffered a fire in February 1987, it has been rebuilt and today is the centerpiece of a residential development of almost one thousand homes bearing the name Rose Hill Plantation.

# Spring Island

Like something out of a story book is picturesque Spring island on the Colleton river, down in Beaufort county. Like story-book characters, too, are Col. and Mrs. W. M. Copp, sole lord and lady of the island, and their several hundred dusky servitors.

From the time one enters their hospitable yacht, Columbia, at Copp's landing on the mainland about fifteen miles from Ridgeland, until one pulls away from the dock on the return trip, watching this genial host and hostess and the shoreline of their island home fade into the distance, one feels under the spell of an enchantment. It is as though one had stepped out of the work-a-day world for a little while and sailed away to a magic isle.

The Copps are graciousness itself. This quality seems to rise intangibly at the first glimpse of the long yellow house with its wide porches and green lawn that slopes down to the seawall, which has been recently built to prevent the wash of the river against the shore. And when the Copps come down their steps and along the dock, waving their hands in greeting, that sense of graciousness becomes a tangible thing.

Col. Copp is not a newcomer to Coastal South Carolina. He discovered it twenty-seven years ago and the lure of it wove its spell upon him, with the result that never again could he be long content away. He came down at first for the hunting and later became a member of the Spring Island Hunting club, which was organized about thirty years ago by Col. Thomas Martin, of Bluffton, who then owned the island.

### Bought at Auction

There was a split-up in the club later, and it was sold at public auction in Charleston in 1912, and Mr. Copp bought it. At first he was interested chiefly in the hunting, but later became concerned in making the island a paying proposition.

He began to clear land until there were 3,000 acres under cultivation and planted it to truck. He did an enormous trucking business, planting potatoes, lettuce, tomatoes and other truck. One season on lettuce alone he cleared $60,000. However, Mr. Copp believes that the day of big truck crops in this section is over. This condition has been

Original title: "The Copps and Spring Island. This Beaufort Isle with Its Single White Couple, Hundreds of Negro Servitors, Numerous Birds, Its Orange Tree and Ruins of an Old Settlement Is Like Something from a Story Book." Publication date: January 4, 1931.

brought about by over-production and keen competition, he thinks. Due to improved machinery, he is now able to make three-fourths of the crop he used to make with one-fourth the number of men. Last year he received only one dollar for whole carloads of truck and shipped some at a total loss.

Now, Mr. Copp has turned his attention to cattle and hogs. He has about 200 head of Black Aberdeen Angus cattle and about 80 Hampshire brood sows. He hopes to ship between 400 and 500 hogs to northern markets in April.

In addition to his cattle, Mr. Copp is interested in planting grain and other food-stuffs. He has 250 acres of oats, 25 of turnips and two of cabbage, which are fed to the cattle, seven acres of pecan trees from which he expects to ship a thousand pounds of nut. He also dug 2,100 bushels of sweet potatoes this year.

The island comprises some six thousand five hundred acres of land and is plentifully stocked with game. Mr. Copp says he believes there are more birds on Spring Island than any other place in the world of its size. Wild turkeys are numerous. Mr. Copp said he saw 58 in one bunch while hunting on Thanksgiving Day. There used to be plenty of deer, but these have gradually left since so many cattle have been brought to the island. Mr. Copp says cattle and deer do not like each other and the deer swim away to other islands. The Copps also raise many chickens, ducks and sheep.

Mr. Copp has his own sawmill and planing mill. Lumber for his house, built four years ago, was cut from trees on the island and finished at his mill. There are also a grist mill and a rice mill. Some rice is raised on the island, but is used mainly for baiting ducks.

Thirty-five negro families live on the island and are all in the employ of Mr. Copp. All of these little tenant houses are painted red and the warm color is pleasant to see here and there among the green of the trees. Mr. and Mrs. Copp know all of the negroes by name, even to the little piccaninnies who curtsy shyly as they pass along the road.

The Copp home is long and rambling and blends picturesquely into its island setting. There are two stories and two large porches which face the water. They have an ice plant which manufactures 600 pounds of ice a day and an excellent cold storage. The walls are lined with row upon row of native meats and game. There are, also, an electric light plant, a speed boat which will take them to their landing, about eight miles away, in ten minutes, automobiles both on the island and on the other side of the water, and even a telephone which connects them with the outside world.

### Large Orange Trees

At one side of their front door is a very large orange tree, from which already this year 14 bushels of oranges have been gathered. The tree is about 22 years old and grew from a seed under the house which stood on this site before Mr. Copp built his new home. It was bitten down by the frost one time but revived and presents a lovely picture now with the brilliant yellow of its fruit gleaming through its waxy green leaves.

Mr. Copp is a man of the world. He is said to have been at one time one of the biggest lawyers in New York city. He is a Yale man, a great athlete and was a colonel in the army. However, he grew tired of wandering about the world and his heart drew him to Coastal South Carolina. Mrs. Copp has lived in Pittsburgh, New York and other northern points but she says she never misses the life of the big city. About twice each year, the Copps leave their island for a visit to the north, and Savannah with its theaters is only a matter of thirty-two miles.

Aside from that they are quite content. Time passes quickly for them here. Mrs. Copp does not care for society nor for the rush and push of many people. When they feel the need of other companionship, they have some friends down. But for the most part, they are happy here together. Mr. Copp is very much interested in his island and travels about it a great deal by horse or afoot or automobile. Mrs. Copp, in breeches and boots, trails after him and is an excellent cattle woman, her husband praises.

They make a distinguished looking pair. Mr. Copp tall and straight with curling gray hair, laughing blue eyes and flashing white teeth. Mrs. Copp is also tall, handsomely modeled, fair and brim-full of vitality.

The Copps live and enjoy life in the modern-day luxury of their island home and the casual visitor would not know that this is only a layer that covers up the luxuriance of a day that is gone.

**Old Tabby Settlement**

The mere parting of a few bushes is the lifting of a curtain, as it were, upon a stage dusty with the years and from which the actors have long since made their final exit.

Over a field and through a wood, and one stands still and, if he has not prepared, rubs his eyes for fear he is dreaming. For there, rising immense and white through the long avenue of oaks and palm trees is the great ruin of an old tabby settlement. The walls of the house are fully 150 feet long and three stories high. From its top windows, it is said, one could see far across the water into the town of Beaufort. There are also the ruins of the servants' quarters, a smoke house and a fourth tall, narrow building which was, presumably, one of the outbuildings. All of these are of tabby and are perfectly intact. They are gaunt and white, except for the dark splashes made here and there by trailing vines. One has a feeling that if some miracle could be performed and the roofs and doors and windows should suddenly drop out of the air into their proper places, the ruins would come alive again. A brooding stillness hangs over the place, that same stillness that lingers about forgotten gravestones.

It is another picture out of the story book.

But time was when the big tabby house was a great mansion and the place teemed with life and was not shut away there across a plowed field and a wood that darkens it now like a heavy curtain.

That was the time when long staple cotton flourished "befo' de war." It was the home of George Edwards who is reported to have made around $100,000 a year on his cotton. Mr. Edwards spent his summers at Saratoga Springs, where he is said to have kept a racing stable. The story goes that he had two barges, one named the General Washington and the other the General Jackson, each manned by the oars, which he used to make trips to Savannah. Sometimes, the old negroes now living on the island have it from their parents, the slaves would steal the barges and make the trip to Savannah, a distance of fifty miles, between dusk and daylight.

### Burned by Sherman

The Edwards' home was burned by Sherman on his march to the sea and then the kindly woods and bushes hung the curtain to shut this gaunt memory of a former splendor away from prying eyes.

Mr. Edwards had one daughter, whom, it is said, he disinherited because of her marriage to a British naval officer by the name of Inwood.

After Mr. Edwards' death, Spring island was sold at public auction and bought by Mrs. Inwood, his daughter. At her death, it went to her son, Trenholm Inwood, who sold it to Colonel Martin.

While it was owned by Mr. Edwards the island was divided into four plantations, Bonny Shore, Goose Pond, Old House and Laurel Point. The Copps live at Bonny Shore and the old Edwards' home is at Old House. The negroes of the island still divide it according to these plantations.

The island, which is seven miles long and three and a half miles wide, was originally a barony grant to Sr. John Colleton. What other stratas of wealth or splendor have been buried here in the interim, no one has recorded. And what will be when time has rusted this civilization, which at the click of a switch can bring the sound of voices thousands of miles away to this island home, there is none to say. ✧

Ruins of Edwards house, Spring Island. *Photograph courtesy of the South Carolina Department of Archives and History*

Originally Spring Island and nearby Callawassie Island were owned by the brothers John (Spring) and James (Callawassie) Cochran, both British dissenters. After their deaths, James's son, also named James, inherited Spring Island, built a home there, and possessed it until his death in 1740. The islands are still connected financially, having been developed since the 1980s by the same company as residential communities.

Burned properties in South Carolina are often blamed on Gen. William T. Sherman, whatever the date of their destruction, and that seems to be the case with the Edwards house. According to historian Lawrence Rowland, it actually burned in a raid by Union troops from Hilton Head Island before Sherman entered the state.

Mrs. Martin mentioned Spring Island again in a March 31, 1935, column, describing it as "a semi-tropical paradise" and repeating that "the Copps and their superintendent [are] the only white people on the island." By that time the old "palatial home" had become "now only four gaunt tabby walls, over which soft green vines are creeping." Mr. Copp, who purchased the island in 1929, died in 1940.

In 2004 Lucile Walker Hays published a small-edition book entitled *Spring Island Plantation: A Remembrance,* which describes life on the plantation during the ownership of her parents, Lucile and Elisha Walker. She explains that there were several owners between the Copps and the Walkers and many untried schemes for the island. One idea dreamed up by a group from Las Vegas would have subdivided the island into nine thousand waterfront lots, to be serviced by shopping centers, hotels, motels, trailer parks, schools, and churches.

The Walkers purchased the island in 1964 for $401,500 from Mrs. Bertha E. Lucas of Charleston, widow of John F. Lucas. The island included about six thousand acres, just over half of which were high land. The Walkers cleared much of the land, stabilized the tabby ruins, hunted there, and eventually rented out the island to other hunters. They held on to the land for about twenty years, until they sold it to Jim Chaffin, Jim Light, and Peter LaMotte.

# Tomotley, Brewton, Bindon, and Castle Hill

Tomotley is one of the very loveliest and most interesting of the old Beaufort county plantations, which have lately come into the hands of wealthy Northern owners.

This plantation, now owned by R. H. McCurdy, in charge of foreign officers of the New York Mutual Life Insurance company, was originally a part of old Tomotley Barony and later belonged to the Bull family. It is situated on the opposite side of the road from the ruins of old Sheldon church and the site of Sheldon Hall.

Tomotley. *From John R. Todd and Francis M. Hutson,* Prince William's Parish and Plantations, *1935*

Original title: "Tomotley, Brewton Plantation, Bindon, Castle Hill—Beaufort Restorations. Trees Hang over Way to Tomotley. R. H. McCurdy, of New York, Now Owns Historic Beaufort Plantation." Publication date: November 23, 1930.

Long before the Confederate War, it was the property of Miss Patience Izard who married General Eustis of Massachusetts, a Northern sympathizer, and it then became known as the Eustis plantation. After that, it was planted to rice for many years by Martin & Hutson and came into Mr. McCurdy's hands about twenty years ago.

Mr. McCurdy, who owns some 5,600 acres in the vicinity, also owns the site of old Sheldon Hall, which is only a short distance from the ruins of the church.

Tomotley is reached by a long, picturesque avenue bordered thickly on each side by immense live oak trees, shrouded with moss. These trees are so large that they overlap above and form a natural arch. There is a similar avenue that leads out from the estate.

Beneath beautiful trees, Mr. McCurdy has erected a charming home. This house, which is of one-story construction, is low and rambling and seems to be nestling on the slight incline, watched over by the silent trees. It presents a delightful picture seen through the green trees. A visitor to Tomotley is impressed by the many chimneys to the house.

On the estate, there are twenty-three buildings, all close together. Edgar Marvin, who is the superintendent, occupies a newly completed cottage, painted white, as are all the buildings on the place.

There is a flock of about 100 turkeys, which add to the picturesqueness of the estate. Mr. Marvin plants about 200 acres, most of it being in grain for birds.

Mr. McCurdy is expected to arrive the last part of this month and he usually remains at Tomotley for about four months each year.

### Brewton Plantation Being Remodeled

Not far from Tomotley is Brewton plantation, owned by John R. Todd, of New York. Here, Mr. Todd is in the process of remodeling an old frame house which had been

Brewton. *Photograph courtesy of the South Carolina Department of Archives and History*

there for about forty years. This house is being raised, a new wing added, furnace heat installed and the entire interior handsomely finished and furnished. It will be a very attractive place when completed some time in December. There will also be new stables, a garage and servants' cottage.

This place was formerly known as Brewton Hall, the Brewton family, among them Miles Brewton, being in possession of the property long before the Revolutionary War. It was later owned by the McPherson family, several of whom are buried in the plantation cemetery at the back of the house. The oldest gravestone is that of Joseph Izard, who, according to the stone, died while visiting at Brewton Hall in 1745. There is another grave marked 1803 and still another, 1816. At another time, Dr. Isaac Gregory was the owner of this plantation, as was W. D. Sanders.

The old fence surrounding this graveyard had fallen down and a huge oak tree had uprooted several of the graves. Mr. Todd has had a new fence built, the tree removed and the stones set up again. When asked why he took all this trouble about an ancient graveyard, which meant nothing to him, he replied, "Well, I imagine there are some fine people buried there."

Three houses have stood on this site since the Revolutionary war, so far as can be learned, this being the third. Mr. Todd came into possession of the plantation about January. It consists of 1,291 acres.

## Bindon

Off the paved highway en route to Yemassee just before the turn is made in Pocotaligo from Beaufort, one comes upon the gates that lead through a grassy meadow, then through a forest of oaks, pines, and holly trees to Bindon, owned by E. E. Lorillard, member of the New York Stock Exchange.

This property, which consists of 1,500 acres, was at different periods owned by the Cuthberts, the Brewtons, the McPhersons and the Screvens. Mr. Lorillard married Miss Bessie Screven, who died recently.

Bindon is located at the top of a little rise in the land, which slopes gently down again to the water. The house, which is of brown stucco with red tiled roof, is partly covered with ivy and fits ideally into the background of lovely trees. The center of the building is a story and a half with low wings on either side. There is a smaller stucco building almost hidden in the trees at one side and the caretaker's cottage and stables are at the back. A wide stretch of well-kept lawn surrounds the whole.

## Castle Hill Estate

Castle Hill, on down the same highway nearer Yemassee, is the last of these large estates. It is at the end of a little road that is entered through tall green gates. There is a square, white house sitting upon a little Hill. At the front are many old-fashioned, newly dug flower beds and at the back a number of freshly painted buildings, all of the group being done in white.

Castle Hill is now owned by Blair S. and John S. Williams, of New York. The plantation comprises 1,800 acres. From the Revolutionary period on it was owned by the

The Williams house at Castle Hill. *From Willis Irvin*, Selections from the Work of Willis Irvin: Architect, Augusta, Ga., *1937*

Cuthberts. It was also at one time the property of Major John Screven. The place is superintended by J. F. Hutto. ✤

Tomotley plantation was laid out on part of the forty-eight-thousand-acre grant given to Edmund Bellinger in 1698. The property remained in that family until 1744. It passed to Ralph Izard a decade later and was in the possession of Izards through the Civil War. Mrs. Abraham Eustis (Patience W. B. Izard) was responsible for the handsome avenue of live oaks, said to have been planted as early as 1820. Mrs. Eustis died in 1860, and her heirs, to satisfy all claims against the estate, sold Tomotley to George Martin and C. J. C. Hutson in 1873. Hutson later became the sole owner.

Henry O. Havemeyer, president of the American Sugar Refining Company, the first northern owner, bought the property in March 1907, but he died in December of the same year and is not known to have ever lived on the plantation. Mr. Havemeyer gained such a hold on the sugar-refining business that he is sometimes named with the nineteenth-century "Robber Barons." The owner of an impressive art collection, he and his wife, Louisine, left almost two thousand pieces of artwork to New York's Metropolitan Museum, including eleven Rembrandts and a great number of impressionist paintings. (Mary Cassatt was his wife's friend and art adviser.) However, Mr. Havemeyer's reputation was tarnished by scandals concerning his business practices. He was charged with contempt and arrested when he refused to appear before a U.S. Senate committee, though he was later acquitted. Two years after his death, the executors of his estate sold the 1,384-acre property to Mrs. Robert McCurdy of New York. Mr. McCurdy was a member of the nearby Okeetee Club.

After a number of subsequent owners (including G. V. Hollins, son of Harry B. Hollins, who organized most of the hunt clubs in the area), the plantation is now the property of Mr. and Mrs. William Mixon.

A March 29, 1932, article in the *Charleston News and Courier* announced Robert M. McCurdy's death and the distribution of some of his estate:

> Daniel D. Woods, 77-year-old farmer and hunter of this community, was informed . . . that he had been bequeathed $10,000 in the will of the late Robert M. McCurdy, an official of the Mutual Life Insurance company.
>
> The aged man, nearly blind now, refused flatly to believe the story at first. He had been informed earlier in the day that he had been chosen by Mr. McCurdy to administer an annuity of $960 for the care of several hunting dogs Mr. McCurdy owned, and he believed this was to be the extent of his inheritance.
>
> Shown a telegram from The News and Courier confirming the $10,000 bequest, Mr. Woods, who has always lived under the most humble conditions, was overcome with joy. He clasped the hands of several friends who were present, and a moment later was "clog dancing," while his son, Rufus, clapped time with his hands.
>
> "Well, it'll be more than hog-and-hominy for me now," he said, smiling broadly.
>
> Mr. McCurdy and Mr. Woods were hunting companions for 33 years until last year when Mr. McCurdy's health forced him to give up the sport. . . .
>
> Mr. Woods during the hunting season was employed by Mr. McCurdy. "I was just a kind of a servant for him, but he called me his 'sports superintendent,'" Mr. Woods said tonight. "We hunted together all of the time, and when we got the bag limit we always quit."
>
> Mr. Woods also related the story of another gift from Mr. McCurdy some years back. Conditions on his small farm were bad and the time was near for the foreclosure on a mortgage on his property.
>
> "So I decided I would try to get some help from Mr. McCurdy. I sent a telegram to him but he was on a boat on the way to Europe. Anyhow his secretary sent him a cable and Mr. McCurdy cabled right back to him to send me the money. It saved my place for me.
>
> "Then next year I raised 13 bales of cotton. When Mr. McCurdy came down, I told him I had the cotton for him and for him to sell it for what he could get. I didn't know how much it would bring, so I told him if there was any left to give it to me and if it came short of the mortgage money, I would pay the balance later.
>
> "'He told me to shut up, that that money was just a little gift from him.
>
> "'He was a fine man and one of the best friends anybody could have. It certainly hurt me when he died. And I missed him a lot when he had to quit coming down here."
>
> Mr. Woods is going to think a while before he decides how he is going to use his new wealth.

Brewton was settled as a plantation of some fourteen hundred acres by 1732, part of John Bull's larger grant. The property passed down in the family to Mary Bull, wife of Miles

Brewton, the wealthy Charleston merchant. The couple and their three children were lost at sea in 1775. By the will of Mary Bull Brewton the property went to her cousin Mary Middleton (Mrs. Pierce Butler), and sometime after 1783 it was sold to the McPherson family. James Elliott McPherson is thought to have been the first owner who made Brewton a principal residence. McPhersons retained ownership until 1860, when Dr. Isaac Gregorie took title.

The old Gregorie house, built in 1893, was there when Mr. John R. Todd bought the place from the Brewton Hunting and Fishing Club, and he retained and improved it as his residence. Early in his career Mr. Todd spent two years teaching in the Middle East; on his return he studied law, passing the New York Bar in 1894. However, his greatest success was in engineering, in which he seems to have had no formal instruction but natural talent. With a friend, Henry C. Irvin, he built a number of large commercial buildings in New York. The most notable one, the Cunard Steamship Building at 25 Broadway, is said by New York architectural historian Gerald Wolfe to be one of the finest office buildings in the world. Mr. Todd later organized the firm of Todd, Robertston, Todd Engineering. With many midtown structures to his credit, he caught the eye of John D. Rockefeller Jr., who engaged him and several associates to represent the family interests in the construction of Rockefeller Center in Manhattan. When the architect Raymond Hood traveled to Europe to select an artist for the murals in the new RCA Building, he asked Mr. Todd to accompany him. Later, as chairman of Todd and Brown, he oversaw the reconstruction of Historic Williamsburg, Virginia.

At Brewton, Mr. Todd is remembered for the oak avenue he laid out and for another avenue opposite the entrance to the plantation, this of oaks (*Quercus acuta*) and hollies, set out in 1929 and recorded on a stone marker just off the road. No lover of the lowcountry's history should forget that Mr. Todd was co-author with Francis Marion Hutson of that valuable resource *Prince William's Parish and Plantations.* A good citizen indeed, Mr. Todd died in 1945.

By 1971 Brewton was rundown when its 363 acres were purchased by heavyweight boxing champion Joe Frazier, who grew up in the nearby Laurel Bay area, for his mother, Dolly. The same year of his Brewton purchase, Mr. Frazier, who had won the championship the year before, defeated Muhammad Ali in one of the most exciting boxing matches of the era. He held the title for three years, trading it with Ali (their 1975 "Thrilla in Manila" was another dramatic battle) and George Foreman. His overall record was 32–4 with one draw; twenty-seven of his wins were by knockout.

Frazier bought Brewton sight unseen. "The first time I saw it," he told the *New York Times,* "I like to about cried. The land was overgrown, fences were down, the ponds all choked up and the big house was something else. I was going to go back and have that lawyer glove up for getting me into this. But then I looked around and thought, 'Hell, I've worked worse land than this. I can make it go.'" He put enough work into the property that when he sold it in 1988 to Paul and Diane Terni, he almost tripled his investment.

On October 16, 1932, the *Charleston News and Courier* reported the death of the shipbuilder E. E. Lorillard of New York, who owned Bindon. Lorillard's wife was Bessie Screven, the daughter of "Major Screven, of Savannah, who owned the land now embraced in

Bindon, Twickenham, Castle Hill, and Brewton plantations, all of which are now winter homes and hunting preserves of northern people." The article boasted that "Mrs. Lorillard always considered herself to be a citizen of Yemassee."

Bindon changed hands several times—Robert Edward Turner Jr., father of Ted Turner, owned it in the early 1960s and committed suicide there—but by 2006 the property still contained thirteen hundred acres, almost its size when Mrs. Martin visited. That year an owners' group sought to develop the property as a residential community and was not satisfied with Beaufort County's zoning plan, which would have allowed 350 homes. Instead the developers worked out an agreement with the town of Yemassee, whose zoning would have allowed 1,300 homes and 450,000 square feet of commercial space. However, because the properties were not contiguous, Yemassee could annex Bindon only by first annexing a strip of land twenty feet wide and more than two miles long. In 2008 the plan was being challenged by the Coastal Conservation League, supported by the South Carolina attorney general.

Castle Hill takes its name from the ancestral home of Dr. James Cuthbert of Inverness, who immigrated to Carolina in 1737. The plantation remained in that family until sometime shortly after 1838, when Col. James Cuthbert, who had borrowed heavily to increase his planting interests, died suddenly of yellow fever, leaving his estate much encumbered. The plantation was sold to Nathaniel Heyward (1766–1851) and by 1849 was sold again to G. M. Wilkins, who bought it as a gift for his daughter, the wife of John Screven. Colonel Screven, as he was later known, planted rice at Castle Hill until his death in 1903.

Blair S. Williams and his son John bought the 1,784-acre property in 1929. The senior Mr. Williams was a partner in the stock-brokerage firm that bore his name and was a former governor of the New York exchange. The architect Willis Irvin is responsible for the Williams house, built in 1935. John Williams lived in Old Chatham, New York, and, like his father, was a New York investment broker. The younger Mr. and Mrs. Williams were particularly good citizens in their new community, providing the funds in 1940 for a new steeple to be added to St. Helena's Church in Beaufort. The church had been without one since before the Civil War, when the original steeple was taken down. The couple spent their winters at Castle Hill until 1948, when they sold the property to P. O. Mead. A major collector of Shaker furniture and farming equipment, Mr. Williams founded the Shaker Museum in Old Chatham. He died in 1982 at age eighty.

Subsequent owners of Castle Hill have included Fred C. Koch, president of the Rock Island Oil and Refining Company, and Dr. H. T. Weaver of Western Reserve University Medical School.

# Twickenham, Hobonny, and Bonny Hall

Turning to the right off the road that leads from the site of old Sheldon Hall and the ruins of the old church at Prince William parish, one enters a long, sandy country road that winds in and out through thickly wooded lands on either side.

The leaves, falling silently through the thick trees, catch upon the cushions of gray moss that festoon the oaks and lie there—gold spilled upon crimson, orange upon green, russet upon brown—until the great forest looks as though it were twined with monstrous strings of confetti for some splendid gala occasion.

One rides for miles feasting upon this gorgeous spectacle. Here, a slim leafy thing stands out sharply like a challenging, scarlet banner. There, all the gold in the world seems to have been melted and poured to make a tree. Yonder, against a dark trunk, a crimson smear traces itself like warm, trickling blood.

Hidden away from the world along this sandy road there is such concentrated beauty as stretches the heart apart.

Then the eyes, paying for the sin of surfeiting, find, gladly, the trailing white fence which leads shortly to a large white house surrounded by neat outbuildings. All of this welcomed whiteness is situated back from the road in a grove of lovely trees.

It is Twickenham, an old rice plantation, owned for the last twenty years by R. J. Turnbull, a New York attorney, who spends about four months of each year at his plantation.

This property, which consists of 1,752 acres of land, was once a part of Tomotley Barony, which was a grant to Edmund Bellinger about 1740. The land later belonged to the Bulls and this particular plantation was next owned by the Heywards, then by Tom Hanckel, of Charleston, who married a Heyward and also at one time by John Screven.

The original house has long since been destroyed and the present home was remodeled only about a year ago from a house which was only about forty years old. This newly remodeled home is said to have cost in the neighborhood of $30,000. It is of two-story

Original title: "Twickenham, Bonny Hall and Hobonny." Publication date: December 19, 1930.

Twickenham. *Photograph courtesy of the South Carolina Historical Society*

construction and contains ten or eleven rooms. It is painted white and stands high off the ground with wide, steep steps leading to the porch from each side.

Very little of the land about Twickenham is under cultivation except what small acreage is planted for bird feed. The estate is used solely for hunting.

McLeod Hutson, superintendent of the places, lives in an attractive little bungalow near the larger house.

### Hobonny

Farther on down the road, near the Combahee river, is Hobonny, which is only a small frame building used as a clubhouse by a group of men from several cities in this state. The club consists of 1,640 acres and was known as the old O. M. Read place. It was also at one time the property of the Middleton family.

Probably the most interesting feature to be seen on this estate is the old brick slave quarters located not far from the clubhouse.

### Bonny Hall

Continuing on down the same little road, one comes finally to Bonny Hall, a tract of 1,700 acres, owned by Arthur Lyman of Boston, Mass.

Bonny Hall was originally owned by Joseph Blake of England, who never saw the place. His son, Walter Blake, planted it up until the Civil war. After this, it was owned by a Mr. Bissell and was then sold to George W. Egan of Charleston, who sold it in turn to Mr. Lyman.

Bonny Hall. *Photograph courtesy of Calvert Huffines*

Bonny Hall is a square two-storied building set attractively beneath a grove of beautiful trees at the top of a little knoll. At the back are the small, neat homes of the superintendent and the stables. ✤

Twickenham was not, as Mrs. Martin supposed, a part of Tomotley Barony. The property was an original grant to Walter Izard Sr. and his son. The Bull and Pringle families were later owners, then the Heywards and Hanckels. At the time of the Civil War it was owned by Sarah Heyward Hanckel. Union troops passing through the area destroyed the main residence and major farm buildings. With the Hanckels' finances depleted by the war, Twickenham was leased in 1871 to J. Bennett Bissell in the hope that enough income would be realized to save the place. When this failed, it was sold in 1879 to Thomas E. Screven, the son of Maj. John Screven. By 1886 Thomas found himself in debt and had to be rescued by his father, who then took title, retaining it until his death in 1903.

The present house is said to have been built in the late 1870s by Major Screven, though he had not yet taken possession of the land. By will it passed to Major Screven's grandson, Robert J. Turnbull, a lawyer in New York, who used the plantation as a winter home until he died in 1951. In recent years Twickenham has been owned by Arnold B. Chace Jr. of Providence, Rhode Island.

Bonny Hall was laid out partly on lands granted to Col. Joseph Blake (1700–1751) in 1732 and partly on lands of Andrew Allen, granted in the same period. Mrs. Martin is mistaken in writing that Blake never lived in Carolina. A landgrave of Carolina and active in local affairs, he probably made his home at Newington on the upper Ashley River. When Blake joined the two parcels is unclear. However, in 1791 William Blake, son of Joseph, purchased from Thomas Middleton the twenty-five-hundred-acre plantation Bonny Hall, "with the strong disapproval and criticism of his family and friends," as Alicia Middleton writes.

At the time of the Civil War, Bonny Hall was owned by the grandson of the original Joseph Blake, also known as Joseph, who resided mostly in England. He had turned over the operation of the plantation to his son, Walter, and it was commonly spoken of as Walter Blake's.

The Union raids at Combahee Ferry in May and June 1863 were bold moves not only to destroy plantation property but also, and especially, to liberate as many enslaved residents as possible, sending them to freedom at Beaufort. More than seven hundred slaves are estimated to have escaped, dealing, as was intended, a crippling loss to the rice planters. (The raid is discussed in this book under Clay Hall and Nieuport.)

Walter Blake died in 1871, and in 1873 the equity court ordered Bonny Hall sold at auction to settle his estate. The highest bidder was J. Bennett Bissell. The Bissell family had owned the largest and most prosperous hardware firm in Charleston. It burned at the close of the war, and Bissell decided to try his hand at rice planting. He secured, either by lease or purchase, at least nine plantations on the Combahee, making him the largest rice planter in the postwar period. However, prosperity did not last. An 1871 description of the rice harvest at Bonny Hall, reprinted in Edward King's *The Great South,* could be confused for an antebellum scene, but debt and especially labor troubles defeated him. He died in 1892. Bonny Hall was sold in 1897 to George Egan, the engineer of the Charleston jetties. The present house dates to that time.

Subsequent owners of note have been Arthur Lyman of Massachusetts (who bought it in 1920) and Nelson and Ellen Doubleday of New York (1932). Lyman (1861–1933), a member of the Pineland Club, was of the Boston family associated with the Appletons, Amorys, Dwights, and Coolidges, sometimes called the "Boston Associates." Lyman was married to a Cabot. After completing studies at Harvard undergraduate and law school, he dedicated more than thirty years of his life to public service, including tenures as mayor of Waltham, Massachusetts, and as the Massachusetts commissioner of natural resources and secretary of corrections. Lyman was a noted horticulturist, and his Waltham estate was one of greater Boston's showplaces.

During their ownership, the Doubledays extended the house, giving it a pleasing elongation and symmetry, and it was they who engaged Umberto Innocenti to lay out the grounds. The firm of Innocenti and Webel of Roslyn, New York, is responsible for a number of handsome gardens and landscaped areas at several lowcountry plantations. In 1941 Doubleday, owner of the publishing house that bore his name, built for his client Somerset Maugham, the novelist, a three-bedroom frame house at Bonny Hall, plus a separate writing studio and a cottage for Maugham's three servants. Companions and literary figures from the North came south from time to time to relieve the isolation of Maugham's rural location. One visitor was Dorothy Parker, who claimed that her visit was "the longest three weeks in my life." During the years he lived there, 1941 to 1946, Maugham finished the novel *The Razor's Edge* and several other projects. Bonny Hall is now owned by John K. Cowperthwaite Jr. The land containing the Maugham buildings has been separated from Bonny Hall.

Hobonny was one of the many plantations on the Beaufort side of the Combahee owned by Gov. Henry Middleton. John Todd and Francis Hutson say that there was an old residence there, though probably not a principal family home, which burned during the Civil War. The substantial slave houses suggest a prosperous plantation at one time. Governor Middleton left Hobonny to his son Williams, but the properties were bequeathed after the war to bring about an equitable division. Williams gave Hobonny in equal shares to his two brothers, Oliver H. Middleton and John Izard Middleton. The O. M. Read mentioned is Mr. Oliver Middleton's grandson.

Hobonny remained a private hunting club, primarily made up of Savannah professionals, for almost fifty years after Mrs. Martin's article appeared. Suzanne Linder notes that the property was divided in 1980 into three parts: "Two sections became part of Twickenham, and T. W. Erickson of Savannah, Georgia, a member of the Hobonny Club, purchased the third."

# *Jasper County* PROPERTIES

Chelsea

Delta

Gregorie Neck

Mackay Point

Maurene (Corlies Estate; also F. K. Barbour Estate and J. A. Coleman Estate)

Okeetee Club

Pillot Hunting Club (also J. L. Wheeler Land, Lindon, Garvey Hall, Red Bluff, Bull's Island, K. B. Schley Lands, and Green Swamp Club)

Pineland Club

Spring Hill

Strawberry Hill (also Old Glover Plantation)

White Hall (also Honey Hill Battleground, Good Hope Camp, and Old House)

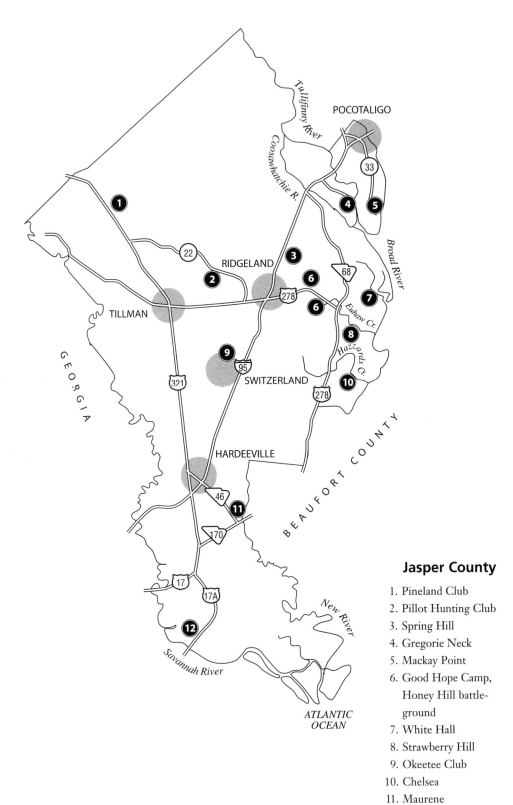

**Jasper County**

1. Pineland Club
2. Pillot Hunting Club
3. Spring Hill
4. Gregorie Neck
5. Mackay Point
6. Good Hope Camp, Honey Hill battle-ground
7. White Hall
8. Strawberry Hill
9. Okeetee Club
10. Chelsea
11. Maurene
12. Delta

# *Chelsea*

Chelsea, down in Jasper county, is perhaps one of the most interesting of the various hunting clubs in Coastal South Carolina. Perhaps one reason that makes for its interest is the fact that the main part of the building is one of the oldest in this part of the country and one of the few left standing here by Sherman during his famous march to the sea.

Chelsea was one of the handsome ante-bellum homes of the coast. It was originally owned by John Heyward, a portrait of whom, made from an old miniature on ivory and said to have cost $2,500, is to be seen on the wall of the living room of the club.

John Heyward died while still a young man, the dates given under his portrait being 1807–1839. The painting was done in 1827 and portrays the young Heyward as the possessor of a rare beauty, feminine like in its delicacy.

John Heyward married a Miss Pritchard and they had only one child, a son, William, who was killed tragically by a man named Dixon, with whom he was associated in a sawmill business. William Heyward was said to have been a man of ungovernable temper and the story handed down by descendants is that he became enraged at Dixon one day and chased him to the attic of the house with an axe. Dixon is said to have armed himself with a gun on his way to the attic and to have barred himself in an effort to avoid trouble. However, the story goes, William Heyward chopped the door down and was killed by Dixon as he (Heyward) crossed the threshold.

After the death of the Heywards, Chelsea was inherited by Dr. Paul Pritchard, brother of Mrs. Heyward.

**Avenue Leads to House**

Chelsea club is about twelve miles from Ridgeland and is reached after a long jog over rough country roads. The approach is made through tall, white gates, which lead up an avenue of splendid oaks, swathed in gray moss. The gate itself is a work of art, tall and

Original title: "Chelsea, Where Northerners Hunt. Old Heyward House Which Escaped Sherman's Burners Serves as Seat of 20,000-acre Game Preserve in Jasper Where Owners Spend $40,000 Yearly." Publication date: June 7, 1931.

The Heyward house at Chelsea. *Photograph courtesy of the South Carolina Historical Society*

white and curving away on either side into a trailing white fence which encircles the club grounds.

The clubhouse, high on its old-fashioned basement foundation, gleams whitely through the tall green trees and invites the visitor with its trim beauty. There are fourteen acres of great live oaks beneath which Italian rye spreads itself in a thick carpet of emerald green.

Entrance is made into a hall whose walls are papered in quaint Colonial design. There is a wide staircase and many lovely old paintings upon the walls.

All of the rooms are papered in the most exquisite designs, the furnishings seeming to catch the very essence of their beings from the colors, now gay, now subdued, of these designs. This papering was designed by the New York artist Theban, authority on interior decoration.

There are great fireplaces in each room and comfortable, beautiful furniture which lends itself perfectly to the atmosphere of the old house.

### Blue China Connection

In the dining room, with its high pine wainscoting, the ledge around the walls is filled with a collection of blue china, which brightens the dark walls enchantingly.

The moldings in the rooms are hand-carved and of solid walnut, but were painted white by some person who did not recognize the value of the natural wood.

The papering in each of the many bedrooms upstairs is different from the others and makes the rooms glow with brightness. Colorful, old-fashioned rag rugs splash the shining floors with gladness and the wide old fireplaces furnish comfort and cheer.

Chelsea club comprises twenty thousand acres of land, a great part of which is used for hunting by its members and their friends.

However, the club is far from being merely a source of pleasure for the few wealthy men who own it. The club lands furnish sustenance to several hundred negroes who live in little cabins here and there and farm little patches of land. It gives protection to game and is continuously restocking the woods to replace the game which has been killed. Woods-riders patrol the lands all the time and constant watch is kept to prevent forest fires. As many of the supplies are bought locally as is possible, the club spending between forty and fifty thousand dollars annually.

**Donate Black Walnuts**

Just now, Chelsea club is aiding the United States Forestry Department in its restocking work being done through the Boy Scouts of America by donating one million black walnuts from the club lands.

The oaks are set at regular intervals and are said to have been put there by an old negro by the name of Barnwell between ninety and a hundred years ago. There are about 250 of these oaks.

On the lawn, sheltered by the house, are two great orange trees. Palm trees here and there add a touch of tropical luxuriance and a thousand pansy plants blossom for Christmas.

On the east is Hazzards creek, this tidal stream being only a few feet from the house. Twelve miles across this water lies Beaufort. By land it is sixty miles.

The basement of the house, which was formerly used as kitchen, laundry, etc., is now utilized mostly for storage space.

Up the large brick chimneys and immaculate walls, tendrils of old English ivy climb caressingly. From shallow steps on either side, one mounts higher stairs to the wide, rambling porch, painted in white with trimmings of green. From the eastern side of this porch, a magnificent view is had of Hazzards creek and the small green islands dotting the coast like the soft daubs of an artist's paints.

Chelsea club is one of the oldest in this section and has the following members: Frederick K. Gaston of New York, connected with the Travelers Insurance company, president; William Crawford of New York, big builder, vice president; George H. Howard, president of United Corporations, secretary and treasurer; George T. Slade, big railroad man, who was sent to France by President Wilson during the time of the World war when all of the railroads were congested; William Kissam; Harold Stanley, New York banker; Mr. White, New York banker; and A. H. Swain, vice president of General Motors.

Each member has his own section in the dog kennels and here are to be found some famous dogs. Stylish Pat, a pointer, the only dog that ever won the high international three times, belongs to Mr. Crawford.

There is also old Mike, famous field dog owned by Mr. Slade. This dog, now ten years old, has almost the appearance of a two-year-old.

Besides Mike, Mr. Slade owns Sligo Castle in Scotland, a salmon stream in Norway and a famous duck pass in North Dakota. ✄

Heyward family records indicate that the old house at Chelsea, described in Mrs. Martin's article, was built about 1818. John Heyward was living there at the time of his death in 1839—he was thrown from his horse while hunting—at thirty-two years of age. The same Heyward records say that he was "known throughout the Carolinas, as the master whose slaves never knew their bondage, so humane was their treatment." Heyward's widow, Constantia Pritchard, with her three children held Chelsea until her death in 1859. Soon after, the Pritchard family called in financial notes and took possession of the property from the Heywards. The notes, already paid off, had never been destroyed, and the Pritchards took advantage of that oversight.

Though 1891 is the date usually mentioned for the founding of the Chelsea Plantation Club, Beaufort County deeds show the earliest land acquisition by the club as 1902. Thereafter the club continued to add to its property, by lease or purchase, through the 1930s.

Among the club members mentioned by Mrs. Martin, Frederick K. Gaston (1896–1966) headed a large insurance company in New York bearing his name. George Howard (1885–1960) was conspicuous in a number of large utility firms in the Northeast, including Commonwealth and Southern, of which he was director, and United Corporation, which he served as president; they were two of the large holding companies put together by Landon Thorne and Alfred Loomis, who owned much land on Hilton Head Island. George Slade (1872–1941) was a railroad man and son-in-law of James J. Hill, the pioneer railroad builder; Slade held executive positions in the Great Northern and the Northern Pacific. During World War I he was named director general for the American Expeditionary Force in France. William A. Kissam (1868–1950), a nephew of Mrs. William H. Vanderbilt, founded an American company to develop gold resources in Ecuador. Harold Stanley (1886–1963) was chief executive of the New York investment firm Morgan Stanley and Company and an officer also in Guaranty Trust Company and J. P. Morgan and Company, all of New York.

In 1936 the old Heyward house burned to the ground, and a year later, during Mr. Stanley's tenure as president of the club, all the property was sold to Marshall Field III (1893–1956) of New York, one of the wealthiest individuals in the country. He headed Field Enterprises, the family holding company for newspapers, magazines, retail stores, banks, and other businesses. In 1937 the architect Albert Simons of Charleston designed Field's new residence in the regency style, which Field referred to as his "Quail Lodge."

Not long after the Civil War, Field's grandfather had established the great Chicago department store that bore his name, laying the foundation for the family's economic success. (The store was acquired by Macy's in 2005.) Marshall Field Jr., son of the patriarch, died of a self-inflicted bullet wound in 1905 at the age of thirty-seven, leaving his son and namesake, then twelve years old, as the future head of the family.

Young Marshall Field III was educated at Eton and Cambridge College in England, where the family had lived for a time. After service in World War I, Field assumed his late father's position in the family business. He settled in New York by 1921, living on a twenty-two-hundred-acre estate at Lloyd's Neck, Long Island. He moved socially among the educated, wealthy, fashionable young people of his class. However, this style of life soon dissatisfied him, and, following a period of critical introspection, he turned his attention to liberal social concerns. Field believed that he should work to benefit society to earn the privileges his money allowed him. His philanthropies extended to museums, colleges, child-care programs, and many other institutions.

He also chose to express his views in newspapers. To that end in 1941 he started *PM,* one of the most liberal papers of its day. *PM* included color illustrations and gave prominence to photography before any other newspaper, accepted no advertising for its first six and a half years, and counted among its staff novelists Ernest Hemingway and Erskine Caldwell, journalist I. F. Stone, photographer Margaret Bourke-White, and illustrator Theodore Geisel (Dr. Seuss). In 1942 Field started the *Chicago Sun* (later the *Sun Times*) in support of President Franklin Roosevelt's New Deal programs and in opposition to Col. Robert McCormack's conservative *Chicago Tribune.*

After Field's death in 1956, his widow, Ruth, continued to make her winter home at Chelsea. Ruth Field died in 1994. Chelsea is now owned by the family's estate.

# Delta

There are probably few estates in coastal South Carolina which excel in magnificence that of H. K. Hudson's "The Delta," located on the Savannah river below Hardeeville. The miracle is that last March the spot where this handsome home stands was a wilderness. Today, when one enters the great gates into the estate, he has a sense of walking straight into the canvas of a stately building, instead of the reality itself.

To the right of the entrance gates is an immense pile of red brick, which, despite its dignity and ornateness, is a mere stable.

Straight ahead at the end of the white road and through an arched gate are the servants' quarters, also of brick, which are themselves something to be exclaimed at.

To the left, between these two, in a grove of beautiful oaks which overshadow a wide sweep of velvety green lawn, rises in all of its warm red splendor, the Hudson mansion, for that it surely is.

The approach from this direction is beautiful enough, one would think, but the part which faces the old rice fields is far more so. Here is a sunken garden as luxuriant and green as though it had been there for years, sloping down to the exquisitely wrought iron gate.

The house is fashioned upon long spacious lines and contains about twenty rooms.

The Delta plantation is made up of a number of antebellum estates. Among these are Delta plantation, containing 2,700 acres; Cane Knoll and Bellinger Hill plantations, containing 1,600 acres; and Hardee plantation, containing 1,000 acres.

These plantations are all on the Savannah river and are bordered by the old Screven Ferry turnpike, which has been abandoned since the building of the Savannah river bridge.

Delta plantation was purchased from Byron Glover, of Savannah, who used it for several years and had it in good shape as a duck preserve. There are some three thousand acres of duck hunting land in the Savannah river rice fields. This rice field area extends

Original title: "The Delta—Home of H. K. Hudson. Member of New York Stock Exchange Clears Wilderness on Savannah River in Beaufort County to Build 20-room Mansion and Construct Sunken Garden." Publication date: January 20, 1931.

Delta. *Photograph courtesy of the South Carolina Department of Archives and History*

for about twenty miles along the river and is about four miles wide, affording an unusually good haven for water birds of all kinds.

The federal government has a bird refuge of several thousand acres several miles above the Delta.

This property was sold to Mr. Hudson by the Christensen Real Estate company, of Beaufort, and Mr. Hudson built his handsome home on a beautiful old home site on the highlands of Delta plantation. Olaf Otto, of Savannah, was the contractor. This house on the exterior is a copy of a very old and famous colonial mansion.

Mr. Hudson is a New York man and a member of the stock exchange. ✑

Since 1931, when Mrs. Martin wrote this article, county lines have moved, and Delta now lies in Jasper, not Beaufort, County. An undated preconstruction clipping found in the South Carolina Historical Society provides more details on the house. Entitled "New York Broker Builds at Delta," it estimates the cost of Hudson's construction plans at $250,000. The clipping reads: "The Manor house, a colonial mansion, in general a copy of Brandon house, on the James river, Virginia, will measure 164 feet over all—though its commodiousness and convenience will be better conveyed to the reader when it is said that it will have nine bath rooms. The barn and garage building will, in size, be only less than the Manor house." The architect Olaf Otto was identified as having also designed the Citizens and Southern Bank building in Charleston at the corner of Broad and Church streets.

Langdon Cheves (1776–1857) returned to South Carolina in 1829 following ten years of service as president of the Bank of the United States in Philadelphia. Leaving the life of a banker for that of a planter, Cheves purchased two adjoining rice plantations on the lower

Savannah River in St. Peter's Parish, Beaufort District: Inverary, or Upper Delta, of 1,250 acres; and the 835-acre Telfair, or Lower Delta. In 1852 Cheves divided his plantation, now thought of as a single property, between his two sons. He gave Langdon Jr. Lower Delta, with Upper Delta going to Charles.

The heirs of Dr. Charles Cheves kept Upper Delta until 1921, when it was sold to Frederick M. Eslick of Jasper County, who three years later sold to J. Byron Glover, a cotton broker of Savannah. H. Keirstede Hudson acquired both sections of Delta in 1929. Hudson (1885–1954) retired from the New York brokerage firm of Whitehouse, Hudson, and Company soon after buying Delta and began building his house and expanding his lands. He brought his holdings to 6,444 acres by 1938, when the plantation was bought by James and Martha Denham of Wilmington, Delaware. The new owner was associated with the DuPont Company as general manager of its photographic products department. The Denhams the same year of their purchase sold 2,940 acres of Delta to Salem Investment Company, also of Wilmington. The company in turn sold that tract to Harry C. Haskell Jr. James Denham and his wife died in 1959 and 1972 respectively, leaving their 3,544 acres of Delta to their daughter, Carolina Taylor.

In 1972 the majority of Hudson's 6,444-acre Delta plantation, comprising the Haskell and Denham tracts, was conveyed to the Delta Plantation Development Corporation. John E. Cay III of Savannah is the present owner of the Hudson house and surrounding property. The Savannah College of Art and Design has purchased much of Lower Delta and built there its athletic center, including fields for soccer, lacrosse, and softball. A nearby residential community has adopted the name Telfair Plantation.

# *Gregorie Neck*

Gregorie Neck plantation, the home of Bayard Dominick, in Jasper county, is one of the most charming of the large northern estates in this section. To begin with, there are very few locations along the entire coast that are lovelier, or more desirable than is Gregorie Neck. This strip of land, about five or six miles from Coosawhatchie, overlooking the Tullifinny river, is an ideal site for a beautiful home.

The handsome home built by Mr. Dominick is situated in a large grove of giant oaks and faces the river. The building and its location are somehow suggestive of Mount Vernon.

The house is a large, spreading two-storied colonial affair, fashioned of brick painted white. At the front, which faces the road, are tall white columns and two wings sloping away on either side of the main part of the building. Open, low flat verandahs face the river at the back and the road at the front. There are fifteen rooms, all furnished with simple but exquisite taste. At one end of the wide porch which looks upon the river, is an old mounted farm bell, which it was said was discovered upon the plantation.

**Three-acre Lawn**

Three acres of Italian rye make a carpet of living green beneath the aged oak trees, one of which is particularly large and venerable looking, its age being estimated at 200 years.

There are many azaleas, japonica and magnolia trees. One very large japonica tree, which has beautifully large red blooms, is highly prized by the Dominicks and is carefully looked after and treated each year.

The Dominick home has steam heat and all the comforts. At one side of the house is an old curving brick wall which adds a picturesque touch to the place. The brick from which this wall was built was bought in Charleston and brought to Gregorie Neck for this purpose.

An interesting piece of work going on at Gregorie Neck plantation is the raising of quail by incubation. These birds will later be turned loose on the estate. There is now

Original title: "Dominick Builds among Giant Oaks. New York Broker's Home in Jasper County Overlooking Tullifinny River Is Fashioned of Brick Painted White—Two Wings Slope Away from Main Building of Colonial Construction." Publication date: February 8, 1931.

Two views of Gregorie Neck in the 1930s: (top) from the garden and (bottom) facing the water.
*Photographs from Willis Irvin*, Selections from the Work of Willis Irvin: Architect, Augusta, Ga., *1937*

a long row of coops, each with its quota of birds. So far, the birds have been raised with success.

W. N. Heyward, Ridgeland attorney, has an interesting surveyor's map of Gregorie Neck plantation dated December 14, 1787, which shows this tract the same as was surveyed to Mrs. Ann Graeme at that time. It shows Pocataligo river, spelled on the map, "Pokotalligo," "Phip" island, Coosawhatchee river and "lands, originally granted to Capt. Anthony Matthews, Esq., and Jonathan Bryan, Esq."

The map reads: "I have measured and laid out unto Mrs. Ann Graeme a tract of salt marsh land, three hammocks of high land, including 1,000 acres situate in said district. Prince William Parish, between rivers Pokotalligo and Coosawatchee." It was signed by Henry Groumiller, surveyor.

Before Mr. Dominick bought the property, it was owned by the Garbade family in Jasper county and one of the family, Henry Garbade, is now superintendent of the place, occupying an attractive little cottage near the Dominick home.

The plantation received its name from the Gregorie family who owned the property at one time. For years it was owned by two Gregorie sisters. This plantation is comprised of 2,184 acres, but Mr. Dominick has also purchased some additional land. He built his home there about three years ago, its cost said to be around $50,000.

Mr. Dominick is one of the biggest brokers in New York City, being a member of the firm which bears his name. This concern is said to employ between four or five hundred people. ✣

A year after this article was printed, another piece on Gregorie Neck appeared in the *News and Courier* on February 7, 1932. Entitled "Japonicas Moved to Gregorie Neck," the article carried no byline but reads like the writings of Mrs. Martin:

> Three double red japonica trees measuring 23 feet in height and more than 19 feet in diameter are being moved twenty-five miles to take places among the giant oaks at Gregorie Neck plantation in Jasper county. The weight of each with its foot dirt is estimated at twenty-five tons.
>
> Bayard Dominick, New York broker, found the three japonicas, believed to be the largest ever transplanted in this state, in an out-of-the-way place in Hampton county. He bought them and then began the task of removing them to his plantation home site that overlooks Tullifinny river in Jasper.
>
> Two of the three have already been moved, each of them requiring the use of a truck, two trailers, five mules, a tractor, 150 feet of one-half inch steel chain, 500 feet of three-quarter inch steel cable, a 50-ton capacity wench [*sic*] and chain hoist, 1,800 feet of oak lumber, 1,500 feet of rope and 200 yards of burlap. . . .
>
> The earth taken up with each japonica is fourteen feet in diameter, five and one-half feet deep and weighs twenty-five tons.
>
> The New Yorker built his winter Mount Vernon–like home in a grove of giant oaks and now he is bringing in shrubs to break the flow of his three-acre lawn of Italian rye.

The Vignoles and Ravenel 1820 survey of Beaufort District, published in *Mills's Atlas of South Carolina* five years later, shows the Gregorie family established at the confluence of the Tullifinny and Coosawhatchie rivers. The Gillison name appears also, a few miles upstream on the Tullifinny.

Mr. Dominick assembled his Gregorie Neck plantation between 1927 and 1931 from five major tracts: Greenwood, the Park and Rose farms, and the Wise and Morrison properties. These along with several minor additions brought the whole to 3,404 acres. The Dominicks engaged Willis Irvin of Augusta, Georgia, to design their house. It was of brick with fifteen rooms, and the exterior was given a coat of whitewash for a mellow appearance.

Bayard Dominick (1873–1941), a native New Yorker, was a partner in the New York stock brokerage firm of Dominick and Dominick, founded by his father in 1899. It was the successor to Bayard's grandfather's earlier firm that dated to 1870. Bayard Dominick was a member of the exchange from 1896 to 1926 and for twelve of those years served on the board of governors. His New York clubs were the Union, University, and Racquet. He was educated at St. Paul's and Yale, graduating in the class of 1894. A forty-thousand-dollar gift to Yale in 1920 was to be used for scientific explorations in the South Pacific oceans. He was a trustee of the New York Zoological Society and the American Museum of Natural History.

A fondness for the sport of quail hunting, shared with most of his fellow northerners in the area, brought him south each winter. Bayard Dominick was not the only member of his family to be drawn to the Carolina lowcountry. His brother Gayer owned Bull's Island near Awendaw in Charleston County, since 1936 a federal wildlife sanctuary.

After Mr. Dominick's death, his widow, Alice, continued to make Gregorie Neck her winter home until 1950, when the plantation was sold to Charles and Katheryn Honeywell. Three years later the property was acquired by J. Spencer Janney, vice president of the Proctor and Gamble Company, and his wife, Elizabeth. The Janney family retained ownership under several titles and deeds for more than four decades.

Robert S. and Alice Jepson of Savannah, Georgia, were deeded Gregorie Neck in 1994. That they feel a particular attachment to the plantation is evident in the care they give it. The main residence is beautifully kept, and the grounds, which are extensive, are in excellent order under the care of Al Altman, Gregorie Neck's manager. The Jepsons divide their time between the country and a home in Savannah, where they are known as generous and enthusiastic supporters of that city's cultural life.

# *Mackay Point*

George Widener, Philadelphia, has just completed a veritable mansion of a hunting lodge near Pocotaligo, Jasper county, at what is known as Mackay Point.

This home, which is one of the show places of the coastal country of South Carolina, is fashioned Colonial style of wooden construction, painted white. The main part of the house is two-storied, while long low wings taper away on either side. There are four great columns supporting the open front porch.

The billiard room faces the entrance into the house. This room adds a splash of brightness at the beginning with its gay colors. There are seventeen rooms, furnished, for the most part, with maple pieces. There is brightness and charm everywhere throughout the house, which make it a delightful place in which to live.

The gun room has walls and ceiling of pine. Every bedroom has an adjoining bath.

At the back there is a splendid view of reclaimed marshlands, which has been made into a sloping lawn. This was brought about by proper piping and draining. The whole of this has been planted to Italian rye, which makes the lawn look like a stretch of rolling green velvet.

From this vantage point, sunsets, which in this section are noted, may be enjoyed to the fullest extent.

This beautiful estate is entered through a large, picturesque white gate, at the entrance of which are two charming white cottages, occupied by the superintendent and caretaker.

A wide, curving driveway circles a grove of splendid oaks, under which green grass is spread. And it is in this beautiful setting that the Widener home is placed.

One tremendous oak almost overhangs the front porch, directly in front of which is an elongated circle of grass and shrubbery.

In the Mackay Point tract there are 5,764 acres of land, used in the main as a hunting preserve.

Original title: "Widener Builds at Mackay Point. Philadelphian Erects Mansion Hunting Lodge on Pocotaligo River in Jasper County." Publication date: December 25, 1930.

Mackay Point. *From John R. Todd and Francis M. Hutson,* Prince William's Parish and Plantations, *1935*

A Philadelphia architect, Charles N. Read, designed the Widener home, but it was built by Clarke and Clarke, Savannah contractors.

The plantation was once known as the Orchards and was planted to figs. The land sold, it is said, for around $200 and $300 per acre about 1914. ✑

Five old properties on the peninsula between the Pocotaligo and Tullifinny rivers make up Mackay Point plantation: Mackay (or Mackey) Point, Jenkins, Rocky Point, Lockwood, and Bull Bluff.

Mr. George D. Widener's grandfather Peter A. B. Widener established the family fortune in Philadelphia after the Civil War, organizing a streetcar firm that he soon expanded to other major northern cities. That business, along with banking and investment interests, made him the wealthiest man in the city. He also began the family tradition of philanthropy and support of the arts. His home, Lynnewood Hall, outside Philadelphia, housed important collections of paintings, sculpture, and other art objects. These were donated to the National Gallery of Art in 1942.

George Widener's father, mother, and young brother were aboard the *Titanic* when it sailed in 1912. Only his mother, Eleanor, who was put in one of the lifeboats, was saved. The White Star Line, owner of the ship, was controlled by the Philadelphia bank of which Peter A. B. Widener was a director.

Years later Mr. Widener assumed management of the Street Car Company and maintained the family's philanthropies and art collection, serving for some years as chairman of the Philadelphia Museum of Art. However, his real love was in breeding and racing thoroughbred horses, an enthusiasm he shared with his wife, Jessie Sloane Widener. He owned two farms in Lexington, Kentucky, and there raised the celebrated colt Jaipur, ridden by Willie Shoemaker to victory in the Belmont Stakes in 1962.

Mr. Widener died in the winter of 1971 at the age of eighty-two. His will identified 6,246 acres of land that he owned in Jasper County. The childless Wildener left Mackay Point to the four grandchildren of his wife, noting, "I think of them as my own grandchildren." The executor of his estate and his trustee and nephew, F. Eugene Dixon Jr. (who owned White Hall on Colleton County), sold the plantation to Wye River Farms in 1972, which conveyed the 4,644-acre property to Stuart Janney Jr. and his wife, Barbara, in August of that year. Mr. Janney's brother owned nearby Gregorie Neck plantation. Mrs. Janney, the daughter of Henry C. Phipps, was one of the wealthiest women in America; many of her male relatives were members of the Okeetee Club. Mr. Janney died in 1988, having survived his wife by a year. He left the plantation to his fourteen grandchildren. The trustees of Janney's estate conveyed Mackay Point to a limited partnership of Delaware in 1986, the property at that time amounting to 6,312 acres.

In recent years Wildener's house at Mackay Point has been taken down and replaced by a new, modern residence. About 325 acres of land on the peninsula are now being developed as the Settings of Mackay Point.

# *Maurene*

(Corlies Estate; also F. K. Barbour Estate and J. A. Coleman Estate)

Arthur Corlies, New York broker, last fall completed one of the handsomest homes in the coastal country. Mr. Corlies' estate, which consists of about two thousand acres of land, with an additional six or seven hundred acres leased for hunting purposes, is what is known as the old Carey property and is located between Hardeeville and Bluffton.

This home is to be more than a mere hunting lodge. It was designed as a winter home for Mr. Corlies and his family, which consists of himself, Mrs. Corlies and one daughter.

Mr. Corlies has been collecting furniture here and there for his home for about five years.

The house, which is of brick veneer, and is four stories high, counting the basement, sits back from the highway.

### Faces Old Rice Field

The building faces an old rice field beyond a little clump of pines and this field will be flooded with six and ten inch artesian wells for a duck pond. The porch is supported by double white columns and the warm red of the brick is heightened by the green of the heavy wooden shutters at the windows.

An interesting feature of this home is the fact that native woods are used for the interior walls and ceilings in some of the rooms. The great living room, for instance, has walls and ceilings of cypress in its unstained state. In the center of this room there is a great fireplace fashioned from oddly shaped stones collected here and there. The stones are all of different sizes and shapes, two of them being brick from the ruins of old Sheldon church. This mantel lends an interesting air to the room.

The gun room is done in unstained pine and each of the bedrooms upstairs, with its connecting bath, is delicately tinted in different colors. Another interesting feature of

Original title: "New York Broker Builds in Jasper. Arthur Corlies Uses Unstained Native Woods in Many Rooms of Four-story Steam Heated and Electrically Lighted Winter Home between Hardeeville and Bluffton." Publication date: July 14, 1931.

Maurene. *Photograph courtesy of Brockington and Associates*

this home is that, with only few exceptions, all of the rooms in the house have adjoining or connecting baths.

### Huge Attic Room

There is a great cedar lined closet for blankets and linens and a huge attic room stretches from one end of the house to the other. This room is reached by a ladder, neatly hidden away in the ceiling, which, when needed, is pulled down. This room will be used for hunting parties.

The kitchen, pantries, storage rooms, etc., have their walls all done in green with floors of white and black checked linoleum.

There are steam heat and an electric light plant and every other comfort and convenience that the heart could wish and money buy.

Both Mr. and Mrs. Corlies are reputed to be expert horse people and will keep a stable of eight to twelve saddle horses.

W. N. Heyward, of Ridgeland, has an old surveyor's map of Mr. Corlies' property, showing where Purrysburg Township, on the water was "surveyed to John Hoover, Esq., land containing 990 acres on the New river, enclosing the buildings formerly occupied by Benjamin Carey, deceased." The survey was made August 3, 1811, and was signed by Philip Lamar, surveyor.

Rex Williams, the superintendent, occupies a picturesque home on the grounds. This house, of two story construction and painted white, is modeled after a type of old farm house seen here and there throughout this section.

### F. K. Barbour Home

Mr. Williams is also superintendent for F. K. Barbour, of Rumson, N.J., linen thread manufacturer, who has a most attractive home between Hardeeville and Savannah. This home too is new. It is a frame building made of cypress and pine and fashioned along Colonial lines with eight white columns supporting the porch. It contains about fifteen rooms, the main room being a great reception hall.

Mr. Barbour's estate consists of about nineteen hundred acres of land. He also has hunting leases on about seven hundred additional acres.

Mr. Barbour is said to have what is probably the most wonderful duck pond to be found anywhere along the coast. This pond is an old rice field of sixty acres flooded with a ten-inch artesian well. It is estimated that there are a thousand ducks at this pond every day.

This property formerly belonged to Washington Pillot.

### Coleman Property

Not far from Mr. Corlies' estate, on down the highway is the property of J. A. Coleman, big turpentine man and banker of Swainsboro, Ga. Mr. Coleman has built a nine-room, two-story frame building on his property. This home, which is painted white, is situated just off the highway near New river, and is approached by a little lane bordered with young palmetto trees.

This tract comprises about twelve thousand acres and was originally known as Bull's Barony, being the property of Governor Stephen Bull. The story is told that he took the slaves off New River plantation to Savannah to help Oglethorpe lay off the city of Savannah.

Through intermarriage, this land came into the hands of Henry Guerrard and his children sold it. J. R. Lassiter & Co. of Hardeeville owned the property when it was sold to Mr. Coleman.

Mr. Coleman does not make his home at this plantation, but has a superintendent, Thomas Warth, who lives close by in a house which is a hundred years old and formerly belonged to the Heyward family. Mr. Coleman uses his land for hunting and also farms to some extent and raises stock. On this property is an old rice plantation of about 400 acres, which he uses as a duck pond. ⚶

The Corlies estate has been known for some time as Maurene plantation. Its name is amalgam of "Maude Irene," the name of Arthur Corlies's wife. The property remains about the same size (now 2,100 acres), and the house has the same appearance as in Arthur Corlies's time.

Arthur Corlies and his brother, Howard, were the sons of Edmund W. Corlies, president of the Bank of America. When Arthur died in 1941, he left the property to his brother. At Howard's death in 1958 the 2,520-acre property passed by his will to Nancy Spaulding Liggett, who held it for almost fifty years. Since her death in 2006 the plantation has been owned jointly by six of her relatives—including Gerry Spaulding, Mrs. Liggett's grandnephew—who farm it for timber.

# Okeetee Club

John King Garnett was the first man in this section who conceived and carried out the idea of the hunting club. He organized several of the largest clubs along the coast, among them being Okeetee, in Jasper county.

Mr. Garnett's father, who lived at Brighton, Hampton county, but was a Virginian by birth, married a Miss Humbert, who owned the property at Okeetee club. He inherited this property from his wife and after his death, his son, John King Garnett, built a club-house near the site of the original home there. This clubhouse was erected in 1894 in memory of the father of John King Garnett and took its name from that of an Indian tribe.

This property was at one time involved in a lawsuit by other heirs, but the suit was discontinued. Sometime after organizing the club, Mr. Garnett sold out his interest.

He also organized Pineland, Good Hope and Chelsea clubs, all in Jasper county, and died about thirty years ago in Savannah. Mr. Garnett was one of the biggest cotton factors in Savannah. The little town of Garnett, on the Seaboard Air Line railroad, in Hampton county was named for him.

## On Coastal Highway

Okeetee club is one of the prettiest in the low country. It is to be seen on the coastal highway just a few miles below Ridgeland toward Savannah. It easily attracts the eyes of motorists because of its wide sweep of smooth green lawn and many live oaks and palmettos.

The approach to the house is up a long, spacious avenue flanked by tall palmetto trees. On either side of this approach is a wide driveway, bordered with large oak trees and on each side of these driveways is a beautifully bordered walk forming a half moon about the grounds, which occupy about six acres.

Smoothly clipped hedges, tall japonica trees, azaleas and magnolias grow luxuriantly here and beneath all is spread a thick carpet of Italian rye.

Original title: "Okeetee Club, 42,000-acre Preserve. Long Avenue Flanked by Tall Palmettos Leads Up to Fifty-room Jasper County House Where Wealthy Northern Sportsmen Come for Three Winter Months." Publication date: May 3, 1931.

Okeetee Club, circa 1910. *Photograph courtesy of Jocelyn Clark*

The clubhouse, fashioned by cypress shingles, stained brown, with its many wide porches supported by the brown of cypress trunks, presents a rustic appearance. There is a main clubhouse with two annexes, which are used for the members of the club. In addition to these is a number of small brown cottages scattered here and there about the club grounds.

### Fifty-room House

The club consists of about fifty rooms and includes, besides the sleeping apartments, a large reception hall, dining room, great living room, ladies' living room, gun room, boot room, kitchen and servants' quarters. The living room, which is immense in its proportions, contains a great open fireplace and divans and deep chairs of red velour which add warmth and brightness to the room.

There is no steam heat at Okeetee club, the members preferring the cheer of the open fireplaces. The club is managed somewhat after the fashion of a hotel, exclusively for the members and their families and friends. The season begins the first of December and closes the first of March. Parties come down continuously throughout these three months, some remaining for only a few days at a time, others longer.

The club lands comprise 42,000 acres and the hunting is said to be excellent. Between thirty-five and forty people are employed regularly about the club. J. B. Bostick has been the general manager of the club for thirty-four of the thirty-six years of its existence. He has as his able assistant, H. H. Coleman.

### Dogs Greet Visitors

From the back of the club during the season one is greeted by the yelping of dogs. Each member brings his own dogs to Okeetee when he comes down to hunt and they are cared for at the club's kennels.

Members of Okeetee club are as follows: Edwin Thorne of New York, retired; Samuel Thorne of New York, lawyer; Charles Steel, Wall street; Robert Goelet of New York, who, however, spends most of his time in Europe; Ben Phipps; John S. Phipps, of Pittsburgh, real estate and building; Howard Phipps; Grafton Payne, of New York and New Jersey; C. H. Mellon, Wall street broker; L. A. Thebaud, retired; A. Pillot, broker; Joseph Grace of New York and Long Island, steamships; John B. Clark, New York and New Jersey, of the well known thread company; Julian B. Clark, of Vermont, banker; Payne Whitney of Long Island; James Still of Long Island; R. H. McCurdy of New York, who also owns Tomotley, a large plantation in Beaufort county; John L. Kemmcrcr of New York and New Jersey, coal mines; H. C. Phipps of Pittsburgh and Long Island; K. B. Schley, New York, broker; Percival Roberts, Jr., of Philadelphia, steel and railroads, retired; Harry Payne Whitney, who recently died, was also a member. ༄

In a history of nearby Groton plantation, James Kilgo reports that the average antebellum plantation in Hampton County was about two thousand to three thousand acres. Okeetee, when established, contained thirty-five thousand acres. As Mrs. Martin explains, it expanded to forty-two thousand acres in 1931 and later to sixty-five thousand acres. According to Kilgo, "When that much land was taken out of production and maintained as a hunting preserve by outsiders for their own use, a significant part of the rural community became fenced off from local activity, creating a private island that operated by customs of its own." He claims that local residents did not resent the clubs, as they had sold the land in the first place, but it is hard to imagine that they did not. The class and cultural differences were great, and only a remarkable man would not have yearned to hunt on such a huge expanse of almost undisturbed land.

However, some Hampton County residents did gain access to the land. Harry Maner, who was first cousin to John King Garnett's wife, was hired as superintendent of the club

Superintendent's house at Okeetee Club, circa 1910. *Photograph courtesy of Jocelyn Clark*

before the turn of the century. Among the members with whom he hunted was Robert Dudley Winthrop, a Harvard graduate who worked on Wall Street as an investor. Many hunting experiences led to a friendship, and when Winthrop abandoned the club to start his own plantation in the area, he asked Maner, also a bachelor, for his help. According to legend, the men of Okeetee voted about 1905 to include their wives and children in their activities, and the bachelor Winthrop felt invaded, asking, "Don't you know of some land for sale where we could hunt birds as we please?" Soon Groton plantation was formed.

Perhaps the story is apocryphal. In her article on the Pineland Club, Mrs. Martin quotes at length from an article in *Sunrise* magazine that tells almost the same story but claims that members George Clark and Samuel Thorne left the men-only Pineland Club to set up the Okeetee Club, to which they could bring their families. When Mrs. Martin wrote about it, the Okeetee Club was made up of some of the most successful businessmen, and richest individuals, in America. Many of them were linked by family ties: cousins Edwin and Samuel Thorne; brothers John S., Howard, and H. C. Phipps; and brothers Payne and Harry Payne Whitney. Robert H. McCurdy was the nephew of Louis Thebaud's wife. (John B. and Julian B. Clark were not related.) Many of the members also owned other properties in the area: Robert H. McCurdy, Tomotley; Julian B. Clark, Spring Hill; A. C. Pillot and John L. Kemmerer, six thousand acres of land in Jasper County; and K. B. Schley, about twenty-two hundred acres in Jasper County. Edwin Thorne's son Landon co-owned most of the land on Hilton Head Island. Many of the members identified by Mrs. Martin were also members of the same clubs in New York and attended the same schools.

Edwin Thorne was a trustee of such companies as the Mutual Life Insurance Company, the Bank of America, Granby Consolidated Copper Company, the Federal Terra Cotta Company, and the New York Dock Company. Samuel Thorne was a senior partner with the law firm Delafield, Thorne, Rogers, and Howe.

Robert W. Goelet was described in his *New York Times* obituary as "a member of one of New York's oldest and wealthiest families." His grandfather was a founder of the Chemical Bank and Trust Company, and he was said to have inherited sixty million dollars. He owned extensive real estate in New York and Newport, Rhode Island, and was a board member of several large corporations. At one time his wealth in New York City was considered second only to that of John Jacob Astor.

The Phipps brothers were sons of Henry Phipps, a steel magnate and business associate of Andrew Carnegie. Together they developed the thirteen-story cooperative apartment building at 1 Sutton Place South in New York City. When built in the 1920s, it was estimated to have cost three million dollars.

Henry Carnegie Phipps, a financier, was most known for his highly successful Wheatley Stable of racehorses. Charles H. Mellon was an investment broker, dog breeder, and tournament golfer. Louis A. Thebaud worked in the import-export business for many years but was best known as a philanthropist and sportsman. He was one of the first to introduce wire-haired pointing griffons and Brittany spaniels to the United States.

Joseph P. Grace was president and chairman of the board of W. R. Grace and Company, which operated the Grace steamship line. In 1929 he helped establish Pan American Grace

Airways, which set up the first international air service down the west coast of South America.

John Balfour Clark was president and director not only of the Clark Thread Company of Newark but of five other companies as well, one of which, also called the Clark Thread Company, was based in Georgia. John L. Kemmerer worked as a lawyer and director of several corporations, including the Kemmerer Coal Company and Whitney and Kemmerer, the latter of which was founded by his father, Mahlon Kemmerer, in 1870 with two other men.

The brothers Harry Payne Whitney (1872–1930) and Payne Whitney (1876–1927) were the sons of William C. Whitney, a wealthy businessman who served as secretary of the navy. They inherited a great deal of money, married money (Harry Payne: Gertrude Vanderbilt; Payne: Helen Hay), and invested well. As a result, they were among the richest men in America. Harry Payne was a major figure in thoroughbred horse racing (his horses won the Kentucky Derby, Preakness, or Belmont Stakes twelve times) and polo. Both were remarkably philanthropic; Payne gave the New York Public Library twelve million dollars during his lifetime, and his will bequeathed more than twenty million dollars to the New York Hospital. The Whitney brothers and, especially, their father were major clients of the architect Stanford White and may have been the club members responsible for hiring White to design the Okeetee clubhouse.

An undated *Charleston News and Courier* article found in the South Carolina Historical Society files (apparently 1959) and entitled "Okeetee Clubhouse, One of State's Oldest Hunting Clubs, Is Rebuilt," includes the following:

> Okeetee Clubhouse, destroyed by fire near here in November 1958, has been rebuilt.
>
> The new, all fireproof clubhouse was completed in mid-January.
>
> Okeetee, one of the oldest hunting clubs in South Carolina, was founded in 1894. The membership consists of 19 sportsmen from New York, New Jersey, New Hampshire, Maryland and Vermont.
>
> The old clubhouse, designed by Stanford White, was built of cypress and pine with cypress shingles.
>
> The new building, which is located on the same site, has 21,000 square feet of floor area.
>
> Construction began on the project last year in March by Daniel Construction Co. of Greenville. The firm of Simons, Lapham and Mitchell are the architects.
>
> The new clubhouse adjoins U.S. Highway 17 and the ACL Railroad, with a double avenue of live oaks leading to it.
>
> It consists of two detached wings, a main building and a service wing. The two wings are one-story and each contains four bedrooms and four baths. They are connected to the main building by covered walks.
>
> The main building has a dining room and a 25 by 40 living room with a bay window overlooking the oak avenues leading to the clubhouse. A corridor leads to the bar, gunroom and locker room. The service wing contains the kitchen, pantry and a freezer room in which to store game.

The second floor of the main building has four bedrooms and four baths for members. Two rooms, with bath, are provided for the housekeeper.

Six bedrooms and baths are provided for domestic help in the service wing.

Each of the members' bedrooms has a fireplace. The building has concrete footing, with brick foundation walls. From the first floor up, a brick facing is used, backed by clay tile. The floors are concrete, covered with square parquetry of oak. The bathroom floors are tile.

The interior is plaster, with the exception of the gunroom which has cypress boards. A central heating plant furnishes heat for the clubhouse.

Membership in the club is limited to 30. Charles Henry Mellon has been president of the club for many years. Other officers include John B. Clark, vice president, W. Allston Flagg, secretary, and Robert Winthrop, treasurer. Cost of constructing the new hunting club has not been announced.

Cultivated land on the plantation raises various crops, however, timber is the principal product of the club. Many thousands of acres have been recently planted with seedlings.

Okeetee remains a private hunting club to this day and serves thirteen members and their guests during its season of Thanksgiving through mid-February. All its members live in the North, with the exception of Jocelyn Clark, son and grandnephew of members, who now lives year round at nearby Spring Hill. The club is made up of about fifty thousand acres. At the Okeetee Club, all the evening meals are formal.

# Pillot Hunting Club

### (also J. L. Wheeler Land, Lindon, Garvey Hall, Red Bluff, Bull's Island, K. B. Schley Lands, and Green Swamp Club)

In Jasper and Beaufort counties there are scattered here and there numbers of tracts of land, both small and large, which are owned by individuals and small clubs and used for hunting. Nearly all of these are without clubhouses, saving small houses or shacks, and the owners are usually members of some of the larger clubs. These tracts, as a general thing, are not so large as the estates which various northern men have purchased and upon which have been erected handsome clubhouses, but the sum total of these smaller tracts adds considerably to the acreage of these counties owned by outside capital.

One of these tracts, consisting of about sixty-five hundred acres, is owned by J. L. Wheeler, a northerner who is now residing in the upper part of this state. This property, which is located in the Savannah river swamp near Tillman, Jasper county, contains only a couple of cabins and is used mostly for lumber purposes. Mr. Wheeler is also understood to have bought land around Hardeeville and it is reported that he contemplates the erection of a clubhouse on this property.

The Pillot hunting club, consisting of 6,479 acres of land between Ridgeland and Tillman, is composed of A. P. Pillot and John L. Kemmerer of New York. Mr. Pillot is a broker and Mr. Kemmerer, a coal baron. They have no clubhouse on this property, both being members of Okeetee club, where they make their headquarters while in this section. They bought this land from C. E. Perry, Sr.

The Lindon plantation near Bluffton is owned by Buck Walter, of Cleveland, Ohio. The tract contains about 1,200 acres of land. There is no house on this property.

The Investment Trust corporation owns the Garvey Hall plantation, made up of Garvey Hall, Oakland and Shubrick plantations. Col. Gaston Allen is said to have been the last of the survivors of the owners of this property. It then passed to the Heywards and the Guerrards, then to H. M. Comer, of Savannah, who sold it to the Pritchards. On this property there is a reclaimed rice field of about 300 acres which is being made

Original title: "Miscellaneous Estates." Publication date: December 31, 1930.

into an excellent duck pond. The residence of W. R. Pritchard on this estate will be enlarged and renovated, it is understood, and will be sold to a club of wealthy northerners.

The Red Bluff plantation at Bellinger Hill, Beaufort county, about twelve miles from Hardeeville and consisting of about twenty-five hundred acres, is owned by J. Byron Glover, of Savannah. The house of this place was burned about six years ago and it is understood that Mr. Glover is contemplating building another. There are several duck ponds here and quail and deer are said to be plentiful.

Percy Huger, of Savannah, owns about 2,200 acres on what is known as Bull's island, Beaufort county.

K. B. Schley owns something like twenty-two hundred acres on Bee's creek, Jasper county. There is no clubhouse. This property was purchased from W. B. Ryan and J. S. Berg, of Ridgeland.

The Green Swamp club in Jasper county consists of about 6,468 acres in the Savannah river swamp and was formerly known as the Ellis property. There are only small houses or shacks on this place.

In addition to these, there are other small tracts owned individually or by small clubs composed of men from Savannah, Charleston and elsewhere in this state. ✄

Some of the men identified here as owning large acreage in the area were members of local hunt clubs. Andre P. Pillot and John L. Kemmerer, both members of Okeetee (as was K. B. Schley), bought six thousand acres of land in Jasper County in 1928 for $12.50 an acre.

Pillot was also a member of the Pineland Club and owned hunting land in Canada. He never erected a clubhouse on his Jasper County property. Since about 1959 most of that land has been occupied by the Nimmer Turf Company.

Joseph L. Wheeler purchased a number of plots in Jasper County between 1923 and his death in 1933, many of them quite large. In 1923 he acquired from the Okeetee Club 16,625 acres of land contiguous with the club's property for $25,000 cash and a promise of $175,000 more. Less than two weeks later he sold the land and the timber rights to that acreage to the Georgia Cypress Company. In 1929 he acquired 6,500 acres from H. N. Torrey, apparently the land that Mrs. Martin refers to in the article.

According to a history of the Joseph Alston Huger family by Clermont Huger Lee, Percival Huger (1881–1950), a Savannah realtor, owned not only Bull's Island in the May River. In about 1928 he also purchased Beef Island "in the same river, renamed it Myrtle Island, built its causeway, planned its development and successfully sold many lots."

# *Pineland Club*

Spoken of reverently as the mother of Okeetee and other hunting clubs in this section and, according to an interview given by Harry B. Hollins, of East Islip, L.I., to Robert Snyder, which appeared in the November issue of the magazine *Sunrise*, the oldest hunting club in South Carolina, Pineland, in Jasper county, is certainly one of the most picturesque.

Situated to the right of the highway between Tillman and Garnett in a grove of beautiful oaks which is cut up into interesting little walks, the clubhouse, fashioned of brown cypress shingles with its accompanying smaller cabins built of logs, is an arresting picture and one which is calculated to cause the passerby to pause for a closer view.

This club was organized somewhere about 1877 through the interest and efforts of the late John K. Garnett of this section. It was through him that Mr. Hollins and others became interested in this section and later formed the club.

Before the clubhouse was built, the members occupied a frame building which is still standing on the grounds and is now occupied by Sam Graves, negro caretaker, who has been connected with the club since 1894.

### House of Shingles

The main part of the clubhouse is built of cypress shingles and has a wide porch supported by cypress trunks. In this main building, one enters first a huge living room with its plain, substantial, but attractive furnishings. All of the walls are of pine with handmade panelings. Besides the living room, there are, in the main part of the clubhouse, the dining room, writing room, kitchen, pantries, etc. Upstairs are six bedrooms. There is also an annex to the club composed of bedrooms. In addition to these, there are five little log cabins of one and two rooms each, with bath.

Friendly little paths connect these cabins with each other, and the clubhouse is approached over circling driveways.

Original title: "Pineland, Mother of Hunting Clubs. Jasper County Organization Was Formed in 1877 with Purchase of 13,157 Acres of Land Which with the Exception of a Few Hundred Are Left to Grow Wilder." Publication date: February 1, 1931.

Pineland Club. *Photograph courtesy of the South Carolina Department of Archives and History*

There are 13,157 acres of land owned by the club and with the exception of two or three hundred acres, which are planted to grain for birds, all of it is used by the various members of the club for hunting. Deer and other game are plentiful on these lands.

Major J. C. Richardson, who has been the general manager of the club since its organization, says there were fifteen members of the club at the beginning. As each member has died, his part has been bought by the other members until now there are only a few. These are: J. R. Clark, Philadelphia attorney; Walter E. Clark, Philadelphia banker; E. J. Baetjer, Baltimore attorney; Dr. L. R. Morris, retired, of New York city; Arthur Lyman, lawyer and real estate man of Boston; and Mr. Getties of New York.

Pineland club does not have electric lights, but is proud of its old-fashioned lamps. The season begins about the first of December and the members continue to come until the first of March.

### "The Coastal Carolinas for Shooting" article

Excerpts from Mr. Snyder's article, entitled, "The Coastal Carolinas for Shooting," might be of interest to readers in this section:

"The development of the Georgia-Carolina Coast country began about 1887 when northern interests took over the Central of Georgia railroad, at which time that famous Southerner, General E. P. Alexander, was made president of the new road.

"Mr. Harry B. Hollins of East Islip, N.Y., with Mr. Edward Dennison of Philadelphia, went on an official tour of the railroad, Mr. Hollins being the vice-president of the Northern banking interest at this time. After the return of the inspection party to

Savannah, General Alexander asked Mr. Dennison and Mr. Hollins if they would like to go on a shooting expedition. They accepted the invitation and traveled in a private car to Ridgeland, about sixty miles north of Savannah, where they visited Mr. John Garnett, one of the directors of the railroad, who was thoroughly familiar and persona grata with all the people. He enlisted the services of Major Henry and Warren Lawton, secured horses at Ridgeland and with nothing but guns, dogs, blankets and light rations the two men started on a trek through the wild region. Here and there they came upon a deserted cabin where it was possible for them to stop, make a fire, cook bacon or the birds that were shot and roll up in their blankets on the floor to sleep.

"After four or five days, Mr. Hollins and Mr. Dennison got a very good idea of the country. They found game plentiful, seeing deer, turkeys, quail, woodcock, doves and snipe in almost limitless numbers.

"Of course, being so soon after the Civil War, their lives wouldn't have been worth a minute's purchase without the guarantee of Mr. Garnett that they were friends of his as well as of the Lawton brothers. Mr. Garnett was related to the Lawtons and this family stood for everything around the country surrounding Robertville, where General Sherman had made his headquarters before his attack on Savannah and from which place he wrote the now famous letters to his daughter.

"'I can't say that the Southerners were very enthusiastic about we Yankees,' said Mr. Hollins to the writer about this journey and subsequent visits, 'but because of our friendship with Mr. Garnett and the Lawtons we were treated civilly.'

"With these gentlemen's guarantees, who realized the benefits of northern interests in this region and the fact that if a club were formed the rights of property would be respected, Mr. Hollins and Mr. Dennison came north to form the first club in South Carolina, the Pineland club, which is so well known today among the country's leading sportsmen.

"The location decided upon was about a mile east of Robertville, which was really only a small village at that time. By the following year a clubhouse was erected which stands today, and the shooting was so good and the members so enthusiastic about the country that it was almost immediately a great success.

"It was thanks to old Major Lawton and Doctor Smith, a clever physician living near, that the feeling against the Yankee changed from one of antagonism to one of friendship. In Mr. Hollins' words: 'I might say that in all these early days we received nothing but hospitality and courtesy at their hands. This was the start of a better feeling between the "hated Yankees" and the Southerners who hadn't known us.'

"Shortly after this, in 1891, Mr. Hollins bought the first private country estate, Good Hope Plantation, which took in the historical Whitehall and other properties belonging to the Heyward family. This estate Mr. Hollins sold to the present owner, Herbert Pratt.

"A few years later, two of the older members of Pineland, Mr. George Clark and Mr. Samuel Thorn, of New York, were desirous of bringing their families down. The Pineland Club being for men only, they put it up to Mr. Garnett at Mr. Hollins' suggestion, to find a suitable location for an additional club, and this led to the formation of the now justly famous Okeetee club with its thousands of acres. This club adjoined the Good Hope Plantation, owned by Mr. Hollins.

"With the natural and healthy growth of the Pineland club, Mr. August Belmont, Mr. Sidney Ripley and Mr. Charles (Charlie) Havemeyer, of the Meadowbrook Club community, felt that they should like to have a club of their own. This resulted in their buying Mr. Garnett's house near the railroad station of Garnett on the Seaboard Line and calling it the Palachucola club, the property comprising about 12,000 acres." ✤

Railroads, banking, and hunting brought Harry Hollins to the Beaufort and Jasper area. He was born in New York in 1854. Showing an early penchant for business, he became an associate with Levi P. Morton and Company before he was twenty years old. He took a position with J. P. Morgan and by 1878 was organizing a banking and brokerage company of his own, H. B. Hollins and Company. Mr. Hollins's other business interests included the Knickerbocker Trust Company, serving as vice president of the Central Rail Road and Banking Company of Georgia, and being director of Central Union Gas and the International Bank of Mexico.

Mr. Hollins spent many winters near Beaufort, an area to which he was much attached, and he passed along those feelings to two of his sons. Jack Hollins is the son most frequently mentioned as an agent in local real estate transactions involving northern sportsmen; he at one time owned Bray's Island and an interest in Paul and Dalton. His brother, Harry Jr., owned Broadmarsh on the Pocotaligo.

Mrs. Martin ran the long excerpt from *Sunrise* without comment, though she was probably well aware of some of its factual errors. For instance, General Sherman's troops traveled through Robertville, burning nearly all of it to the ground, *after* leaving Savannah, not on the way there.

Though the subtitle of this article identifies Pineland as the "Mother of Hunting Clubs," apparently the parentage was unclear; a 1936 article by Mrs. Martin dubs it the "Father of Hunting Clubs." (In that later article she also changed the founding date of the Pineland Club, pointing to 1887. The earliest deed found by the editors is dated 1884.)

As she explains in the article above, when the members of the club died, they were not replaced, so the Pineland could not long continue as a private institution. Before long the clubhouse and its land were sold. A number of people held the property before 1971, when Savannah businessman David Bormes, driving past the entrance, saw a large sign announcing its auction through the Federal Deposit Insurance Corporation. The previous owners, three local men, had gone bankrupt. Bormes says that he was the only bidder and was awarded the property.

A renovation that he expected to take six months stretched to more than three years, but the results are remarkable to see. The property probably looks better than it ever has: lovingly restored, with all of the original wood preserved; the rustic kitchen replaced with a modern one that fits well into the building; grounds carefully tended. Of the five log cabins on the property, Bormes was able to save two and has restored them as guesthouses. A summerhouse that once stood beside the main house has been replaced with an art studio. Though most of the contents of the house were removed by previous owners,

Bormes has retained a beautiful side table, now used for dining; a couple of iron and brass beds; and a set of encyclopedias.

In the more than thirty years that he has owned the land Bormes has also done much research on the property. He reports that the old club, which always excluded women, even as guests, required tuxedos at dinner—but only above the waist. Guests dined in tuxedo jackets, shirts, and ties, while legs in waders and boots stretched beneath the table. Among the guests were Theodore Roosevelt, Herbert Hoover, and Dwight D. Eisenhower. Bormes questions the last paragraph in the *Sunrise* article that Mrs. Martin quotes, doubting that Belmont, Ripley, and Havemeyer were ever members of the club. The shingles, he says, were made of eastern white cedar, rather than brown cypress, as she writes. The main house, including the floor above the kitchen, included nine bedrooms, and the annex had another six plus a sitting room. Bormes remembers Sam Graves, mentioned in Mrs. Martin's article. He was known as "Slim" and died in the early 1980s, ninety years after he was first associated with the club.

# Spring Hill

"But we don't consider ourselves strangers in this section. We live here. Why, we've been living here for fifteen years!"

The slim woman standing before the glowing logs in the wide fireplace, removed her cigarette and laughed a throaty laugh in greeting to her newspaper visitor.

And her two young sons, building airplanes on the rug at her feet, lifted their bright faces and grinned at the idea of anybody's thinking they were strangers in that part of the world, shut away by a pine forest though they are.

One of the lads is fair and has a smile that is flashing and sweet like the sunshine between rifts in the clouds. The other is dark and sober. Both sturdy and strong and glowing with vitality and beauty, they offer a sharp contrast for study.

The lovely, spacious home does have a lived-in look. In the atmosphere is that intangible something which is lacking in the immaculate order of rooms that are rarely visited.

## Many Books in Library

In the big, sunny living room books and magazines lie carelessly here and there, tumbled cushions look as though some beloved head had rested for a little while—and there is all that little disarray which makes a mere house into a home.

The walls of the large library, just back of the living room, have row upon row of built in shelves and these are filled with many books, whose bright jackets add gaiety to the room. The wide windows give upon a restful view of great trees, moss-draped, and quiet woods beyond.

Not only do Mr. and Mrs. J. B. Clark, of Spring Hill plantation, make it their home, with exception of the summer months, which they spend in New England, but they make of their plantation of thirty-five hundred acres a self-supporting venture.

The house, of Colonial type of architecture with a long, low wing at each side, is situated off the Coastal highway between Yemassee and Ridgeland. It cannot be seen from

Original title: "Spring Hill Plantation Days. New Englander Makes His 3,500 Acres of Jasper County Land Self-supporting Venture—Mr. and Mrs. J. B. Clark Spend All but Summer Months There, Employ Tutor for Boys." Publication date: December 29, 1930.

Spring Hill. *Photograph courtesy of Robert B. Cuthbert*

the highway, but is reached over a little road which winds through a pine forest. The great white house of fifteen rooms, with its wide porch and tall white columns, is at the very end of a long picturesque avenue of large oaks, from which the gray moss streams in long, mournful ribbons.

A privet hedge forms a circle in front of the house and a fence at either side, one of which hides a charming small garden which is Mrs. Clark's very own. She is much interested in this garden and in getting flowers, which she loves, to grow in it. She says she is not a very successful gardener, but the results, so far, are creditable. There are azaleas and japonicas and magnolias, besides numerous small shrubbery and flowers adaptable to this soil and climate.

### Natives of Vermont

The Clarks are from Vermont, where Mr. Clark is interested in banking. However, they come south to their Jasper county plantation about the close of cotton picking time each year, remaining until summer has come.

Spring Hill plantation is made to pay for its keep. The land is farmed at a profit, negroes operating it under Mr. Clark's directions. In addition to the farm, Mr. Clark raises Hereford cattle. He used to raise pigs, but he discontinued this phase of farming activity.

Although the place is very large, Mrs. Clark says there is not enough room for their requirements when they have guests so they are planning to build a school house, which will include two guest rooms for the visitors to this hospitable plantation.

Besides these two energetic little sons, there is a five year old daughter, who is the baby. These children have a private tutor and seem to enjoy life and thrive in the coastal atmosphere.

Spring Hill plantation was owned at one time by Dr. W. D. Gillison and his sister, who married Dr. Thomas H. Gregorie. The original tract of land was said to contain about two thousand acres, but Mr. Clark also bought the place of W. O. Buckner, thereby increasing his holdings. The old Gillison home stood on this site at one time, but there had been no home here for years until Mr. Clark built his.

After the Gillisons, the property came into the hands of Tom Miller, negro lawyer, who was prominent in politics here just after the Confederate war. He is still living in either Charleston or Philadelphia and has a daughter, Mary Miller Earle, who is prominent in educational work among the negroes in Jasper county. ✄

Members of the Clark family of Vermont have had the distinction of being winter residents of Jasper County since 1915, when Julian B. Clark bought property between the Coosawhatchie River and Bees Creek for his Spring Hill plantation. However, Mr. Clark was not

Julian B. Clark, circa 1910.
*Photograph courtesy of Jocelyn Clark*

the first of his family to come to the area; his uncle George C. Clark was a charter member of the Okeetee Club, which Julian B. Clark soon joined and members of the family have belonged to ever since.

Today Jocelyn Clark, Julian's son, owns Spring Hill and lives there full time. (In Mrs. Martin's assessment he was the dark and brooding one in 1931, though those are hardly the terms one would use to describe him now.) He explains that his father contracted polio at an early age and got about in a wheelchair. Tutored at home as a child, he graduated from Harvard in 1914 and that year was given a membership in the Okeetee Club. He worked in the family investment house, Clark Dodge and Company, and ran a dairy farm in Vermont. His infirmity hardly limited him as he was an avid bird hunter and spent much time in the fields and marshes.

Initially, Spring Hill comprised two tracts, said to have been Huguenin family property prior to the Civil War. These were Fairfield and Waterloo, together amounting to 3,568 acres.

Julian B. Clark bought the land from Thomas E. Miller, who had acquired it in 1908 from the Combahee Lumber Company. Miller (1848–1938) led a challenged life. Raised by black parents, he had a fair complexion that suggested a mixed heritage. He came to prominence in the post–Civil War period with his advocacy for the political and educational rights of his race. Miller studied and practiced law, served in the South Carolina legislature, and briefly held a seat in Congress before in 1896 accepting the office of president of the new South Carolina Agricultural and Mechanical College (now South Carolina State University) in Orangeburg. His goal was to train black youths to improve their position in life as teachers, farmers, and mechanics. However, the white Democratic leaders in the state—Gov. Coleman Blease was Miller's most vitriolic opponent—interpreted his efforts as moves toward social equality and undermined him at every turn. Miller moved to Philadelphia in 1923 and lived there until 1934, when he returned south and settled in Charleston.

Today the main house at Spring Hill looks much as it did in 1931; central heat and air conditioning were not added until 2007. The approach to the house includes a handsome double allée of live oaks, the first row planted by the Huguenins, the second by Julian B. Clark. The garden laid out by Clark's wife, Louise Jocelyn Clark, still stands, and it belies Mrs. Martin's description of it as merely "creditable." In fact Mrs. Clark laid out gardens for many others, including Mrs. Bayard Dominick at Gregorie Neck. Spring Hill today contains about four thousand acres. Many of the fields have been planted in pine, which provides most of the income from the property. Mr. Clark, a lifelong sportsman, still hunts almost every day. He is assisted in the management of the property by his son, Julian Clark, who drives down from his home in Charleston.

# Strawberry Hill

(also Old Glover Plantation)

Strawberry Hill plantation, while not elaborate nor ostentatious in the least, is one of the most picturesque of the estates owned by Northern men in Jasper county.

Strawberry Hill is the property of Mrs. Martha S. Wade, of Waterbury, Conn., widow of the head of a large watch company of that place. At his death, this property in Jasper county went to his widow.

Mrs. Wade rarely ever visits her property here, but the place is popular with her son-in-law, William Henry White, who uses it as a hunting preserve.

Strawberry Hill is so hidden away that it is found with difficulty. Even after one has entered the thick grove of trees, in which one is told the lodge is located, the low brown house is very hard to distinguish from the trunks of surrounding trees.

The clubhouse, which is of two story or a story and a half construction, and fashioned upon simple lines, is made of brown shingles and blends chameleon-like with the thick surrounding forest. The rustic atmosphere is carried out in the minutest detail, even the fence and gate being made of cypress trunks and limbs.

Italian rye relieves the brownness of the place, just now.

The house is reached over a winding road, heavily carpeted with pine needles, and branches here and there, serving to throw a stranger into confusion as to which of the many little curving roads will eventually lead to the clubhouse.

Another simply constructed place in this vicinity is the home of John F. Harris at Grahamville. This is the old Glover plantation, Joseph Glover having lived there for years before the Confederate war. Sherman's troops burned the old Glover home and a pole house was built after the war close by. This house is still standing and in good repairs, although the poles have been covered and the house otherwise modernized. It is now occupied by J. C. Tison, superintendent of the Harris place.

Original title: "Strawberry Hill, Hidden in Jasper. Winding Roads Lead to Property of Waterbury, Conn., Watch Magnate's Widow—John F. Harris, of Chicago, Controls 3,000 Acres near Grahamville." Publication date: April 19, 1931.

The house now used by the Harris family upon its visits to Coastal South Carolina is a house which was built by Mr. Glover on or near the site of the old home. This home, however, has been enlarged and elaborated so that it is now a modern, handsome home. It is situated in a large grove of trees with a wide sweep of lawn, enclosed by a fence just off the main road, which leads through the little village of Grahamville. The tract contains about three thousand acres. Mr. Harris, who is a railroad magnate, lives in Chicago. ◈

Henry L. Wade was actually the co-owner of Strawberry Hill. He bought half of the 450-acre plantation in 1910 from Noah Wallace of Farmington, Connecticut, who had purchased the property in 1891 from Louis Reinstein for nine hundred dollars. Wallace, a manufacturer of lightning rods, owned considerable property in Jasper County (including the lands that would become Good Hope Camp), much of it in partnership with Mr. Wade. In 1911 they purchased 2,337 acres in the vicinity of the Pineland and Okeetee clubs. When Wallace died in the 1930s, he endowed his local Connecticut school with a bequest of more than a quarter-million dollars.

Wade was born in 1842 in Rhode Island. He was educated in the public schools of Connecticut and at Eastman Business College. In 1862 he enlisted in the Eighteenth Regiment of the Connecticut Volunteers.

Wade was engaged in the business of clock manufacturing by 1871, when he was elected secretary of the Waterbury Clock Company. Through subsequent reorganization the Standard Electric Time Company was formed, and Wade advanced from treasurer and general manager to president of the company in 1885. The company manufactured self-winding clocks, battery-powered clocks, and electric tower clocks, all profitable innovations. Mr. Wade was dead by 1914, and his widow, Martha, conveyed to Noah Wallace a large part of the lands her husband and Wallace had owned jointly. Wade left his interest in his Beaufort and Hampton county lands to Martha in a will signed in 1911. When she died in 1946, she left Strawberry Hill to her four grandchildren, who in 1983 sold the property, more than 349 acres, to E. R. Ginn III. William Henry White, described by Mrs. Martin as Wade's son-in-law, continued buying lands in Jasper County until 1938.

The original Strawberry Hill has been divided since Mrs. Martin wrote her article: the fields and high land have been separated from the area along Euhaw Creek by a paved road. The name Strawberry Hill now is applied to the fields: good high, open land with oak and pine, meadows and fields planted for dove and quail. Mr. Wade's brown shingle house was located on the creek and was torn down years ago because of termites. The present owner's house has been erected on Wade's foundation and uses the original chimney, with the date 1906 inscribed at the top.

# White Hall

## (also Honey Hill Battleground, Good Hope Camp, and Old House)

About ten miles from Ridgeland, past historic old Grahamville, past Old House, where is buried still more of history, at the end of a long, narrow, nerve-trying country road—is White Hall, home of Thomas Heyward, Jr., signer of the Declaration of Independence.

Before coming up to that large old white gate, a visitor who has never seen White Hall finds himself wondering if a few old ruins could possibly recompense him for such an arduous trip. Once at that gate, however, there is a certain end to doubt. One stops dead, almost forgetting to breathe for a little.

Whether it be a painting or a piece of sculpture or a burst of music, the work of a Master always takes the breath. And that splendid avenue, fashioned of a double row of gigantic live oaks draped heavily with long streamers of gray moss, is truly the work of a Master. A man's hand measured out those regular spaces and set the small trees there many and many a year ago, but only a Master could have brought them to such immense, proud splendor.

Caretakers at White Hall planted the ground beneath these oaks several weeks ago and just now it is like an emerald carpet for the feet, while far overhead the beautiful old trees form three perfect arches, like softly-stirring green canopies. On sunny days, the blue of the sky slips through, exquisitely patterned, and the sunshine touches the gray moss into shining scarves, tossed in the wind. When a moon is in the heavens, the green canopies are like great sieves distilling liquid silver over the world.

This avenue of trees is about a quarter-mile in length and about 100 yards in width and is a spectacle to take away the breath and bend the knee.

### Ruin Up the Avenue

At the end of the avenue is the ruin of the once wonderful home of the Heywards. It was built by Thomas Heyward, Jr., as his plantation home. It was twice burned, the first

Original title: "Oaks Remain of Glory That Was 'White Hall' in Jasper. Tourist Hunters Now Give Life to Place Where Once Carolina Society Gathered, Where Washington and Lafayette Stopped." Publication date: December 2, 1928.

White Hall, circa 1910 (top) and circa 2005 (bottom).
*Photographs courtesy of Jocelyn Clark (top) and Charles Philips (bottom)*

time by the Tories during the Revolutionary war and was later rebuilt. The second fire occurred about ten years after the Civil war and the home has never been rebuilt, although it is understood that plans have been underfoot for some time by the present owner, H. L. Pratt of New York, president of the Standard Oil company, to have White Hall reproduced just as it was originally. No authentic information is available on this matter, although rumor has it that well-known architects and artists have made trips to White Hall for the purpose of making investigation.

Of the ruins, the two large wings facing the avenue are still intact, while part of the foundation of the body of the house remains, the bases of the great columns which stood at the front of the house also being in evidence. One of these wings was used as the kitchen and servant quarters. Two immense fireplaces in this wing may still be seen.

The old building was fashioned of tabby and brick, was four stories high and more than 100 feet in length.

It was situated in what was known as St. Luke's parish and was the center of much social activity and gaiety. It was here that George Washington stopped to break the then long journey from Charleston and Savannah. It was not Washington's custom to stop at private homes, but he made an exception at White Hall. Lafayette was also entertained by Judge Heyward at White Hall, when he visited this section.

### Guests for Ball Arrive

The story is told that days before a big ball was to be given, handsome carriages from all over the country would draw up to White Hall.

Mrs. Heyward, who was Elizabeth Savage, was the social arbiter of the parish in those days and the story goes that she held a very high standard. It was thumbs down for those who did not attain that standard.

It is said that Judge Heyward was very fond of peacocks and guinea fowls and raised great droves of them. Once in a while an owl would get in among them and on those occasions the pandemonium raised at peaceful White Hall could be heard for miles.

Hazzards creek, a tidal water, skirts the ruins of White Hall and the grounds of the estate, dotted with oaks and large magnolia trees, slope down gracefully to the water's edge. Standing upon a high point in the grounds, the narrow inlet can be seen curving and gliding along the bank like a silver band.

Straight across the water is Hilton Head and it is said that a great ball was in progress at White Hall on the night that Sherman landed his army on Hilton Head. The dancers crowded into the cupola of the house and watched the army disembark. Excitement and speculation must have been rife at White Hall on that night.

Thomas Heyward, Jr., was the son of Daniel Heyward, who lived at Old House, about five miles from White Hall. Near the site of the old Heyward home at Old House is the Heyward graveyard and it is here that the signer of the Declaration of Independence lies buried.

### Heyward Graveyard

The old graveyard is approached by a long curving avenue of moss-draped live oaks. It is enclosed within an iron fence and the ancient tombs are moldy and blackened with the years. Grass and tangled undergrowth trip the step and the words on some of the old tombs have faded so that they are indistinguishable. The earliest date found on a tomb was to the memory of John Heyward, who died in January of 1795.

Beside his gravestone, the state of South Carolina placed a monument to the memory of Thomas Heyward, Jr., in 1922. This is a granite shaft about eight feet high, surmounted by a bronze bust of the man who helped to write his country's history.

Thomas Heyward, Jr., was born in 1746 and died 1809. On the granite shaft, which the state erected to his memory are the words: "Patriot, statesman, soldier, jurist, member of the Continental Congress, 1775; member of the Council of Safety of S.C., 1775; Signer of the Declaration of Independence, July 4, 1776; Signer of Articles of American Federation in behalf of state of South Carolina, July 9, 1778; Judge of Court of Common Pleas, 1778; at the siege of Charleston, May 12, 1780; in command Charleston Battalion of Volunteers and in the surrender of the city was taken prisoner and confined St. Augustine, Fla., one year; member of the Constitutional Convention of South Carolina, 1790; was son of Daniel Heyward by Maria; erected by state of South Carolina."

When White Hall passed out of the hands of the Heywards, it became the property of Gen. John Howard, who bought the place from Thomas Savage Heyward, grandfather of W. N. Heyward, the present magistrate at Ridgeland.

## Honey Hill Battle Ground

Between Old House and Grahamville is the famous Honey Hill battle ground. Breastworks thrown up by the Confederate troops are still there. The little stream that flows near this historic spot is the same stream that on that day ran blood instead of water, and whose gurgling progress to the sea was dammed by dead bodies. The federal troops landed at Old House and the story goes that they gathered the negroes from the plantations they passed and forced them to march ahead of them. The Confederate troops, according to the story handed down, picked off the leaders of the federal troops as they marched and mowed the negroes down before them.

Good Hope. *Photograph courtesy of the South Carolina Department of Archives and History*

### Good Hope Camp

The property now belongs to Mr. Pratt, who owns considerable land in this section. Among his holdings is Good Hope camp, located not far from White Hall. This is one of the most picturesque estates in Jasper county. To this spot Mr. Pratt comes, when the notion strikes him, bringing parties of friends for hunting.

Five hunting lodges made entirely of logs make up this settlement. About fifteen negroes are employed regularly to care for the place. W. C. Sipple serves as superintendent of the property and he is assisted by C. R. Smith. The estate comprises about sixteen or eighteen thousand acres of land. Between fifty and seventy-five dogs, well-trained, are kept in readiness for the hunt.

It is a section rich in romance, in history, in undeveloped resources, a section with past, an eager present and a future—little Jasper county, hugging the coast of South Carolina. ৴ፊ

Rather than burning "about ten years after the Civil war," as Mrs. Martin writes, according to the Ellis Papers at the South Carolina Historical Society, White Hall burned in 1885, during the ownership of General Howard. Despite the rumors about Mr. Pratt's plans, it was never rebuilt.

Years later Mrs. Martin discovered, as she wrote in *Winds of Change in Gullah Land,* that her maternal grandfather had fought in the Battle of Honey Hill at the age of sixteen. She interviewed a Confederate veteran named Capt. Ben Williams of Brunson, who took part in the battle and described to her "the little stream that ran through this section and how it was red with blood and clogged with bodies." Recent histories of the battle do not include the story Mrs. Martin recounted about Confederate soldiers killing plantation blacks as they marched ahead of Union troops.

Before Herbert L. Pratt purchased Good Hope Camp from H. B. Hollins in 1910, the land for the club had been assembled in 1902 by Noah Wallace, who also owned Strawberry Hill and several other area properties. J. L. Cadwalader, president of the New York Bar Association and onetime assistant secretary of state, was in 1909 an interim owner of Good Hope. He was also a close friend of the architect Charles F. McKim, partner of Stanford White, who designed the Okeetee Club.

Pratt was a son of Charles Pratt, founder of Astra Oil, a kerosene company. When the company was acquired by John D. Rockefeller Sr. in the late 1870s, Mr. Pratt became a business associate in the parent company, later Standard Oil. Advancing in the business, Herbert Pratt was made vice president of Standard Oil of New York (Socony) in 1911, rising to president in 1923. When Socony merged with the Vacuum Oil Company in 1931, he became chairman in what was then the second-largest oil firm in America. The Pratt family held, after the Rockefellers' interest, the largest block of stock in Socony-Vacuum Oil. Pratt retired from active business in 1935 and died a decade later.

The main lodge at Good Hope Camp burned in the late 1930s and was replaced in 1944, according to a Jasper County survey produced by Brockington and Associates in 1996. A 1946 newspaper article stated that fifty-four African Americans were then employed on

Old House. Image made by Basil Hall with a camera lucida in 1828.
*Courtesy of the Lilly Library, Indiana University, Bloomington*

the property and occupying houses built by Mr. Pratt, who also erected a school attended by 325 students.

In recent years Good Hope served as the winter home of Mr. and Mrs. Richard Webel of Glen Cove, Long Island. Mrs. Webel was the widow of Herbert Pratt. Her second husband, Mr. Webel, who died in November 2000 at age one hundred, was a partner in Innocenti and Webel, the distinguished landscape firm that laid out the grounds of a number of lowcountry plantations, as well as Furman University's Greenville campus.

When the English couple Basil Hall and his wife traveled from Charleston to Savannah in 1828, they spent several days at Old House. Mr. Hall made a drawing of the residence with his camera lucida, the only likeness that is known. The county has erected a marker at the site, located beside the Heyward gravesite.

# Hampton County PROPERTIES

Buckfield

Gravel Hill

Palachucola Club

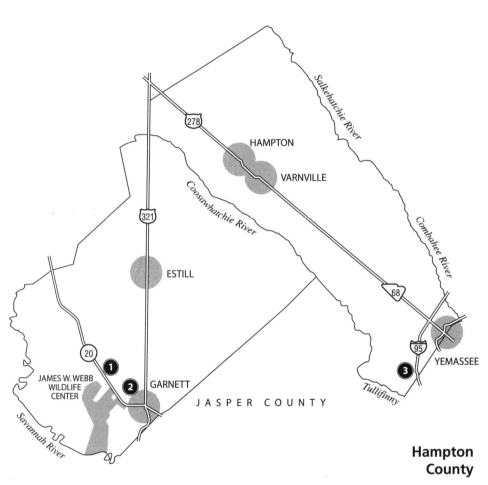

**Hampton County**

1. Gravel Hill
2. Palachucola Club
3. Buckfield

# *Buckfield*

Buckfield plantation, just a few miles off the Coastal highway, at Pocotaligo, home of C. W. Kress, is probably one of the best known estates owned by Northern men in this entire section. Particular interest is attached to this place because it is where the famous paperwhite narcissus bulbs are raised on reclaimed rice fields to supply the chain of Kress Five and Ten Cents stores scattered over the country.

Mr. Kress, who is president of the S. H. Kress company, became interested in this section about twenty years ago because of the hunting possibilities and has owned this property since that time. His interest in bulb growing came later, about the same time that A. Felix du Pont, down on the Combahee, undertook the experiment of growing truck crops on the reclaimed rice lands of the coast. Mr. Du Pont's experiment has been abandoned, but Mr. Kress is now producing at Buckfield plantation about half of this country's supply of the paperwhite narcissus.

Mr. Kress and his family use Buckfield plantation as a winter home. He and Mrs. Kress and their two daughters, both of whom are grown, come down throughout the winter months. Mr. Kress usually spends about a month of the winter here.

He has had a home here for about as long as he has owned these lands, but three years ago remodeled this place and has made of it one of the most interesting and lovely along the coast. The house is a large two-storied white frame building, containing about fifteen rooms. It is built along the lines of early American architecture and is furnished throughout in keeping with this period. There are tall, white columns, and a little upstairs balcony. The green roof blends harmoniously with the green of the surrounding trees and the wide sloping lawn. The home, which is beautiful but simple and in keeping with the coastal country, is enclosed with an iron fence.

## Avenue of Magnolias

At the time of this visit, Mr. Kress, one of his daughters and two little grandchildren were down. The little grandson was out on the lawn in the sunshine enjoying the new

Original title: "Buckfield, Kress Narcissus Farm. Reclaimed Rice Fields near Yemassee Produce Half of Nation's Supply of 'Paper White' Bulbs Sold in Chain Five and Ten-Cent Stores—Hunting Preserve There Develops into One of State's Best." Publication date: April 12, 1931.

Buckfield, 1993. *Photograph courtesy of Robert B. Cuthbert*

automobile which old Santa had brought him and the little granddaughter of nine months was dozing in her carriage, opening her blue eyes to smile sleepily once in a while, as she was wheeled up and down the walk in her carriage.

The Kress estate is approached across a railroad track at the little station called by that name and up an avenue bordered on each side by magnolia trees. On the grounds, which comprise about ten acres, there are pines, magnolias and palmettos. There are many winding walks and driveways through the estate all bordered by privet hedges of boxwood. Mixed with this is also some native shrubbery.

The employees of the estate live in attractive cottages scattered here and there about the grounds.

Buckfield plantation is made up of four old plantations. These are the Savannah, Retreat, Recess and Stokes plantations. The first three were owned by the Gregorie family, descendants of whom now live at McPhersonville, a picturesque little village near Yemassee. The fourth plantation belonged to the Stokes family.

### Operates Quail Hatchery

About twelve hundred acres of this large estate are under cultivation and the remainder is used as a hunting preserve. This preserve has been developed into one of the best in the entire state. Particular attention is given to quail and the breeding of quail. At Buckfield are to be found probably the best quail hatching facilities in the state. About one thousand of these birds are turned loose in the forests of the state each year.

In addition to this phase of the work, a great deal of attention is given to keeping down the natural enemies of game, such as rats, foxes, snakes, varmints of all kinds and poachers.

Some attention has also been given to the preservation of the timber on the Kress lands. This has been done by thinning out undesirable growth and allowing the young timber, which it is desired to preserve, to remain. No timber has been cut on Mr. Kress's lands and it is generally understood that none will be cut for years to come.

E. W. Goldenstar is superintendent of this property. ✣

Claude W. Kress (1876–1940) acquired his first properties in Beaufort and Hampton counties in 1907 with the purchase of Gregorie, Savannah, and Recess plantations, totaling 4,378 acres. He subsequently, in 1910, bought three additional tracts known as the Pine Land, Lapham Lands, and Stokes, and in 1912 he purchased Retreat plantation, giving him control of more than 11,000 acres by 1927.

Kress's brother Samuel purchased a stationery store in Nanticoke, Pennsylvania, in 1887, changed the name to S. H. Kress & Co., and soon opened a number of others. They were known as "five and dime stores," which says something about the economy in those days. Eventually the business grew to 241 stores in twenty-nine states. Claude worked closely with his brother in both the retail business and in the foundation that they eventually established.

Claude W. Kress was an avid quail hunter and skeet shooter and wrote the book *The Point System of Wing Shooting.* When Mrs. Martin visited Buckfield, she met "one of his daughters and two little grandchildren," including a small boy playing with a toy car. That boy was Daniel E. Huger Jr., who has lived in Charleston for many years and shares stories of his grandfather and his plantation. He says that the Kress home was usually filled with the aroma of narcissus plants. Quail was often on the menu.

In 1935, he explains, his mother remarried. When his mother and stepfather left for their honeymoon, he and his sister were sent to Buckfield, and Mr. Huger assumed that, as usual, they would reside in their grandfather's home. Instead, they stayed with their governess in a new five-bedroom home that Mr. Kress had built for his daughter and her family. He constructed a similar home for his other daughter, without telling either of them of his plans. The two daughters and their families enjoyed Buckfield for part of almost every year for decades.

During World War II the Kress family sold the timber on their land to the government, which used German prisoners from a nearby prisoner-of-war camp to clear the trees. When more men were sent than were needed for the timbering, they helped care for the grounds of Buckfield. Until they were sent back home after the war, these men maintained that Germany had won.

A 1927 article in the *Beaufort Gazette* suggests the great amount of land at Buckfield given over to the cultivation of the narcissus: "There are hundreds and hundreds of acres. . . . [O]n our left our eyes look out upon these Narcissus Bulb fields and out and out 'till our vision ceases in the far distance." During weeks when the labor in the fields was most demanding, additional workers were brought to the plantation from the neighboring communities of Yemassee and Sheldon.

In addition to the Kress railroad station, where freight trains picked up bulbs for transport around the country, Kress maintained a narrow-gauge railroad line on the property.

Workers in the narcissus fields at Buckfield. *Photograph courtesy of Daniel and Katherine Huger*

This was used to haul narcissus bulbs and plants between the fields, the sheds, and the station.

Mr. Kress was a trustee of the Harvard Graduate School of Business, and to that institution he gave his valuable business and economics library. His agricultural papers and books were donated to Clemson. At his death in 1940 a third of his estate was designated for the S. H. Kress Foundation for charitable work. The Kress stores were sold in 1964 to Genesco Inc., and the chain liquidated in 1980.

In 1952 the bulk of Buckfield, slightly more than eleven thousand acres, was sold to the Camp family and their associates, which held on to it until 1964, when John D. Hollingsworth Jr. purchased the land for about one million dollars. Hollingsworth, of Greenville, South Carolina, had inherited a small textile-machinery company founded by his grandfather and built it into a major international corporation. During his ownership of Buckfield, Hollingsworth bought much nearby property, expanding the plantation to twenty thousand acres and selling the land's timber and hunting rights. After his death in 2000, an obituary explained, "Although he was one of the world's richest men, he lived for more than 30 years in a trailer behind his flagship plant."

By all accounts John Hollingsworth was an eccentric individual. He routinely attended company affairs dressed in overalls and a flannel shirt. In business transactions he wanted payments in cash. For many years separated from his wife and daughter, whom he refused to see, Hollingsworth never met his six grandchildren. Most people doing business with him (and Mr. Huger, who with his sister retained their mother's portion of Buckfield for decades) never saw him. However, many agreed with Mr. Huger that "he was a genius." He controlled 70 percent of the market for card clothing, "the teeth that comb fiber to make cloth." Eccentric or not, Hollingsworth began sharing his wealth in the late 1960s.

Well over one billion dollars was given to education: Massachusetts Institute of Technology, Vanderbilt, Emory, and Furman were major beneficiaries. His real estate holdings alone were estimated at four hundred million dollars.

Buckfield was left to Furman University, which sold the plantation to Richard L. Chilton Jr. of Connecticut, president and chief executive officer of the Chilton Investment Company. In addition to his business activities, Chilton collects antiques and, because of his interest in historic preservation and American decorative arts, is a board member of Winterthur. He also owns White Hall in Colleton County.

# Gravel Hill

"They insist on making me a Yankee down here and I resent it. I'm a Southerner and one side of my family came from South Carolina."

R. P. Huntington, of Gravel Hill, Garnett, smiled when he said that, but he really was serious. He is proud of being a Southerner and once he admitted it a visitor is at a loss to understand why that fact wasn't self-evident, not that Yankees aren't just as nice as Southerners, but there is something that marks a person from the South . . . something that is like an instant bond when two Southerners meet, particularly somewhere that isn't the South.

Mr. Huntington's South Carolina ancestors were Palmers and on the other side they came from Virginia. Mr. Huntington himself is a Kentuckian, although he has been a resident of New York for some time.

It is a singular coincidence that Gravel Hill belonged to Mr. Huntington's ancestors sometime about 1680. Mr. Huntington did not dream this when he bought the place, but he has since concluded from records and old maps that the Gravel Hill which he now owns is the very same mentioned in connection with his family.

## Veteran Winter Visitor

Mr. Huntington has been coming to Coastal South Carolina for thirty years and has owned Gravel Hill for twenty-one of those years. He is also president of Palachucola club at Garnett.

Gravel Hill is the home of the Lawtons. Their home was burned during the Confederate war and was never rebuilt until Mr. Huntington erected his home there. This house is unique in appearance and arrangement. Mr. Huntington, who is a retired architect, designed it himself, after a home which he has in the Adirondack mountains. It is a series of rambling cabins, built of cypress shingles, painted a grayish brown. The roof is low and sloping and reminds of the roofs of huts of tropical countries. Cypress

Original title: "Gravel Hill, R. P. Huntington Home. Retired Architect Fashions Hampton County House after His Summer Dwelling in Adirondack Mountains—Prefers Grounds of Clean White Sand." Publication date: April 5, 1931.

Gravel Hill main house (top) and guest cottage (bottom), 2007. *Photographs courtesy of Dan Vivian*

posts are used on the porches and smaller cypress trees, split, form mouldings on the interior of the house. The little cabins or wings are all connected by a crooked, rambling porch. The material for the house was cut in the woods of Gravel Hill.

The house is situated in a grove of trees, the grounds comprising about twenty acres. Directly in front of the house there is a small evergreen garden, in the center of which is a fountain. There is a very little grass, Mr. Huntington preferring to have his grounds as they are naturally, a wide stretch of clean white sand. There is a picturesque aged negress whose sole duty it is to keep these grounds clean and she is continuously sweeping with her brush broom.

### Dozen Smaller Cabins

There are about twelve or thirteen smaller cabins, all made of cypress shingles. These are used for various purposes. Some are occupied by employees, a cold storage plant is housed in one, another is used as a dog kennel and so on.

The interior of the house is artistic and comfortable. The immense living room occupies the main part of the house. This has a tremendous window across almost the entire front in a single piece of glass. This glass is kept sparkling and perfect so that it gives the effect of having a piece of the out-of-doors in the big room all the time. There is also a great fireplace which burns very large logs, and many divans and comfortable chairs, tables and shelves of books. The room is wainscoted until within a short distance of the ceiling, which space is filled in with a dull blue burlap all around the wall.

The dining room, which, with the kitchen, pantry, and servants' dining room, occupies another wing, also has a very large window like that in the dining room and where the burlap on the walls in the living room is blue, it is green here.

The bedrooms occupy still another wing off from the big living room, these all being attractively and comfortably furnished.

Another large cabin on the grounds, which was used for the three Huntington children and their governess when they were small, has now been turned into a guest cabin. This, too, is charmingly arranged.

### 2,500 Acres in Estate

There are about twenty-five hundred acres in Mr. Huntington's estate, about a thousand of it under cultivation. He likes hunting, but finds the trees and plantings of more interest. He is very fond of dogs and has three or four Springer spaniels at his heels every step he takes.

There is a landing field at Gravel Hill, used mostly by Mr. Huntington's son, Richard, who is very much interested in aviation. He was in the navy for a while and is now connected with a firm of boat builders.

Mr. Huntington believes that one of the big advantages that this section of the country has is its deep flowing wells. All of the water used at Gravel Hill comes from a driven well and Mr. Huntington is very proud of it.

Hampton county offers a change from those counties which border directly on the coast. Giant pines are numerous here, where the great live oak predominates in the counties lower down. This is one of the finest quail sections in the country, according to hunters. ⚜

Gravel Hill is located near the town of Robertville, not far from the Savannah River. Robertville was the first community in South Carolina reached by Gen. William T. Sherman during the Civil War, and most of it was burned to the ground, including Gravel Hill. Owned by John Goldwire Lawton, it was, according to a history of the Lawton family, "two stories tall on a high English basement. It featured a columned portico, an octagonal entrance hall with circular stairway, and scenes representing the four seasons painted on the walls."

Robert Palmer Huntington began putting together his Gravel Hill plantation in 1909 with the purchase of the 41-acre Gravel Hill tract. Over time he acquired adjoining land, eventually owning some 2,644 acres. The gray-shingled, Adirondack-style lodge he built for himself is a pleasure to the eye today. Huntington also designed the "rambling white building," as Mrs. Martin describes it, at the Palachucola Club, of which he was president. Like Gravel Hill, it was built of cypress shingles.

Huntington was a partner in the New York architectural firm of Hoppin, Koen, and Huntington, which was responsible for several notable buildings in the city. His own home was the spacious Hopeland House in Staatsburg, New York, which the *New York Times* called "one of the most beautiful year-round country places in America." It adjoined Ferncliffe, the Astor estate at Rhinebeck. This proximity no doubt helped nurture the romance between Huntington's daughter Helen Dinsmore Huntington and Vincent Astor, who wed in a major society ceremony in 1914.

Outdoor activities held Huntington's interest as much as architecture. He was an avid hunter, and his pointer Gravel Hill Bob won the 1932 bird dog competition held by a large number of the northern plantation owners at the Hamilton Ridge Club, mentioned in the introduction to this volume. He sailed with the New York Yacht Club and played tennis on a competitive level; his doubles team won the national championship in 1891 and 1892.

He kept Gravel Hill until 1948, when, his mental health having deteriorated, the property was sold at the direction of his guardian. Jacob G. Howard, the buyer, held the place until 1962, in which year two area banks took title. Gravel Hill became the property of John M. Richardson of Brookfield, Massachusetts, in 1964, remaining in his family for several decades, until J. W. Yonce of Johnson, South Carolina, acquired the land. Yonce used the property for hunting and timbered all of the fields. In 2000 he hired Joe Chapman to begin controlled burning of the then-overgrown lands.

Chapman has stayed with the property ever since, continuing with new owner Stephen C. Tobias of Norfolk, who purchased the property in 2007. The Yonces kept about eight hundred acres, on which they constructed two hunting lodges. Under the direction of Tobias, an executive with Norfolk Southern, Chapman has been renovating the buildings in Huntington's compound, all eleven of which still remain, and managing the plantation's 2,700 acres. In addition to the main house and guest cottage, the other structures include the manager's house, a carriage house, a gatehouse, an icehouse / meat locker, a laundry, and a stable. The interiors of the main house have all been updated, but much of the original building material remains, including about 90 percent of the cedar siding. Tobias is a graduate of the Citadel and is active in alumni activities, so he returns often to his property in South Carolina. At the end of 2009 he was scheduled to retire and was planning to move permanently to Gravel Hill, where he will build a new house that complements the design of the nearby Huntington complex.

# *Palachucola Club*

Palachucola Club at Garnett, in Hampton county, is small, but picturesque and charming with its buildings set at the end of a long driveway of young oaks.

It is said that this spot was the camp of the Indian chief, Palachucola, the tribe camping farther down on the waterfront at Palachucola Bluff.

The original clubhouse which stood on this site was the home of the late John King Garnett, who was instrumental in organizing a number of hunting clubs in this section. Mr. Garnett sold his home to a club of wealthy northerners and the house was used as the clubhouse until it was destroyed by fire about 1916. During the World war, the present rambling white building was erected.

This clubhouse, which is unique in appearance, is shaped somewhat in the form of a semi-circle, with a main part and four wings. Two of the wings circle out from the main part of the building and the other two wings are at the back, three of them being used as sleeping rooms and the fourth as kitchen, pantry, and servants' dining room.

## House of Shingles

The house is fashioned of cypress shingles and painted white. The lumber for this building was obtained from timber on the lands of the club. The house has a slate gray roof and gray trimmings with a long wide porch. The chimneys are white and trailed with English ivy.

The center of the building contains the large living and dining room and gun room. There are great windows across the front of these rooms which give upon a lovely view. In the dining room the large windows are draped with yellow that is like warm splashes of sunshine, relieving the somberness of the dark furniture and walls. There is a large brick fireplace here.

Blue is the predominating color in the large living room, this bright shade picking itself out of the draperies and the covers on couches and chairs. In the bedrooms, too, of which there are six, gaiety is rampant at the windows with their bright draperies. The

Original title: "Palachucola Club in Hampton. Indian Chief Pitched His Camp, Tradition Says, Where House Erected by Northern Sportsmen Now Stands, the Seat of Twelve Thousand–acre Hunting Estate." Publication date: February 22, 1931.

rooms are wainscoted in native cypress and the living room is heavily beamed. The clubhouse is furnished throughout in simple but elegant taste. There is a long-distance telephone, also, for the convenience of the members.

The house was designed by the president of Palachucola Club, R. P. Huntington, of New York, who is an architect, now retired.

In addition to the main clubhouse, there is also a charming little log cabin on the club grounds. This cabin contains a living room, several bedrooms and a bath. This, also, was built with pine cut on the club lands. It is finished roughly on the interior, but is attractive and comfortable. This cabin is used by the club members and their guests.

The houses of the various employees, all painted white, are scattered here and there around the grounds at the back.

### Grounds of White Sand

As a usual thing, the hunting clubs along the coast and other large estates delight in Italian rye, which makes an ideal carpet of brilliant green, but the members of Palachucola Club evidently desired something different, for, with the exception of one large circle and two small ones in which grass has been planted at the front of the clubhouse, all of the grounds are of white sand. This is effective and carries out more vividly the shining whiteness of the club. This sand is hard and white and is kept gleaming with constant sweeping and care.

At the front are some pretty japonica trees. The long driveway of oaks was planted about twenty-five years ago by the superintendent of the club, J. W. Stevens.

The club steward is Thomas Hansen who has been with the club for thirty-two of the thirty-three years of its existence. He is as proud of the club as any member could be.

The club lands comprise about twelve thousand acres and furnish excellent hunting. The members come down off and on throughout the winter months, singly or in parties to enjoy the shooting. A small portion of the land is planted to feed for birds and the stock on the place.

The club boasts an excellent cold storage plant, where the various game killed by the club members is kept in perfect condition.

The club members and its officers are as follows: R. P. Huntington, New York, president; E. J. Shadwick, New York real estate man, vice-president; Henry Morgan, Wall street, secretary; Morgan Belmont, New York banker, treasurer; G. S. Brewster, New York oil man; Alonzo Potter, New York; Rudolph Well, Boston cotton factor; Lawrence Hemingway, Boston pottery manufacturer; Gorham Brooks, Boston; Amory Coolidge, Boston Cotton mill man. ✎

Robert Palmer Huntington designed not only the main building of the Palachucola Club but also his own Hampton County home, Gravel Hill, which was also built of cypress shingles. As Mrs. Martin makes clear, the club was made up of members from New York and Boston. Henry Morgan, a graduate of the Harvard Engineering School, was senior partner of the New York Stock Exchange firm of Henry Morgan and Company.

Morgan Belmont's father and grandfather, both named August Belmont, were noted for their extensive wealth generated by the banks they owned. Much of that money was invested in thoroughbred horse racing. Morgan Belmont continued in the family banking business, serving as president of August Belmont and Company of New York. His membership in the Palachucola Club was typical of this active man: he was an avid polo player, exhibited retrievers and was a member of the Westminster Kennel Club, hunted big game throughout the world, and served in both World Wars I and II. He bought land near Palachucola for his own plantation, which he named Belmont. Among the horses that he is said to have trained there is Triple Crown winner Citation.

Alonzo Potter was the son of an Episcopal bishop, worked with the banking businesses William Solomon and Company and Blair and Company in New York, and served as president of the Big Brother Movement in that city. Amory Coolidge (scion of two Boston Brahmin families) was a director and former executive vice president of the Pepperell Manufacturing Company.

John King Garnett (1853–1903), who sold his own home to the club members, bought and sold more than one hundred thousand acres of land in the area, much of it to northern sportsmen, according to an article in the November–December 2003 issue of *South Carolina Wildlife*. The article calls Garnett "The Plantation Broker." It explains that by 1993 Palachucola's land was 6,757 acres, a little more than half of what it had been when Mrs. Martin wrote her article. That year and the next the land was added to that of the adjoining Belmont plantation as part of the James W. Webb Wildlife Center, managed by the South Carolina Department of Natural Resources. This was done "under an agreement with

Hamilton Ridge, 2007. *Photograph by Robert R. Cuthbert*

the U.S. Army Corps of Engineers as mitigation for wildlife habitat lost in the impounding of Lake Richard B. Russell, farther up the Savannah River. Today, [the lands of] both plantations are open to the public, providing quality outdoor recreation for the people of South Carolina."

Part of the Webb Center is now known as the Palachucola Wildlife Mangement Area. A fine antebellum dwelling on the property, once lived in by Reuben Henry Tison, houses a Webb Center technician. The main house at Belmont (built in 1890 by Col. John Allen Tison) serves as the Webb Center lodge; its shingle siding was replaced with standard boards. A shingle-sided building at the Webb Center that does remain is Hamilton Ridge, thought to have been built about 1908 as a hunt club. During the days when the clubhouse was in use, fireplaces provided the only heat; on one of the seven chimneys that rise above the roof is the figure of a standing man, delineated by a different shade of brick. It is a relic of the past now and in poor repair. The Huntington-designed structures no longer exist. The *South Carolina Wildlife* article reads: "Palachucola hunting club is now only a memory and a live-oak lane to nowhere."

# *Colleton County* PROPERTIES

Bradley Estate

Cheeha-Combahee

Combahee and Bluff

Hope

Laurel Spring (also Lowndes)

Long Brow

Myrtle Grove

White Hall (also Paul and Dalton)

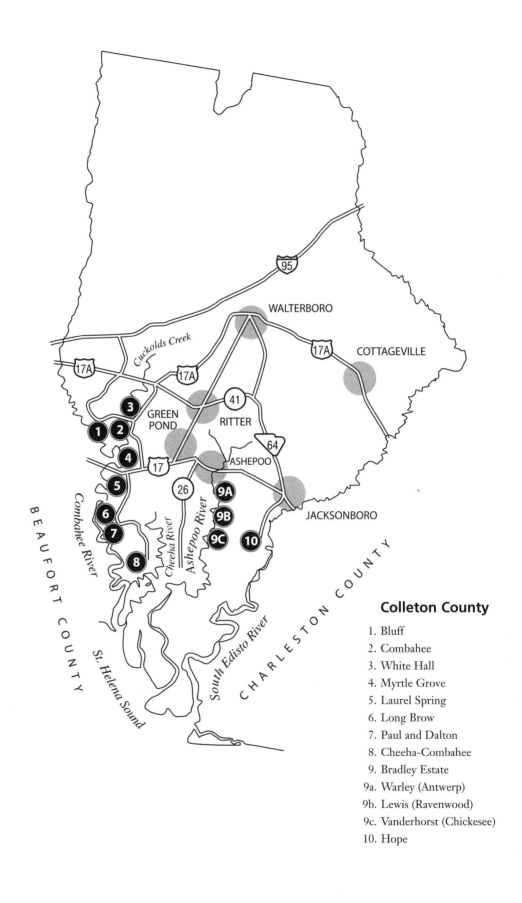

## Colleton County

1. Bluff
2. Combahee
3. White Hall
4. Myrtle Grove
5. Laurel Spring
6. Long Brow
7. Paul and Dalton
8. Cheeha-Combahee
9. Bradley Estate
9a. Warley (Antwerp)
9b. Lewis (Ravenwood)
9c. Vanderhorst (Chickesee)
10. Hope

# Bradley Estate

At Asheboro, in Colleton county, is one of the biggest saw mills in this section. There are more than a hundred modern cottages, equipped with baths, hot and cold water, electric lights and all conveniences, a twenty-four-room hotel and a shed measuring 200 by 430 feet—but a dead silence hangs over the little town, for it is without a single inhabitant save the people who take turns at keeping the engines fired. And this silence has reigned for six years, for the Bradley Lumber and Manufacturing company has not been in operation during that time.

This mill once cut eighteen million feet of lumber a year and employed about four hundred people. The company owns around 34,000 acres of land, running from the Ashepoo to the Edisto rivers. It is thought there are still around a hundred million feet of timber yet to be cut and it is expected that this mill will operate again at some future date.

The mill is owned by Peter B. Bradley, of Hingham, Mass., and his brother, Robert S. Bradley.

In addition to his interests in connection with the mill, Peter B. Bradley owns between sixteen and seventeen thousand acres of land in Colleton county and in a grove of trees, just across from the mill, has an attractive, substantial two-story house which is occupied by his superintendent, W. J. Moore, Sr., and where Mr. Bradley himself stays while in this county. However, Mr. Bradley has a winter home in Charleston county at Bulow mines in St. Andrew's Parish, where he spends all of the winter months. He has a home there of about twelve rooms and in addition there are about six or eight cottages where he entertains his guests. There are ten thousand acres in this Charleston tract where he raises stock.

## Bradley Not Newcomer

Mr. Bradley is not by any means a newcomer to coastal South Carolina. His father, William Bradley, was interested in phosphates in this section long years ago and

Original title: "Peter B. Bradley's Colleton Holdings. One of Massachusetts Man's Estates, Containing 16,000 Acres, Becomes Haven for Wild Life as Owner Hunts Little and Allows No Trespassers." Publication date: March 8, 1931.

Peter B. Bradley's winter home at Rantowles, 1950. *Photograph courtesy of Dr. and Mrs. Jack Rhodes*

acquired a good bit of property along the coast, so that Mr. Bradley has been coming to this section since he was a boy. His father founded the A-A Chemical company, which was first known as the Bradley Fertilizer company, with which Mr. Bradley has been connected. Now, however, he has severed his connection with this company and has retired.

Mr. Bradley's Colleton county property is made up of several old plantations, the main ones being Warley (on which Mr. Moore lives not far from the ruins of the original old home, which was situated farther back in the woods upon the river), Lewis and Vanderhorst. Beyond Vanderhorst are several other smaller plantations.

At the Lewis plantation, the approach to the old home site is up an avenue of trees, sentineled by two small magnolias. Here are to be seen the remains of the great steps which led up to the porch and also the ruins of two large brick chimneys. The old kitchen, which has been made into a tenant house, is still standing with its original floors. It is made of yellow cypress. The old bakery shop, commissary and carriage house are also still standing. There are three thousand acres in this plantation.

Beyond Lewis plantation and separated by a gate, as are all the other plantations, is Vanderhorst (called by some Vandroft) plantation. This plantation home was evidently the most magnificent of them all and there is evidence of a tremendous formal garden of ten or fifteen acres which surrounded the house. Here and there, according to various designs, are still to be seen numerous mounds in different shapes, oval, hexagonal, round and square. These are believed to have been large flower beds. There is a border in the shape of a great horseshoe which runs around to the back of where the house stood. There are also four or five long borders, which were evidently walks through the garden. The ruins of the two large brick chimneys and an old jug-shaped well, now bricked up, are still to be seen.

### Rice Canals Remain

Where once were stately grandeur and wealth and culture is now only a young forest of scrub oaks, interspersed thickly with young magnolia trees. Down from the house and passing in front of it is a long avenue of great oaks.

Many old rice canals with their picturesque trunks are still to be seen here and there on this plantation. One canal runs straight through from the Ashepoo river to Deer creek, making of Vanderhorst plantation an artificial island. At the elbow of land approaching the site of the old home is to be had a rare view of the Ashepoo river, fringed with a heavy growth of trees which splash the silver length of the river with velvety shadows.

All of this property is in the form of a peninsular which follows the river until it intersects with Deer creek.

Some years ago Mr. Bradley conducted an interesting experiment on about twenty acres of the old rice fields to see what crops could be made to grow here. The experiment was a great success so far as growth of truck crops was concerned. The crops were prolific, it being found that 700 bushels of onions could be raised on one acre. Lettuce was also a success. However, it was found that considerable expense was entailed in keeping the water back, so the experiment was abandoned.

Farming was also tried until it became unprofitable and now Mr. Bradley has devoted his large tracts of land to the raising of cattle. The breeds which he has are the Black, Aberdeen Angus, Ayershire and the Hereford for beef and the Jersey for milk. Here and there through the woods these cattle graze in great numbers. There are from four to five hundred acres of natural carpet grass pasture and the cattle are never fed with the exception of the Jerseys.

### Flood Gates Kept Up

The old flood gates are still kept up on these lands so as to allow the fields to be irrigated for the cattle. There are also many sheep on the lands.

It has heretofore been the practice to sell the calves, but it is the plan now on the Bradley estate to put them into baby beeves and sell them in that form.

A drive over the old plantation roads that wind here and there through the Bradley estate is most interesting. Mr. Bradley hunts scarcely at all and no hunting is allowed on the place, so that it is a veritable haven for wildlife. Mr. Moore says nearly any morning deer can be seen on the lawn around his home and that it is not unusual at all to come upon as many as six or eight deer along the roads in the late afternoons. In fields where vetch is growing, he says deer tracks are as thick as hog tracks.

The woods on the Bradley estate are beautiful and Mr. Bradley prizes them so much that Mr. Moore does not believe he will ever cut timber there. The old plantation roads are about thirty feet wide and Mr. Moore believes that they were built long before the trees grew up. The age of these trees is estimated at 75 years. Where are now thick woods on either side of the roads were once rolling fields of cotton and corn, as is proven by the ridges still to be seen through the woods.

Bradley's mill office, later the Ashepoo town hall and post office, now owned by Triarco. *Photograph by Robert B. Cuthbert*

Mr. Moore believes that Mr. Bradley's plantations are probably the oldest in this part of the country, although that is difficult to determine due to the destruction of records when the county courthouse was burned many years ago, one time by an Irishman by the name of Gahagan, who appears to have been a character in this section.

Mr. Bradley has a beautiful estate at Hingham, Mass., and has there a very large greenhouse, which he started as a hobby, but which has recently been commercialized. ✣

Though phosphate beds were discovered in the Charleston area, along the Ashley River, prior to the Civil War, it was not until 1861, just after the war began, when Dr. St. Julian Ravenel made his chemical analysis of the nodules. Only then was their value as a fertilizer understood. After the war local efforts to raise the capital to take advantage of his discovery were unsuccessful. Northern businessmen, however, had both the money and the foresight to see the profit in the new industry. Peter B. Bradley's father, William, who had organized the Bradley Fertilizer Company in Boston in 1861, was one of the first northern investors to locate a plant in Charleston. In partnership with George W. Williams, perhaps the most successful businessman in postwar Charleston, and others, Bradley organized the Marine and River Phosphate Mining and Manufacturing Company, which in 1870 obtained from the government of South Carolina the exclusive rights to mine the rock in all the navigable rivers and streams of the state. During the same period Bradley acquired the Bulow property near Charleston.

When William Bradley died in 1894, his two sons, Peter (1850–1933) and Robert (1855–1945), inherited the business and quickly expanded it to block the rapid and monopolistic growth of the Virginia-Carolina Chemical Company (also controlled by northern interests). The Bradleys put together a merger of twenty-two northern fertilizer concerns to form the

American Agricultural Chemical Company, the largest fertilizer company in the country. Peter B. Bradley became its president and chairman; Robert Bradley took over as chairman in 1906. Peter B. Bradley's own South Carolina holdings included Ashepoo Fertilizer, the Bulow and Bolton mines, and Bradley Lumber and Manufacturing at Ashepoo, with ten thousand acres of timberland.

By 1900 South Carolina's phosphate industry—already devastated by the 1893 hurricane—was superseded by that in Florida, where the rock was less expensive to recover and was not subject to the tax required in South Carolina. The Bradleys followed the phosphate move south to the area around Port Charlotte on the Gulf of Mexico. Their plan was to establish a deep-water terminal where phosphate brought in by rail could be shipped out to world markets. Bradley also saw the area as a site for a future resort town.

Of the large complex of buildings described by Mrs. Martin, only one structure remains on its original site: the mill office, which has been restored and serves as an office for Triarco Industries, a food-suppliment company. In the 1930s many of the buildings were photographed by Marion Post Wolcott, one of the Farm Security Administration's most acclaimed photographers.

In addition to sheep and cattle, Peter B. Bradley maintained for thirty years a thorough-bred line of Arabian horses, the Davenport, that had been brought to America in 1893 for the Chicago World's Fair. He brought a group of them south to a tract of land on the west side of Rantowle's Creek, which is still referred to by people in the area as Bradley's Horse Pasture. This account comes from Mrs. Jack Rhodes, whose father, the lumberman Malcolm L. McCleod, knew Bradley well, bought timberland from him, and at one time owned Bradley's house on Rantowle's Creek. When Mr. Bradley decided to sell his Charleston property in the early 1930s and move to Florida, he asked Mr. McCleod to take care of the horses, explains Mrs. Rhodes. Her father moved them—perhaps as many as a dozen—to the Old Tea Farm, which he owned, and then to his farm at Ravenel. After a hurricane, the pasture was flooded; when the land dried and the horses were turned out to graze again, they developed "blind staggers," a disease of the central nervous system, and had to be destroyed.

Peter B. Bradley was a winter resident of Charleston for sixty years. Two years after Mrs. Martin's article appeared, he was killed in an auto-pedestrian accident in Massachusetts. The family business, phosphates and fertilizer, continued under the management of his brother, Robert, who had been an active partner since graduating from Harvard in 1876. He also became president of his father's old company, Bradley Fertilizer of Boston, and vice president of Bradley Lumber and Manufacturing. In Florida he headed the development and operation of the Charlotte Harbor and Northern Railway and the terminal at Boca Grande.

The three Colleton County plantations mentioned in Mrs. Martin's article were in the area where rice was successfully grown along the east side of the Ashepoo River, south of Highway 17. All are now within the perimeter of the ACE Basin. Warley, or Antwerp, as it is better known, is the uppermost of the three. It takes the Warley name from the family of Felix Warley (1747–1814), a Charleston merchant and onetime clerk of Henry Laurens. His son Charles (1797–1877) was planting rice at Antwerp in time to be included in the 1850 agricultural census. His workforce of 134 enslaved blacks suggests his prosperity. The plantation dwelling was burned by Union troops during the war, and no doubt his out-buildings, including barns and mills, were destroyed as well. Charles Warley was almost eighty at the end of hostilities and unable to recover his losses. Antwerp, left at his death to his two sons, neither of whom saw a future in planting, was sold to outside interests in the late 1880s.

South of Antwerp is Lewis, or Ravenwood. When in 1850 John Williams Lewis (1820–1873) took a second wife, Anna Raven Vanderhorst, he named his plantation in her honor. She was the daughter of his neighbor Elias Vanderhorst of Chickesee. Lewis owned some 3,750 acres, most of it woodlands, with 353 planted in rice. His workforce numbered 154. He too lost heavily in the war and was forced to borrow capital to resume planting. When he died, the mortgage he had been given was yet unsatisfied, and Ravenwood was sold at public auction.

Mrs. Martin describes the ruins of a large dwelling at Vanderhorst or Chickesee, but a drawing of the old house at Chickesee, reproduced in Suzanne Linder's *Historical Atlas of the Rice Plantations of the ACE River Basin—1860* shows a surprisingly small building. The property belonged to Elias Vanderhorst (1791–1874), whose principal home was on Kiawah Island. There were about 2,700 acres in Chickesee, with 550 in rice. The 1860 census gives Vanderhorst 210 black workers. He had the misfortune of outliving five of his six children. In the settling of his estate, Chickesee was awarded to the children of his daughter Anna Raven Lewis.

# Cheeha-Combahee

Just a few years ago Wiggins, in Colleton county, was a bustling saw mill village and boasted more than a hundred homes. Only five years ago this mill was in operation and was probably the biggest mill of its kind in this section.

Now there is only silence where once the days were filled with the whine and drone of machinery. And where once, under the great trees, were the worn paths made by the constant tread of many feet, there is now only a rolling carpet of grass. Of all the buildings, only the superintendent's house, the company store, and, down a little slope, two little white cabins remain.

This is now Chee-ha-Combahee plantation, owned by Frederic Pratt, of Long Island, and his children. The superintendent of the large properties lives in the big yellow house which was once the home of the superintendent of the Wiggins mill. He is E. A. Boynton. The old company store has been turned into a stable for the Pratt horses and the Pratts themselves, when they make visits to Chee-ha-Combahee during the winter months, occupy the two little white cabins down the slope.

This mill village was torn down about a year ago after the mill had been in operation for about thirty years. It closed down after its timber holdings had been exhausted.

## Owns Long Island Estate

This property was purchased by Mr. Pratt, who formed a company and divided it up among his children very much after the fashion of the large Pratt estate, Dosoris Park, at Glen Cove, Long Island. An illustrated article about this estate appeared in the last June issue of *The Sportsman* written by Guy H. Lee under the title: "Estate of American Sportsmen."

This park is a community estate of the Pratt family and is owned and operated by the Pratt estate for the benefit of its various members. It was originally a thousand-acre

Original title: "Chee-ha-Combahee Plantation. Frederic Pratt, of Glen Cove, Long Island, Outfits Two Little White Cabins, Once Part of Huge Colleton Saw Mill Village, as Living Quarters, When He and Children Come to Hunt on Eleven Thousand Acre Estate." Publication date: February 15, 1931.

Cheeha-Combahee. Photograph from *Carologue* (Autumn 1999). *Courtesy of the South Carolina Historical Society*

farm bought by Charles Pratt about 1875. It has been inherited by his children and grandchildren, who have built homes of their own on the various pieces of property, but the bathhouse, yacht pier, stables, dairy, trout pool, bridle paths, etc., are all owned by the estate and used jointly by the members of the Pratt family. Among these are Frederic B. Pratt, John T. Pratt, George D. Pratt, Herbert L. Pratt, and Harold I. Pratt.

The Pratts who come to Chee-ha-Combahee do not care for anything elaborate in the way of living quarters and thoroughly enjoy "roughing it" in their little cabins. And their treatments of these cabins show what may be done to a simple frame cottage at little expense to secure a great amount of comfort and pleasure.

### Gay Window Draperies

One of the cabins, containing a large living room, dining room, kitchen, pantry and gun room, is used as the living quarters. The living room, which extends the full length of the house, is aglow with warmth and color. The simplest of wicker chairs and couches are used with small, inexpensive tables. Rich colors can be found in the fabrics that are placed upon the couches and chairs, bright jacketed books on painted shelves and a small tea table holding warmly colored dishes.

The dining room is even simpler with its painted kitchen chairs and long table covered with bright checkered oil cloth, but the cabin is cozy and happy and vastly comfortable when days are gray and cold.

Above the mantel in the living room is a pictorial map of the Pratt estate, showing in colored pictures just where the various game may be found.

There are about eleven thousand acres in the tract, which is made up of a number of old plantations. Among these are: Magwood, Wickman, Woodburn, Oak Hill, Middleton, Minot, Whaley, Townsend, Tarr Bluff, Riverside and Fields Point. These lands border the Chee-ha and Combahee rivers, which meet at the sound here.

## Great Round Tin Tubs

The other cabin is used for sleeping quarters. There are no baths, but each room has its great round tin tub with its built-in seat and when the guests feel the need of a bath, the tubs are brought into the bedrooms and filled with hot water by the maid. Each bedroom is furnished very simply with hospital cots and only the other necessary pieces of furniture. However, the severity is relieved in each room by dashes of color, furnished by the window draperies and the bedspreads.

The Pratts are a jolly, happy bunch and have great times here. Mr. and Mrs. Charles Pratt and their three children, of Long Island, Mr. and Mrs. Christian A. Herter of Boston and Mr. and Mrs. R. S. Emmet are frequent visitors here.

Mr. Herter is editor of the *Independent* and associate editor of *The Sportsman*. The November issue of *Sunrise* carries interesting snapshots of his two children, Adele and Frederic Pratt Herter.

The Pratts founded and are still operating the Pratt Institute of Brooklyn, N.Y. One of the family, Herbert L. Pratt, president of the Standard Oil company of New York, also owns a large estate, Good Hope Camp, in Jasper county. ✦

The Pratt Institute, which Charles Pratt founded in 1887, occupied more than five square blocks in Brooklyn and focused on useful skills in art, engineering, architecture, and science. Charles's son Frederic served for much of his life as president of the institute.

Charles Pratt assembled Cheeha-Combahee (the usual spelling today) in 1929 and 1930. The majority of the properties had previously been owned by the Savannah River Lumber Company and had been timbered at the time of Pratt's purchase. These were Magwood, Woodburn, Middleton, Oak Hill, Whaley, Brick House, Tar Bluff, and Riverside. Field Point and Walnut Hill were bought from Caroline Cowl of Great Neck, New York. Cheeha-Combahee amounted to more than ten thousand acres.

In 1932 Pratt persuaded James Henry Rice Jr. to prepare a history of the Cheeha-Combahee area, a copy of which can be found at the South Carolina Historical Society. Rice explains that Thomas Rhett Smith, an Englishman finishing at Cambridge University at the time of the Revolutionary War, married Anne Hutchinson and obtained from her family twenty acres of land on Chee-ha Neck, which they called Study Hill. They added to their acreage and eventually built on the site "a miniature Versailles garden at the Bluff on Chee-Ha Neck. This included a ten-acre rosary, where roses bloomed under his study window the year round." Smith had spent much time at Versailles and engaged one of the royal gardeners to help him lay out the garden. When William Makepeace Thackeray visited, he declared the gardens "the daintiest bit of earth I ever set eyes on."

Richard S. Emmet, grandson of Charles Pratt, describes his family's involvement in the plantation in a 1999 article in the South Carolina Historical Society's magazine *Carologue.*

"Life at Cheeha Combahhee was strenuous," he writes. "Every day started early, hunting fox or duck or turkey. There was barely time for a second breakfast before we rode out for lunch and a long afternoon of hunting quail. An evening hunt for coon and possum was a regular feature of the week, with a bonfire on the road and members of the local population singing spirituals and telling stories. Other evenings were devoted to charades, games, or dancing."

In 1936, five years after Mrs. Martin's visit, the Pratts built a new house on the property, designed by the New York architect William Platt. Emmet has written that the house "combines simplicity with classical grace. The separation of the two wings echoes the two buildings of the former housing and isolates the sleeping areas from some of the early morning bustle and nighttime festivities of the other wing. . . . [T]he two bathrooms were a welcome addition, and they were supplemented by labor-intensive tin tubs that were placed in front of the fireplaces in the bedrooms each evening and filled with pitchers of hot water by the maids."

One of the plantation's most distinguished shareholders was Christian Herter, a career diplomat, Massachusetts governor, secretary of state during the Eisenhower administration, and son-in-law of Charles Pratt. Emmet writes that Herter "was whisked off from Cheeha-Combahee by military helicopter, to be sworn in by the President in Georgia, and he returned in time for lunch at Middleton Bluff." Although badly crippled by arthritis, Governor Herter was "an avid duck hunter . . . on his South Carolina plantation," according to the *New York Times* on Mr. Herter's death in 1967.

After World War II the family sought to cut its costs at the plantation by planting rice, cutting lumber (one million board feet in 1950), and raising cattle. In the late 1960s corn and soybeans were planted. Eventually some of the land was sold off, and more acreage was leased to area farmers.

Starting in 1980 many individuals outside the family bought shares of the plantation. With the help of Ducks Unlimited, a stringent conservation restriction has been imposed on the plantation. Today it is mostly owned by sportsmen from Charleston.

# Combahee and Bluff

Combahee plantation, made up of several ante-bellum estates, is owned by A. Felix du Pont of DuPont Company, Wilmington, Del. Among Mr. Du Pont's properties in Colleton county are several old Heyward estates, among these being the home of D. C. Heyward, former governor of South Carolina.

Mr. Du Pont became interested in this section through Mr. Heyward in a rice field experiment proposition some years ago and the Combahee company was formed for the purpose of ascertaining whether or not the old abandoned rice fields along the coast might not be planted profitably again, with other crops. This experiment was conducted from about 1915 to about 1923, but was discontinued because it was found that the expense of draining the rice fields made the venture impracticable.

After the company was dissolved, Mr. Du Pont bought the plantations and has owned them since. He uses his properties, which contain more than ten thousand acres, as a hunting preserve. He also raises Hereford cattle, there being about six hundred head of this breed of cattle on the place. The cattle have about seven thousand acres of pasture land over which to roam. They are raised for market.

## Uses Old Southern Home

Mr. Du Pont uses as his home, when he is here off and on during the winter months, the lovely old southern plantation home which he found on one of his plantations. This house, which is a square, two-story frame building, painted yellow, has been changed but little and the interior and furnishings are ample, but most attractive and comfortable. There is nothing elaborate nor ostentatious about the Du Ponts' home. It is just what it always was, a hospitable old plantation home, fashioned so as to enable its occupants to enjoy to the utmost the simple things of life.

Original title: "Du Pont Lands Border on Combahee. Delaware Millionaire Controls Old Heyward Family Estates in Colleton—Herd of Herefords Roam Seven Thousand Acres and Game Multiplies." Publication date: September 27, 1931.

Combahee plantation. *Photograph courtesy of the Historic Beaufort Foundation*

The approach to this house is from the back through a gate and around one of the two circling driveways which wind between a veritable wilderness of periwinkle, green now, like a thick heavily embroidered carpet, but in summer, a mass of purple. Overhead are many aged oaks. At the front and sides a green lawn slopes down to the rice fields, through which a canal winds its way directly in front of the house. There are white columns in front and the heavy shutters are painted green. The house contains ten or twelve rooms. There is no steam heat, yet the house is comfortable from a big stove which is installed in the little hall at the foot of the stairs. The large living and dining rooms are furnished simply but in exquisite taste and the bedrooms upstairs depend upon the selections of colors and arrangements for their charm rather than upon the elaborateness of their furnishings.

At the back of the Du Pont home, a little to one side, is the quaint, picturesque home of the superintendent and his wife, Mr. and Mrs. Charles Turner. This house, which was an old servant's home, is approached up a tiny path made of old mill stones. The house has two small rooms upstairs and is white-washed. Inside Mrs. Turner has made it like a picture that reminds of those of the early life of young America, even to the red checked oil cloth on the dining table of painted pine, placed in one corner of the kitchen.

This plantation is said to have belonged to the Gibbes family originally and later came into the hands of the Heywards and the Haskells.

**Bluff Plantation**

On down the road a little way is Bluff plantation, also Mr. Du Pont's property. This is one of the very loveliest home sites in this entire section. It is high on a bluff overlooking a wide expanse of the Combahee and is reached through an avenue that cuts through a grove of magnificent trees set upon a rolling stretch of land.

On the plantation is one of the "streets" of slavery time, which negroes living in the cabins now say have been there since that time. These cabins are all neatly white-washed and are in an excellent state of preservation. However, their age could not be verified at the time.

At Bluff plantation were also seen a large number of sheep from which wool is clipped to make blankets for the Du Pont beds. Some of these blankets were seen sunning on a wide piazza on the day this home was visited and they were soft and fleecy and dyed in dainty, pastel shades.

Nathaniel Heyward was the owner of Bluff plantation and his tomb is there, just a little to one side of the attractive modern bungalow which takes the place of the stately old southern home which once dominated this noble estate.

Upon this tomb, gray now from the ravages of wind and storm and the heat of sun through many years, is an epitaph, which to have graven above him, any man might be well content to lay himself down.

"Sacred to the memory of Nathaniel Heyward, who departed this life April 10th, 1851, aged 85 years. While yet a youth, he shared in the vicissitudes and privations of the Revolution and having thus imbibed the principles of constitutional liberty, he unhesitatingly adhered to them.

"A planter on an extensive scale for more than sixty years, he illustrated by his prosperity and success the attainment of a green and honoured old age the truth of the classic maxim (this is followed by a Latin quotation).

"His firmness and even stoicism as a man were tempered by his urbanity and liberality as a gentleman and he fulfilled with moderation, dignity and wisdom the various duties of life.

"A residence here of half a century with its associations and attachments induced him to select this spot as a resting place for his remains."

At Bluff plantation is a landing field where, during the winter months, there is often to be seen a plane or two. The Du Ponts and their friends fly down from the north for visits occasionally and this field has been turned over to the United States department of commerce for emergency use. ✣

Capt. Nathaniel Heyward (1766–1851) was the largest South Carolina rice planter of the antebellum era. According to historian D. D. Wallace, Heyward was also the richest individual in South Carolina, with a fortune of about two million dollars. The Latin quotation on his tomb reads "Nihil est agricultura melius, / Nihil uberius, nihil dulcius, / Nihil homine libero dignius." As roughly translated by Dr. Darryl A. Phillips of the College of Charleston, it reads: "Nothing is better than agriculture. Nothing is more productive, nothing is sweeter. Nothing is more worthy of a free man."

Heyward's great-grandson, Gov. Duncan Clinch Heyward (1864–1943), began planting rice on the Combahee in 1888. Overcoming numerous adversities, he persevered until a final ruinous storm in 1911. Over that long period he managed to acquire a number of the old family properties, some few in partnership with W. E. Haskell. Eventually they owned Amsterdam, Lewisburg, Rotterdam, Vineyard, and Myrtle Grove.

By 1915 he found commercial rice planting no longer profitable, and to make the former rice fields suitable for upland crops he organized the Combahee Corporation. The expense of rebuilding the riverbanks, ditching the land, and constructing pumping stations required outside capital. Mr. A. Felix du Pont provided the funding, becoming the largest stockholder and mortgager, but after three years of effort the experiment proved a failure, with a debt of more than $618,000. The court ordered all the lands of the corporation sold at auction in 1923, and Mr. Du Pont acquired the corporation holdings. He kept the property until 1946, selling it then to the Lane family of Savannah.

Both plantations have been purchased by groups of sportsmen over much of the last half century. Today, Combahee is owned by Jacquiline Moore of Cincinnati. Bluff is the property of attorney Bobby Hood of Charleston.

Hood joined a partnership of sportsmen that purchased the Bluff from Earl Fain Jr. in 1978. Later Hood bought the interests of a couple of members, then divided the remaining property with fellow members J. Henry Fair Jr., whose land included Rose Hill, and Dr. Harry B. Gregorie Jr., whose acreage is now known as Plum Hill. Today the Bluff consists of twelve hundred acres. Hood has been able to reestablish the old rice fields and construct new trunks to attract waterfowl. The "attractive modern bungalow" that Mrs. Martin described is long gone. Using some materials from the land, Hood has built a new three-story house facing the sunset over the Combahee River. In 1995, soon after he purchased the Bluff, he was walking across the property's old airfield when a plane swooped in, missing his head by just a few feet. The dirt landing strip is now planted in corn, with trees standing at either end like sentries. Hood has granted an easement to the land to Ducks Unlimited, limiting future construction.

Capt. Nathaniel Heyward's monument still stands, as does one of the many slave cabins on the property, restored as a guest house. Heyward's long and substantial avenue of oaks remains and was used as a major set during the filming of the movie *Forrest Gump*. The Gump house at the end of the avenue was just a stage set and was torn down after the film was completed. The Vietnam scenes were shot in the duck fields, with the alligators herded away before Tom Hanks entered the water.

# *Hope*

The wealthy northern men who buy old, ante-bellum plantations in Coastal South Carolina have varying ideas of developing them. Some prefer ornate mansions of brick or stone, others rustic hunting lodges and there are a few who, gifted with a sixth sense, have caught the spirit of the old south and possess a fine sense of the fitness of things.

Belonging to this last named group is Z. Marshall Crane, of Dalton, Mass., and the famous Crane Paper company, which makes government bank note paper for forty-two different countries, including the United States.

Mr. Crane, who owns Hope plantation, near Jacksonboro, in Colleton county, did more than merely catch the spirit of the old days and seek to preserve it. He created beauty and charm and dignity where there were none. He looked at the ugly hulk of a house which he found on his plantation and shuddered. He had Simons and Lapham, Charleston architects, design that which he needed and with such success that a visitor approaching the house through the gate at the side, comes slowly, staring in surprise. Looking for a handsome new home, one is puzzled but somehow delighted. Why this is one of those real, old plantation homes. Not a new imitation—the real thing!

**Lantern Winks Welcome**

And so it is. Yet it has not been there long. This is like being home. A newspaper reporter feels none of that trepidation that he does when he mounts the grand steps of some of the more elaborate homes. Happily he runs up the friendly steps that bring him close to a picturesque old lantern which seems to wink a welcome.

Square and two-storied, this is a nice house. One likes it at once. People may not have loved and been born and died here, but it reaches out arms that seem to have held all that. Perhaps it is because there is really part of an old house here, after all, and that the house is not entirely new except as to appearance. Or, perhaps it isn't that at all, just that its owner saw that kind of a house in his dreams and made it come true.

Original title: "Crane House Reflects Old South. Millionaire Massachusetts Paper Manufacturer Achieves Real Plantation Atmosphere with His Two-Storied Dwelling among Oaks and Magnolias." Publication date: March 1, 1931.

Hope plantation. *Photograph courtesy of Budd Price*

Anyway, it is simple and stately and enfolding with warmth and understanding. It stands in a grove of great old oaks, interspersed with splendid magnolias. There is a rolling green lawn of twelve acres. Straight out in front is a long avenue of oaks, set at regular intervals, and beneath them the grass spreads itself an unbroken carpet.

About this time, Mr. Crane himself comes to the door. He doesn't send a butler nor a maid. That fits into the picture perfectly. A man who had so unerringly drawn for himself a picture of the old south could not possibly be the kind of a man who would spoil it so. Hospitable, gracious, delightful, Mr. Crane may be a Yankee, but he knows how to behave exactly like that far-famed "Southern Gentleman."

### Shelf of Carolina Books

One enters a large hall with its wide boarded flooring put together with pegs, its interesting green and white wallpaper and its swinging chandelier fashioned lantern style. The large living room, with the dining room beyond, take up the entire length of the house. These rooms are furnished simply, but charmingly. There are sofa, comfortable divans and chairs and tables in the living room. On the walls are some interesting Currier and Ives sporting prints. There is a shelf of Carolina books, too.

Above the mantel in the dining room is a pictorial graphic map of the properties of Mr. Crane done by Edward I. R. Jennings, of Charleston, showing the various hunting preserves and where the game is to be found. On the walls of this room is a series of four rare sporting prints painted by Dean Wolstenholme and published in London in 1817.

There are several bedrooms across the hall downstairs, Mr. Crane's being one of them. Here, the shiny floors reflect the brightness of rag rugs. There is an old-fashioned quilt upon the bed and on the bedside tables, old farmhouse bottle lamps. Tin lamps are used in the kitchen and servants' quarters.

Two upstairs bedrooms are done in green and gold and their windows frame pictures that are varying and breathtakingly lovely, like dainty etchings sharply drawn with vivid strokes of blue and green and gold-blue of sky, green of trees and gold of shimmering sunshine. Upstairs, too, is a bright little sitting room for women guests. The furniture is all of maple.

### Shrubbery All Native

The shrubbery about the house is practically all native. There is to be found the myrtle, holly and the lowly ink berry, Mr. Crane being the first one known so far to make use of this common but effective (with its black berries and green leaves) native shrub.

At the back of the house is a little road leading away into the distance. It was once "the street" of slavery days and when Mr. Crane bought the place there were still standing about three hundred little cabins. However, he tore them down to open up the view. There still remain, too, traces of the old race track which the Bischoff family enjoyed. It is said that races here were always attended by large crowds from far and near. There are also many beautiful bridle paths over the place.

At the side is the attractive little white cottage where lives Mr. Crane's superintendent, W. R. Marvin. Still farther back are the kennels with a number of finely bred pointers of the Muscle Shoals strain.

The history of this plantation dates back beyond 1850. Mr. Crane has a plat of his property, dated 1874, which shows a survey made on January 1, 1850. It was formerly known as the Bischoff property, being owned by a Charleston family of that name from just after the Confederate war for about sixty years, it is said. About 1908 a company acquired the plantation. Mr. Crane bought about three thousand acres and the remaining portion was bought by Donald D. Dodge. Mr. Crane also has the Pringle Field and the DuPre properties, five thousand acres at Jacksonboro and two thousand acres of quail shooting near Walterboro. In addition, he leases about five thousand acres. He comes down three times during the winter months, stopping two weeks each time and usually brings with him a group of congenial friends.

The hunting possibilities attracted Mr. Crane to Coastal South Carolina and the ideal climate adds considerably to the holding qualities of this section, he says. There is excellent hunting to be found on his estates, deer, wild turkey, quail and ducks being plentiful. ☙

Z. Marshall Crane purchased three plantations—Hope, Rotterdam, and Baynard—in 1927 from three Charleston men who had used the lands for duck preserves. Together the plantations totaled three thousand acres.

A year after this article appeared, Mr. Crane convinced Charleston Museum director Laura Bragg to move to Massachusetts to organize his family's art museum, in part by providing the museum with twenty thousand dollars more than his usual annual contribution. At the time it was called the Pittsfield Museum, but the name was soon changed to the Berkshire Museum. Crane may have been introduced to Bragg by Edward I. R. Jennings, known as "Ned," the Charleston Museum's curator of art, who painted the map of Mr.

Crane's properties; or perhaps the introduction came through the architect Albert Simons, also a friend of Bragg.

Bragg modernized and professionalized the museum and greatly increased attendance, but she also faced major confrontations with Crane. She sold paintings that he thought were important parts of the museum's collection, and she refused to hire architects whom he specifically selected. At Crane's death in 1936, $675,000 was left in public gifts, including $200,000 for the Berkshire Museum, $100,000 to Yale Divinity School, and $10,000 to the Charles E. Dorn Hospital in Walterboro.

The manager of Hope plantation in 1931, W. R. Marvin, later managed Bonny Hall plantation in Beaufort County. He was the father of the noted landscape architect Robert Marvin of Walterboro and related to two other property managers mentioned by Mrs. Martin: Edgar Marvin (Tomotley) and Hal Marvin (Myrtle Grove).

Max Fleischmann (1877–1951), chairman of the Fleischmann Yeast Company, bought Hope plantation in 1939. He said he wanted the five-thousand-acre property for partridge shooting. The new owner, a native of Ohio, had entered the family yeast business at age eighteen, advancing from superintendent of manufacturing to chairman of the board by 1925. Four years later he sold the company to Standard Brands, of which he became a director. To his friends he was "Major" Fleischmann, a title earned as commander of a balloon corps in World War I.

Fleischmann's principal homes were in southern California and Nevada. In the latter, on the shore of Lake Tahoe, he built one of the most imposing dwellings in the state. Nevada, finding the "Major" a congenial resident, commissioned him as an honorary police officer, a position he treated somewhat seriously. According to his *New York Times* obituary, he liked to patrol the area near his home dressed in "an unmatched coat and trousers and a plaid shirt with a .38 pistol or two strapped to his waist," pursuing speeders and those who would disrupt the order and peace of the neighborhood.

For many years Fleischmann was a member of the Cincinnati Reds baseball team board of directors, and he was the individual responsible for an agreement between the National and American leagues that prevented each from stealing players from the other. Diagnosed with an incurable malignancy at age seventy-four, Fleischmann took his own life. His estate of seventy-three million dollars in large part was left to a foundation bearing his name.

After the property went through various owners, media mogul Ted Turner of Atlanta bought it in 1978 from Northrup R. Knox of Buffalo, New York, businessman and owner of the Buffalo Sabres hockey team. Turner had previously spent much time at his father's Cotton Hall and Bindon plantations in Beaufort County. He also owns Kinloch plantation in Georgetown County. Most of the five thousand acres have been placed under conservation easements so that the timber can never be clear-cut and the land will not be developed. Buffalo now roam the property.

# Laurel Spring

(also Lowndes)

Of all the lovely estates owned by Northern men along the Combahee river, that of E. F. Hutton, of New York, is one of the most desirable and picturesque.

Mr. Hutton has large holdings in both Colleton and Beaufort counties and has built a low, white rambling bungalow in the shape of a "Z" at Laurel Spring plantation, near Green Pond. This plantation was owned by T. D. Ravenel, who sold it to Mr. Hutton. Mr. Ravenel planted rice on his plantation up until a few years ago and was about the last man who planted this crop for commercial purposes in this section.

Mr. Hutton's properties in Colleton county comprise some 10,000 acres and are made up of a number of ante-bellum plantations, all rich with memories and history. One of the most interesting of these is the old Lowndes plantation, which is not far from Laurel Spring and it is here that his superintendent J. A. Gibbes lives.

This plantation belonged to the Lowndes family, the only surviving member of whom, Mrs. Caroline Lowndes Mullally, the widow of Dr. Lane Mullally, lives in Charleston.

## Spared by Sherman

The house on this plantation is said to be the only ante-bellum home on the Combahee that was spared during Sherman's march to the sea and the reason given for this is that a brother-in-law of Mr. Lowndes, a Mr. Courtenay, was an officer in the federal army. A story is told that charred embers in the attic bore testimony to the fact that it was planned to burn this house and that it was saved only at the last minute.

"Daddy Scipio," an aged negro who still lives in one of the little cabins of "the Street," standing from the days of slavery, says the "big house" was used by the Yankees during the war and describes vividly how the ground about the house was strewn with

Original title: "The Hutton Estate of 16,000 Acres. New Yorker Builds Rambling Bungalow at Laurel Spring Plantation in Colleton—Two Thousand Acres of Rice Fields Furnishes Best Duck Shooting along Coast." Publication date: January 25, 1931.

The photograph of Laurel Spring that accompanied the original *Charleston News and Courier* article. *Photograph courtesy of the Charleston County Public Library*

the bodies of dead soldiers, which, he says, were later dug up and removed to the National Cemetery in Beaufort.

Asked how old he was at that time, Daddy Scipio shook his head. "We bin so busy dose days we couldn't keep score of chillun's age, but I bin big niggah den."

When he was questioned as to the age of the Lowndes house, the old darkey replied: "When I had sense, dat house bin dere."

### Hundred Years Old

If anybody in Colleton county is a hundred years old, residents say that Daddy Scipio is that person. Slightly stooped, with a gray thatch of hair and beard, he walks with a cane gropingly because he is almost blind. However, he hears perfectly and is in good health, even to his teeth. He begged for a dime with which to buy tobacco. "I on the pore list now," he explained, but his costume was topped with a high silk hat as though in jaunty defiance of both poverty and age. His aged and palsy-shaken wife in the little cabin appeared older than he, but he smiled at the idea that she was so old. "Dat my four wife," he boasted.

The Lowndes house is large and square and white, as were most of the old Southern homes. There are ten or twelve big rooms. The mantels and mouldings are lovely and some of them are believed to have been imported. The house is made of cypress and heart pine and has a graceful mahogany stair, midway of which is a charming window.

The house is situated in a beautiful setting of trees, including a number of camellias and azaleas, which are said to have been planted by the Rev. John Grimké Drayton of Magnolia garden fame, a friend of the Lowndes family.

In addition to the home, there is an ancient carriage house, stables, barn and a queer looking old building with outside stairs that go into the attic, which was the kitchen. All of these buildings are estimated as being from 175 to 200 yeas old.

### Experiments with Quail

At this plantation an interesting experiment is being conducted, the raising of quail, which will later be set loose in the woods. There are numerous coops where 600 quail are being cared for.

Plantations included in Mr. Hutton's estate are: Rose Hill, Anderson, part of Hickory Hill and Oakland, Cypress, March, Stocks, Hazelwood, part of Seddon and Minot plantations. In addition, he has about 6,000 acres in Beaufort county, which includes old Coosaw, Dale, Briars, part of Cotton Hall, Oak Point and part of the Spann property.

Mr. Hutton has owned this property a little more than three years. It has about 15 or 17 miles of river bank and about 2,000 acres of rice field area which is said to furnish probably the best duck shooting of any estate along the coast. A visit to this duck field area is well worth the effort. On good days the ducks can be seen backed up for half a mile. The water seems literally black with them. A visit is all the stranger is able to accomplish for there are guards stationed along the road to act as a damper in case anybody should feel too strongly the temptation to take a shot at the ducks.

The Hutton bungalow, situated on a little knoll, amid a wide expanse of green lawn, spreads itself out contentedly in the shadows of the great trees like a fat white puppy, enjoying its view of the rice fields beyond. It is painted white with a warm red roof and trimmings of green. Low-growing shrubbery banks closely against the building.

### Tomb of Dr. Lynah

At the back is the old Ravenel house and beside this is a tall white tomb, almost entirely covered with English ivy, beneath which rest the remains of Dr. James Lynah, at one time physician-general of all the military hospitals in South Carolina.

At Cypress plantation, just across the highway, there is still to be seen an old rice mill, fast falling into decay with its canal and old flood gates.

Only a few hundred acres of the Hutton property are planted, this being used for grain for birds. However, next year Mr. Hutton is allowing Dale and Coosaw to be planted in truck.

Mr. Hutton is head of General Foods and was head of the Postum company until it recently bought out a number of other companies, changing its name.

Franklin Hutton, brother of E. F. Hutton, also owns a few hundred acres in Colleton county.

The November issue of *Sunrise*, in connection with an article about Coastal South Carolina, carried a snapshot of E. F. Hutton at his Laurel Spring home, together with scenes on the properties of both E. F. and Franklin Hutton.

### Village Disappears

On down the road from the Hutton estate, one comes to a spot which was once the thriving village of Ballouville. At one time this place boasted a big mill, store and number of houses. Mrs. Sallie Speights, who lives in Walterboro, remembers it vividly from her little girl days and says this village used to seem as big to her as Charleston does now.

Now, however, unless the spot were pointed out, no one could find it, for there is not a vestige of anything to mark it as once the scene of human habitation.  ✥

Mr. Theodore D. Ravenel was among the most knowledgeable and successful rice planters in the state. He began his career as a planter in 1881 on the Cooper River, moving later to the Edisto at Willtown and coming to the Combahee in 1908, when he bought Laurel Spring from Arthur Nowell. He was still engaged with rice in 1927, "giving him the distinction of being the last large rice planter in South Carolina," according to Milby Burton's introduction to David Doar's *Rice and Rice Planting in the South Carolina Low Country.* In addition to Laurel Spring, Mr. Ravenel acquired neighboring properties and in 1923, with three business partners, bought Cypress.

When Laurel Spring was sold to Edward Francis Hutton in 1927, the property consisted of Lynah (as Laurel Spring was formerly called), Cypress, Smithfield, Hickory Hill, and Rose Hill. At the same time he purchased the nearby March and Stock plantations. In 1928 Mr. Hutton added Oakland and several other properties.

Mr. Hutton (1875–1962) started in the securities business at age seventeen as a mail boy. At twenty he was a partner in Harris-Hutton and Company, stockbrokers in New York. That firm was dissolved, and in 1904 he organized E. F. Hutton and Company. He later joined the Postum Cereal Company and was named its chairman in 1923. (From 1920 until 1935 he was married to Marjorie Merriweather Post, owner of the Postum company, which her father, C. W. Post, had founded.) Postum Cereals merged with other food companies to become the General Foods Corporation.

In March 1934 Mr. Hutton's home at Laurel Spring was destroyed by a fire thought to have been caused by defective wiring. Among his losses was a valuable collection of guns and antiques. By December of that year his new twenty-room house, built with fireproof materials, was ready for occupancy.

Mr. Hutton sold his Combahee River holdings, some 8,031 acres, in 1942 to Oswald and Norris Lightsey, lumbermen from Miley, South Carolina. Most of the property is still owned by those families, consolidated under the name Laurel Spring.

The old Lowndes house at Oakland, described by Mrs. Martin, burned about 1942. Ballouville was on the Union Road, now called the White Hall Road, opposite Smithfield. All signs of it have disappeared, but at one time a large commissary there served the needs of the rice-field workers. It was there that J. B. Bissell's laborers went on strike in May 1876 in a dispute over low wages and Bissell's practice of paying his men in scrip that could be redeemed only at his own store. The strike spread throughout the rice fields. Republican politicians tried to mediate the strike and eventually convinced the black workers to return to their jobs, but three months later the strikers again left their work when more disputes arose. Black replacements were called out from Walterboro under the protection of a white Democratic rifle club. The original workers ridiculed the Walterboro men as traitors and prevented them from going into the fields. Though there were many short-term victories for the laborers—scrip replaced with cash, wages raised, and arrested strikers released— ultimately the strike was unsuccessful as the Republicans soon lost their political power to reemerging Democratic rule.

# *Long Brow*

Few people in Colleton county know that all through the winter months there slips quietly in and out among them a personage, more or less unknown here, but famous and honored in England. He occupies, while in Coastal South Carolina, a simple, unpretentious, but neat and attractive farm house.

A passerby would see nothing except an ordinary, single story dwelling, painted cream with trimmings of green and a warm red roof. He might be struck with the beauty of the two immense and stately old oaks in the front yard and admire the heavily budded small japonica trees and the grape vine that forms an arch and makes an entrance into the yard. If he had any thoughts at all about the place, he might say: "Here lives a hardworking and prosperous farmer." And that is about all he would think before passing on to forget.

However, one who is so fortunate as to learn that Harold Ashton Richardson, inventor of the Richardson armour plate, spends about four months of the year in this house and has for his guests such as Irvin S. Cobb, one pauses to see what he can see.

**House Filled with Antiques**

Peering closer at that object on the porch, he discovers that it is an old spinning wheel and learns that the house is filled with priceless antiques, sent down by the Richardsons from their home in Canada. He would also hear about the collection of knives from various countries over the world which Mrs. Richardson has made.

These knives have been mounted upon a board and photographs made of the board, with descriptions and explanations beside each. This collection is most interesting, the knives varying all the way from the most harmless appearing to those that are positively alarming merely to look at.

This is Long Brow plantation, containing about 785 acres. The house is a remodeled and enlarged farm house. Although appearing to be small from the front view, it stretches out at some distance in the rear and contains nineteen rooms.

Original title: "Inventor Lives Quietly in Colleton. Harold Ashton Richardson Spends Four Months of Year at Simple Farm House and Sometimes Entertains Distinguished Guests, Such as Irvin S. Cobb." Publication date: March 29, 1931.

The photograph of Long Brow that accompanied the original *Charleston News and Courier* article. *Photograph courtesy of the Charleston County Public Library*

Mr. Richardson and his family, which include Mrs. Richardson, two daughters and two sons, all of the children being grown, like coastal South Carolina very much. They have been coming down here for twelve years, but have owned Long Brow only four years. Previously to that, Mr. Richardson leased Nieuport plantation in Beaufort county.

### Hails from Montreal

Mr. Richardson is a Canadian, hailing from Montreal. However he and his family spend their summers in France.

They were at Long Brow for Thanksgiving and had Mr. Cobb as their guest.

Most of the Long Brow land is used for hunting, a small acreage being planted to grain for birds. This year fifty acres were planted in rice for ducks.

There is an excellent garden at the back, just now green with a great variety of vegetables. Beneath the house is a collection of four huge copper pots, which Mr. Richardson found somewhere and sent down to his plantation home. These great utensils are blackened and much in need of cleaning and polishing. They were obviously used for cooking at some time.

Down the road a little way is the river and the scene of the old plantation rice field. The brick from this mill were used in the foundation of the house, which is now occupied by the Richardsons. The giant old mill wheel is lying on the ground, surrounded by bushes and small trees, which have grown there since the old wheel was forced to take its long and rusting rest.

The wheel is made of cast steel and weighs about two tons. Effort has been made to tear it to pieces so that it could be turned to other uses, but so far no one has been able to make more than a dent in its solidity, so it lies there and dreams of days of former usefulness. The Richardsons are proud of their flowing well, which is 615 feet deep and has a flow of fifteen gallons a minute.

An appreciation of Harold Ashton Richardson, reprinted in a booklet by J. Theodore Lawrence from the *Interest Monthly* magazine for July 1911, is entitled "Canadian Patriotism" and throws an interesting light upon Mr. Richardson. It speaks of Mr. Richardson in part: "The invention by a Canadian scientist of the best six-inch armour plate that has ever been produced . . . he was born at Halifax, Nova Scotia, in 1872, the son of the Venerable Archdeacon Richardson, D.D., of the Diocese of Huron, Ontario, and a cousin of Admiral King Hall, director of naval mobilization of the British admiralty. . . . A Richardson six-inch armour plate has resisted a 9-2 inch shell at a high velocity, while the standard Krupp six-inch armour plate, used by every country in the world, including England, has always attained its standard by impact from a six-inch shell . . . the great importance of Mr. Richardson's invention can be realized. . . . Mr. Richardson offered the British admiralty the preferential rights of his invention, which has been fully patented and in 1910 the Richardson armour plate officially tested. . . . "

In 1931 Mrs. Martin felt no need to identify Irvin S. Cobb, a popular humorist, newspaper columnist, and author of hundreds of books. He died in 1944.

At the time of Dr. James Lynah's death in 1809, he owned all the rice lands bordering the east side of the Combahee River from his Lynah or Laurel Spring plantation south to the line of Paul plantation (now part of Paul and Dalton). This would have included Rose Hill and part of the later Long Brow.

In 1849 William Kirkland Jr. (1828–1864) of Rose Hill, great-grandson of Dr. Lynah, added to his 600-acre share of Rose Hill an additional 380 acres of Dr. Arthur Parker's adjoining Long Brow property. Kirkland took the name Long Brow for his combined 980 acres. In 1859, to settle a family debt, Kirkland exchanged plantations with Joshua Nichols of Rose Hill. Nichols, though just nine years older than Kirkland, had married Kirkland's mother in 1848.

During the Combahee raid of June 1863, Nichols was caught on Long Brow when the Union troops landed. Concealing himself in the woods, he witnessed the burning of his house and farm buildings and the escape of the black laborers at Long Brow and Rose Hill. He reported similar destruction upriver as far as Cypress. It was Joshua Nichols who spoke of the unidentified passenger on the Union boat whom many of the black people greeted as they stepped aboard. Almost certainly this was Harriet Tubman. Nichols's account of the raid was printed in the *Charleston Mercury* on June 21, 1863. Long Brow remained in the Nichols-Kirkland family until 1869, when the Kirkland heirs lost the property in a mortgage foreclosure to James L. Glover.

For the 1926–27 season Harold Richardson leased Nieuport plantation, just across the Combahee from Long Brow. In 1929 he bought the Long Brow property from the widow of Frank Q. O'Neill of Charleston.

Mrs. Martin returned to Long Brow for another interview in 1936. In that article she explains, "Mr. and Mrs. Richardson are enthusiastic home-makers. From the four original rooms of the plantation house, they have added other airy rooms and long halls, in keeping with the house. They designed and built the addition to the house themselves with the aid of local carpenters. They also laid out and planted the gardens and grounds." She describes in more detail the antiques owned by the Richardsons: in addition to the knives, they showed her their collections of falcon hoods, Audubon prints, paintings of race horses, old English trays, porcelain pub kegs, and hand-woven rugs that reproduced hunting scenes and hung on their pine-paneled walls. The Richardsons continued to live on Long Brow's 750 acres until 1941. In the deed of sale Richardson is listed as "of Augusta, Ga."

After a number of owners who held onto the property for a decade or less, the Santee Portland Cement Company purchased the land in 1967 and retained ownership for several years. The present owner is Mr. Edgar T. Cato, cofounder with his brother Wayland T. Cato Jr. of the Cato women's clothing store chain, which has more than one thousand stores in thirty-two states. Among his other holdings is Paul and Dalton plantation.

# Myrtle Grove

Joseph S. Stevens, New York stock broker, owns Myrtle Grove plantation, a tract of about fourteen hundred and fifty acres not far from the E. F. Hutton estate in Colleton county.

On the home site here, Mr. Stevens has built a little rambling bungalow of brick, said to be old English bricks, and brought here from Savannah.

The house is placed on a wide sloping green lawn made more beautiful with low-growing shrubbery and cedars. Bordering the lawn at one side is a row of stately oaks

Myrtle Grove. Engraving by Elizabeth O'Neill Verner (from a postcard). *Courtesy of Budd Price*

Original title: "Myrtle Grove Plantation in Colleton. New York Stock Broker Builds Little Rambling Bungalow of Brick Brought from Savannah—House Faces Rice Field That Furnishes Excellent Duck Shooting." Publication date: May 31, 1931.

set at intervals. The house faces an old rice field, which furnishes excellent duck shooting. At one side of the house is a small pond where tame ducks are raised for decoys.

**Ducks and Turkeys**

Turkeys disport themselves upon the lawn, their cheerful gobble-gobble being mingled with the hearty quack-quack of the ducks in the pond.

The bungalow is located some distance from the large entrance gates of brick, which match the house.

The interior of the Stevens' home is most attractive. Besides the large living room, there are several bedrooms in the main part of the house, kitchen, dining room, guest rooms and a cottage for servants. The interior walls are of pine and the living room is heavily beamed. In each room is a wide fireplace with a leather seat entirely surrounding it so that guests may enjoy the fire and toast their toes cozily. In the living room is an interesting old Welsh dresser and also a large old drop leaf table.

Ancient black Jim Frazier, watchman on the Stevens' place, is immensely proud of his job and his boss. "Mr. Stevens say he gonna took me to New York and show me how dey makes money," he bragged. "He say dey piles de gold up in one pile so and de silber up in anudder pile dere. I sho does wanta see dat much money."

Hal Marvin is superintendent of Mr. Stevens' property, which he has owned for about three years.

Myrtle Grove plantation was the property of Charlie Heyward and afterwards it was bought from the Heyward estate by a group of men from this section, among them being W. E. Jaycocks, B. Josselson, Oscar Speights and others. They, in turn, sold it to Mr. Stevens. ⚕

This brief article did not include a byline for Mrs. Martin but reads like her writings.

The Colleton County side of the Combahee River is Heyward territory. Daniel Heyward (1720–1777), the first of the family to acquire property here, came before the American Revolution with a sharp eye for the best tidal rice land. Myrtle Grove was put together from the Grove tract and a part of Vinyard (usually spelled Vineyard today).

Nathaniel Barnwell Heyward (1816–1891) was an early owner. He sold the property to his brother, James Barnwell Heyward (1817–1886), on the eve of the Civil War. The property remained with his descendants until 1909, when they conveyed it to their cousin Duncan Clinch Heyward (1864–1943), who was later a governor of the state, and W. E. Haskell Jr. By that time the days of growing and marketing Carolina rice at a profit were coming to an end. Nevertheless, Heyward's attachment to these ancestral lands was powerful (at various times he also owned Amsterdam, Lewisburg, and Rotterdam), and he determined to make the old fields yield the golden grain again. He did so until the destructive hurricane of 1913. He wrote tellingly of his struggle in these years in his book *Seed from Madagascar*.

Heyward and Haskell sold Myrtle Grove in 1918 to W. E. Jaycocks and several other local men. The property then contained 1,200 acres, with 250 on adjoining Vineyard Reserve. The two places were considered as one.

Joseph S. Stevens of Jericho, New York, bought the plantation in 1927 and built the brick house referred to suitably as his "shooting box." The son of a noted New York banker, he was a sportsman most of his life: polo star, golfer, and duck and grouse hunter. He often rode to the hounds and traveled in the social set appropriate to the sport. In his youth he served as a Rough Rider with Teddy Roosevelt. He took ill on the Cuban campaign of 1898 and went to France to recover. In the last several years of his life he spent much of his time in Paris and also at Aiken.

It is unclear if Stevens ever took Jim Frazier to New York to see his piles of gold and silver. Stevens died March 23, 1935, in Charleston. At his death, he left the Myrtle Grove property to his Aiken friend H. S. Taintor "for his life." (Taintor was among the participants in the 1932 Hamilton Ridge Club dog trials mentioned in the introduction to this volume.) Exercising his executorial powers, Taintor deeded Myrtle Grove to the Charleston Museum following Stevens's wish to maintain the plantation as a game preserve. The museum in turn sold the place to Austin and Susanne Igleheart of New York in 1936.

When General Foods acquired the Igleheart Brothers' milling operation in Evansville, Indiana, in 1926, Austin Igleheart (1890–1979) stayed on with the new parent company. He had worked in the family business since graduating from the University of Wisconsin in 1912 and was familiar with packaged foods, the company's specialty. Honing his marketing skills, he steadily advanced in the ranks of management, serving as corporate vice president and then executive vice president, in 1943 being named president of General Foods, and becoming chairman in 1954.

Igleheart's success at General Foods brought him to the attention of other business leaders in New York, earning him a position on the boards of several major firms, including Chase Manhattan Bank, International Steel, and Meade, Johnson, and Company. An early member of the Carolina Plantation Society, he, along with his wife, spent many winters at Myrtle Grove.

Mrs. Igleheart and her children held on to the property until her death in 1982, after which it was sold several times, most often to timbering interests. The present owner, Eugene Slivka, a Texan, has taken down Mr. Stevens's "shooting box" and plans to erect a handsome brick house, said to be some thirteen thousand square feet. The surrounding area will be transformed into an elaborate garden.

# White Hall and Paul and Dalton

About six miles from the little village of Hendersonville, Colleton county, Charles L. Lawrance, of Islip, L.I., who is credited with having designed the motor in the Spirit of St. Louis, in which Lindbergh made his famous flight, has fashioned for himself a charming home at White Hall plantation.

This house, which is remodeled from an old one which stood there, is approached through arched brick gates and a grove of oaks set in a wide sweep of rolling green. The house is a white frame building, two storied in the main part, with flanking wings on either side. It is not pretentious, but rather built along simple lines. The front porch, flat on the ground, is supported by small white wooden columns. It has a red roof with trimmings of green.

Nathaniel Heyward, said to have owned about twenty-eight hundred slaves and credited with having been the largest slaveholder in the state, once owned this plantation, which contains something over three thousand acres. It is said that he himself, aided by slaves, set out the great oaks on the home site. Of a certain group of oaks on the place, the story is told that a love-lorn youth set them to form the initials of the girl he loved.

### Interest in Paul and Dalton

Another plantation in which Mr. Lawrance holds an interest is Paul and Dalton. This he owns in conjunction with J. K. Hollins, of Beaufort and New York.

On the plantation is one of the oddest and most original clubhouses in this section. This house is fashioned somewhat in the form of a semicircle on a high basement. The front of the house, which faces the Combahee, is made of brick which were taken from an old rice barn on the place. The wings, which taper back from the main part, are made of brick and shingle, the latter being painted gray. The trimmings are white. There is a belfry up over the center of the building and an old bell. The interior of the house is reached by outside stairs on each wing.

Original title: "Engine Designer Plays in Colleton. Charles L. Lawrance, of Long Island, Credited with Having Fashioned Motor for Spirit of St. Louis, Owns White Hall and Interest in Paul and Dalton." Publication date: March 15, 1931.

White Hall. From *Colleton County South Carolina: A Pictorial History.*
*Courtesy of the Colleton County Historical and Preservation Society*

The living room extends the entire length of the main part of the house. It has two great chimneys built inside with niches midway of one in which are set great lanterns of the Paul Revere type. This same type of lantern, of a smaller size, hangs on each side of the outside walls at the back just above the basement, with one also in the center. The basement is used as a garage and dog kennels.

On the hearths are odd, old andirons, an ancient black kettle and long handled skillet. In this room with its walls resembling pine and its high beamed ceiling, there is an interesting old Welsh dresser. The other furnishings of the room are severely simple, including only substantial benches and tables. Interesting sporting prints hang upon the walls.

The bedrooms, which occupy the wings, are plainly furnished. One of these has two old corner cupboards. There is a grandfather clock in the hall and the entrance door is said to have been taken from the jail at old Jacksonboro, at one time the capital of Colleton county and the scene of one convention of the general assembly of South Carolina. This door, which is tremendously heavy, is about two inches thick and the great iron key which unlocks it hangs on a nail close by.

Paul and Dalton was once owned by Payne Whitney, who sold it to Mr. Hollins who in turn sold part of his interest to Mr. Lawrance.

At one corner of the club house is a great oak which is highly prized by the owners of the plantation.

The December issue of *The Red Book* carries a full page photograph of Mr. Lawrance at his desk and beneath it the inscription, in part . . . "The hand and the mind of Charles L. Lawrance, engineer designer, is in many of the great airplane motors today."

The November issue of *Sunrise* also shows a snapshot of Mr. Lawrance looking at the ruins of White Hall, famous Heyward home in Jasper county, part of Good Hope plantation, owned by Herbert L. Pratt.  ✳

Charles L. Lawrance (1883–1950) bought the 756-acre White Hall (the preferred spelling) plantation on Cuckold Creek in 1927. It had been owned by the Heyward family since the early nineteenth century. It belonged first to Nathaniel Heyward (1790–1819) and then to his son Nathaniel Barnwell Heyward (1816–1891). Contrary to what Mrs. Martin tells us, it seems never to have been held by the family patriarch, Capt. Nathaniel Heyward (1766–1851).

Lawrance served as president of Wright Aeronautic Corporation between 1924 and 1929 and later was head of Lawrance Engineering and Research Corporation. His invention and development of the air-cooled radial aircraft engine, known as the Wright Whirlwind Engine, made early transcontinental flight possible, first successfully tested in 1926 by Adm. Richard Byrd's trip to the North Pole. Other exploits followed: both Charles Lindbergh and Amelia Earhart used the Whirlwind engine. For his pioneering work in the industry, both Yale and Harvard awarded Lawrance honorary degrees, and the French government made him a chevalier of the Legion of Honor.

In addition to White Hall, Lawrance bought the Hamilton Ridge Club in Hampton County with Jack Hollins in 1928, selling it in 1936 to George Warren, an attorney in Hampton, South Carolina. Hamilton Ridge is now a part of the Webb Wildlife Management Area.

After Mr. Lawrance's death, Mrs. Lawrance sold White Hall in 1937 to Fitz Eugene Dixon Jr. (1923–2006), whose uncle George D. Widener lived nearby at Mackay Point in Jasper County. Like his uncle, Dixon inherited a fortune from his family's investments in the White Star Line as well as the steel, tobacco, and streetcar industries. Though he had no need for a regular income, Dixon taught for many years at the Episcopal Academy in Philadelphia. In 1976 he was often in the news. That year Robert Indiana removed his sculpture of the word *Love* from New York City after the city refused to purchase it for $45,000; Dixon offered $35,000 and had it returned to the city. That same year he also bought the Phila-delphia 76ers basketball team and signed Julius "Dr. J" Irving, one of the most spectacu-lar players in the history of the game. (A major supporter of Philadelphia sports teams, Dixon invested as well in the Eagles, Phillies, and Flyers.) Dixon held onto White Hall until 1958, when he sold it to stockbroker Anson McCook Beard of Tuxedo Park, New York. Beard's uncle George Slade was a member of the Chelsea Club in Jasper County. Subse-quent owners included John E. Meyer (who also owned Botany Bay on Edisto Island) and J. Peter Grace (CEO for almost fifty years of the chemical company W. R. Grace). In 1985 Mrs. Loretta H. Cockrum renovated the building extensively. The current owner, Richard L. Chilton Jr., who also holds the deed to Buckfield in Hampton County, has assembled a truly picturesque estate with the erection of new award-winning stables and outbuildings, lines of white fencing, and many red roofs.

The Combahee Land and Rice Company is credited with uniting Paul and Dalton plan-tations, previously independent properties, into a single identity in 1898. They both had been part of the large property acquired by the Stock family prior to 1800.

Paul took its name from James L. Paul, who in 1859 bought the 775-acre Palmetto plantation of Arthur and Francis Parker, renaming it after himself. The Union raid on the Combahee in June 1863 freed his black workers; his house and farm buildings were burned. Paul died in 1866, and his plantation was sold for debts. W. Dalton Warren (1839–1896), buying several distressed properties at the close of the war, owned Paul until 1875, when he sold it to James Adger and Company. The Combahee Land and Rice Company acquired Paul plantation in 1898.

The land that would be named Dalton was inherited by Ann Burgh Smith, wife of Andrew Burnet, and Ann's sister Margaret Stock Smith from their mother, Ann Stock Smith. They were the owners in 1860. The plantation was managed by Burnet, who claimed 175 black laborers on this tract of 775 acres (127 of those acres had been added in 1854 by purchase from the Parkers' Palmetto plantation). Dalton was burned in the Combahee raid, the slaves departing with the Union vessels. Left without means to make a new beginning, the owners lost the land to mortgage foreclosure in 1875. W. Dalton Warren became the new owner, but four years later he signed it over to James Adger and Company. Like Paul, it was added to the Combahee Land and Rice Company holdings in 1898.

Payne Whitney of New York bought Dalton's 828 acres and Paul's 1,275 acres in 1926. A member of the Okeetee Club in Jasper County, he had owned land on the Combahee since 1923, when he bought William C. Heyward's old plantation, Cypress. He sold Cypress in 1927, the year he died in New York at age fifty-one.

Whitney's estate amounted to almost $240 million. A major bequest of $23 million was made to New York Hospital; the psychiatric ward, at his request, bears his name. He was in 1924 the third-largest taxpayer in America, according to the notice of his death in the *New York Times,* outranked only by John D. Rockefeller and Henry Ford. Some of his wealth was inherited from his uncle, Col. Oliver Payne, one of the founders of Standard Oil, but Whitney was an astute businessman, investing in New York banking and real estate. His many philanthropies were anonymous. One of his chief pleasures, shared with his wife, was breeding thoroughbred horses and all the activities of the turf.

The trustees of Whitney's estate sold Paul and Dalton (1,976 acres) in October 1927 to John K. Hollins. In 1930 the property amounted to 2,103 acres, and Hollins transferred almost all of it to Charles L. Lawrance. Lawrance had studied architecture for three years at the Ecole des Beaux Arts in Paris following his graduation from Yale in 1905 and before he took up his serious interest in aviation. The dwelling at Paul and Dalton is said to be his design.

Lawrance and Hollins sold Paul and Dalton to the Combahee Land Company in 1933. Among later owners were Theodore Maybank (1962) and Anthony Merck (1991). A conservation easement for the 2,122-acre property was donated to the Lowcountry Open Land Trust in 1998. Today, Paul and Dalton is owned by Edgar T. Cato, who also holds the title to Long Brow.

# *Berkeley County* PROPERTIES

Cypress Gardens (also Dean Hall)

Medway

Mepkin

Mulberry Castle (also South Mulberry)

Pimlico

Wappaoolah

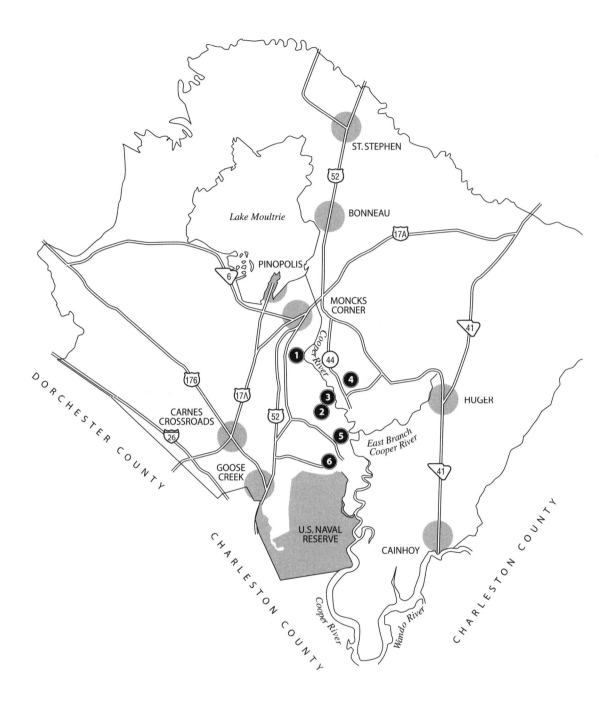

**Berkeley County**

1. Mulberry
2. Wappaoolah
3. Pimlico
4. Mepkin
5. Cypress Gardens (Dean Hall)
6. Medway

# Cypress Gardens

(also Dean Hall)

The world boasts a number of beautiful gardens, but it has remained for Benjamin R. Kittredge of New York and South Carolina to create something entirely new along this line.

Sunken gardens, hanging gardens, azalea gardens—the list is long—and now Mr. Kittredge has added to it a garden fashioned of cypress trees and water. He calls his creation—for it is that—The Cypress Gardens. The Cypress Gardens are located in Berkeley county, not far from Charleston, and although they have been enjoyed by Mr. Kittredge and his family and a few friends for several years, they have just been opened to the public.

These gardens, containing two hundred acres, were once a reservoir for old rice fields and were so thickly overgrown with trees and underbrush that the work of clearing was an undertaking worthy of the stoutest heart. Six years of tedious labor and thought were required to perfect the gardens and bring them to their present loveliness.

Mr. Kittredge was a great hunter and used to be particularly fond of duck shooting. He would spend hours at a time in the great, dense swamp and while there grew more and more under the charm of the weird beauty of the cypress trees, moss hung, reflecting themselves for miles along the lacquer-like surface of the water. His imagination delighted in plans for enhancing all this and making it available to others.

## Canals and Boat Landings

Then he became seriously active. As a first step, he drained the immense swamp, had its bottom scraped and all the trash and refuse burned. This particular phase of the activity in itself created such a strange loveliness in the wilds of the swamp that several

Original title: "The Cypress Gardens, in Berkeley. Benjamin R. Kittredge, of New York and South Carolina, Creates Another Coastal Beauty Spot with 200 Acres of Moss Hung Trees and Water." Publication date: July 19, 1931.

artists reveled in the opportunity of putting upon canvas the long plumes of gray smoke that curled upward from numerous, small flame-licked piles in the bed of the swamp.

This scraping and burning took place every summer and all during the time the underbrush and unsightly growth were being cleared away. Sometimes there were as many as a hundred men engaged in this work.

Canals were dug all through the pond and many novel boat landings built so that visitors to the gardens may paddle the shiny black, red-lined boats here and there over the water, leaving them where and when they choose.

Narrow winding paths were trailed all through the gardens and a number of picturesque, rustic bridges placed where the paths lead across the pond. Each of the rustic bridges is different from the other. One has a tree growing out of the very center, an iron rod having been run through the tree as a support for the bridge. Another is supported entirely by the trunk of a large tree. Thirty men were required to lift the trunk. They set it in the crooks of two trees and the bridge was built across it. Still another bridge rests on the arch of a great live oak.

### Flowers Border Paths

All of the little paths are bordered with narcissus and daffodils and the quaintly designed tiny islands which were thrown up at intervals in the water are planted thickly with azaleas and other flowering plants. Bulbs and flowers of various kinds are also planted through the woods so that, in spring, the garden is a mass of rioting color, which breaks the thick green of the foliage into entrancing patterns that are reflected for miles in the still, black water.

The charm of Cypress Gardens is that they are entirely natural. Mr. Kittredge has had the good taste to leave nature unchanged, merely adding color and vividness with the thousands and thousands of bulbs which he has scattered throughout the woods. The place is always green; numerous bays, sweet myrtles, palmettos and ferns making this possible.

One gets a different scene at every turn of a path. Here, in a border of yellow jasmine; around the corner, sweet olive; wistaria vines climb high and add their purple blurs of gorgeousness. A new plant to this section of the country, Daphne, has been set in great quantities through the gardens. This plant bears a resemblance to the arbutus and has a reddish purple bloom, which fills the air with a most penetrating sweetness. There are also the iris, the Kurume or Japanese variety of the azalea, and the Belgian azalea. The gardens spread a shifting panorama of delight, a veritable ocular feast, before the eyes.

### Flower Nursery

Mr. Kittredge has his own nursery back of the gardens and here he has thousands of plants, such as the azalea, Daphne, magnolia, sweet olive, gardenia, Carolina cherry, japonica, laurel, and many others, which he transplants to the Cypress Gardens from time to time.

Some of the cypress trees with their long, drooping banners of gray moss and their great smooth trunks are believed to be between two and three hundred years old.

Two views of Dean Hall before it was moved to Gardens Corner.
*Top: Historic American Buildings Survey, photograph # SC8-P16RD. V. 1-3;*
*bottom: photograph courtesy of the South Carolina Historical Society*

Down a little slope in the garden is an artesian well which flows out of the trunk of one of these immense old trees. There are benches scattered here and there, where visitors wearied with much walking and feasting on beauty may drop down for a little rest. Some of these are built in a reclining position, so that one may gaze up through the lacy tree tops into the patches of sky that sift through.

Maps are placed at intervals along the paths so that visitors may keep check on their location and not get lost, as they might very easily do, undirected.

There are two entrances, the main one, which is sufficiently picturesque, and the east entrance, which has gates fashioned of great stone posts taken from the old rice fields. These posts were used as special flood gates before the day of steam, the purpose of them being to create water power.

In the old days white herons and egrets were wont to rest in this swamp, but the coming of men has frightened them away.

These gardens, which are at their best during April and May, are Mr. Kittredge's hobby. His home, Dean Hall, one of the famous old ante-bellum plantations of the coast, is not far away. Mr. Kittredge is not a new-comer to the south. He has owned Dean Hall for about twenty years and his wife, the former Elizabeth Marshall, is a Charleston woman.

This old plantation was once famous for its rice planting. Now, these abandoned fields furnish splendid duck preserves. Deer and other game are also plentiful here.

James P. Carson, whose family once owned this plantation, throws some light on the life of a rice planter in these woods, credited to his pen. "My father, William A. Carson, was a rice planter who wore out his life watching a salty river, and died at the age of 56, when I was ten years old."

Although the place is rich in history, the age of the house itself is not definite. John B. Irving, M.D., wrote in his book, "A Day on Cooper River," printed in 1842: "Dean Hall . . . former residence of Sir John Nisbett, a Scotch Baronet . . . but now the estate of Col. Carson." It is said to have been advertised for sale in *The South Carolina Gazette* in 1757.

### Square, Picturesque House

The house, which is square and picturesque, is fashioned of brick and set high on an arched basement. A wide piazza extends entirely around the building. It is approached by high, wide entrance stairs on either side of the porch in front. There is a wide hall which divides the house directly through the middle. The rooms are enormous and have very large fireplaces. During the Confederate war there were said to have been as many as 500 slaves on the plantation. Some of the old slave cabins are still to be seen there and some of the descendants of these slaves live there yet. The Kittredges' butler is one of a family which has lived there for four generations.

The story is told that when William Carson died just before the war, his executors sold the place and accepted Confederate money in exchange. Mrs. Carson was at that time living in Rome, Italy, with her two minor sons. Before the transaction was completed, or about the time, Confederate money lost its value and Mrs. Carson repudiated the sale. The case was taken to the courts and the property was in litigation from that time until 1883, when the United States supreme court reestablished Mrs. Carson in her property on the grounds that her executors had no right to accept anything except legal tender in exchange for the property.

The Kittredges spend the winter months at Dean Hall and Mr. Kittredge has built an excellent road from the highway to Cypress Gardens and his home.  ✴

The dwelling at Dean Hall was built shortly after William Carson bought the property from Sir John Nesbit, Baronet, of Dean, Scotland, in 1821. Sir John was grandson to Alexander Nesbit, who had acquired the land in 1725. Writing of Dean Hall in 1842, Dr. John Irving said, "The residence of the proprietor, the condition of the fields, the banks, the white and cleanly appearance of the negro houses, the mill and threshing machine in complete order, all excite a strong feeling of admiration and stamp at once the proprietor as an experienced and skilled planter." The only surviving building from the Nesbit (sometimes spelled Nisbett) ownership is a two-and-one-half-story house, thought to have been the overseer's residence. It was moved to Moncks Corner after Cypress Gardens was deeded to the city of Charleston in 1963 and now serves as the office of the Chamber of Commerce.

Mr. Benjamin R. Kittredge bought the three-thousand-acre plantation in 1907. The new owner was born in Ohio in 1859 but was brought up on his father's place at Peekskill, New York. Privately tutored as a youth, he graduated cum laude from Harvard College in 1882. His early business venture was in the San Joaquin Valley of California in partnership with George West and Son, a firm with extensive vineyards and wineries. His success was such that in 1910 the California Wine Association named him its president. The wine business, however, did not survive the new prohibition laws of 1915.

His introduction to South Carolina came with his marriage to Miss Elizabeth Marshall of Charleston in 1899. He spent much time in the state and joined Yeamans Hall in North Charleston, and yet his financial interests remained in the North and the West. In 1900 Mr. Kittredge acquired seven thousand picturesque acres of woodlands and lakes in Putnam County, New York, just north of his old home at Peekskill, which he undertook to develop as residential property. The Carmel Country Club now occupies one of his houses.

The garden at Dean Hall, begun in 1926, covered about 250 acres and required the labor of two hundred men to complete. It was laid out around an old freshwater reserve from the period of rice planting—an irregular lake of dark water and mature cypress trees. Essentially a water garden, it was best viewed as a passenger in one of the wooden boats provided for the purpose. Passing through this silent and shaded swamp, bordered with the brilliant blossoms of the Japanese azalea, is a unique experience. As Mrs. Martin writes, it has attracted a great number of artists, including Alice Ravenel Huger Smith of Charleston, who painted at least four scenes. The grounds were advertised nationally as one of the three famous Charleston gardens, the others being Middleton Place and Magnolia Gardens.

Mr. Kittredge died in Charleston in 1951 and, with his wife and three favorite dogs, is buried on the grounds. His family continued to operate Cypress Gardens until 1963, when Benjamin Kittredge Jr. deeded it to the city of Charleston. The high ground of Dean Hall, including the old house and some two thousand acres, was sold to the DuPont Company in 1970 for an industrial plant. What was to be done with the historic dwelling, which could hardly be pulled down without stirring up the wrath of preservationists, was a dilemma. Cmdr. C. C. Boggs, a retired officer in the SeaBees and a native of Allendale, proposed dismantling the house and moving it to a twenty-five-acre site he owned at Gardens Corner in Beaufort County. The DuPont Company agreed to give the commander the house, and the work of removal began in 1971. By 1976 Dean Hall was resurrected on its new site.

Hurricane Hugo in September 1989 caused enormous damage to the gardens. Some twelve thousand trees were thought to have been destroyed, including the larger part of the mature cypresses whose shading canopy was essential to the gardens' deep swamp atmosphere. The clearing of debris and repair work on the grounds necessitated the closure of Cypress Gardens for two years. In 1996 ownership of the gardens was transferred to Berkeley County, and a number of new attractions there have since opened.

# *Medway*

Medway, located on Back river, in Berkeley county, is said to be the first brick house in South Carolina built out of Charleston. Various dates have been credited to it, all the way from 1682 to 1695. The house was built by Thomas Smith, one of the landgraves of South Carolina and governor of the province, who died in 1694. His grave, a brick, ivy covered vault, is just a short distance from the house.

Dr. John B. Irving in his book "A Day on Cooper River," printed in 1842, says: "According to a patent dated May the 13th, 1691, Thomas Smith was created a perpetual and hereditary noble and peer of the province under the title of Landgrave . . . the old family mansion . . . could not have been built previously to the date of the patent, 1691, as the house is upon a part of one of the four baronies of 12,000 acres each given to the newly constituted Landgraves."

A footnote in pencil in this old book says in reference to the house: "Built by the second Landgrave, lived in it, 1695."

## Rice Claims Disputed

At another place, Dr. Irving says: "It is not generally known perhaps but the fact is well established that in the low grounds attached to this residence, Landgrave Smith cultivated his first patch of rice and that from this small beginning introduced it. . . . "

However there are some who dispute this, contending that rice had become a considerable industry in the province before Landgrave Smith came into it.

Medway, located twenty-four miles from Charleston, and nineteen miles from Moncks Corner, and at the end of a long dreary country road in Berkeley county, certainly gives the appearance of age. Solitary and gaunt in its lonely spot, far removed from other houses or roads "where the race of men go by," one can easily imagine it the haunt of ghosts, if there be any at all. And there are tales of ghosts that come and go in the old mansion.

Original title: "Medway, Historic Brick House. Mr. and Mrs. Sidney J. Legendre, of New York, New Owners of Building Erected in Berkeley County by Landgrave Smith, Modernize Interior and Beautify Grounds." Publication date: April 26, 1931.

Medway. *Photograph courtesy of the South Carolina Historical Society*

The house is built of brick, which has since been stuccoed, and was originally only one story. It has been added to and changed a number of times in the course of its history, but is said still to retain its essential appearance. The queerly shaped roof is broken by Dutch gables. There are three stories and twelve rooms; all of the rooms, it is claimed, still have their original floorings.

Medway, until a short while ago, was owned by the Stoney family, being the estate of Samuel G. Stoney. Recently it was purchased by Mr. and Mrs. Sidney J. Legendre, of New York. The new owners have done the interior of the house over, put in bathrooms and otherwise modernized it without detracting from the charm of the place. The grounds have also been beautified and made into a more picturesque setting for the old house.

The estate comprises about 2,500 acres of land. ✤

Of the new northern plantation owners, few ingratiated themselves with the local community as did the Legendres. Sidney, who died in 1948 at age forty-seven, was from New Orleans. Gertrude, who died in 2000 at ninety-seven, grew up in New York, where her family ran the carpet manufacturing company John Sanford and Son and the Hurricana horse-breeding farm.

The Legendres learned of Medway in October 1929 through their friends Benjamin and Elizabeth Kittredge, owners of Dean Hall plantation nearby. (Mr. Kittredge had already begun the massive task of developing Cypress Gardens, but it was not opened to the public for a few years.) After a horseback ride to Medway for a picnic with the Kittredges, the Legendres bought the rundown plantation the next year. Soon after that they began the renovations and improvements that Mrs. Martin mentions above. As she wrote this article, the Legendres were just beginning a task that would continue for decades, as Medway became one of the showplaces of the lowcountry. They were careful to reuse materials from the plantation: the rice mill gave up its bricks for a garden fence; its slate shingles went on the stable; and the beams and floorboards ended up in the garden arch and walls. They welcomed as guests dignitaries, celebrities, and artists from around the world, so Medway was widely photographed and described. Mrs. Legendre's parties, especially her New Year's Eve costume balls, were legendary.

The couple influenced the surrounding communities in many ways. Sidney Legendre co-owned a local grocery store and a number of movie theaters. They hung their safari trophies on the wall of a theater in Summerville and renamed it the Jungle Theatre. Gertrude wrote in her autobiography, "Sidney had wanted to organize a parade with everyone in African skins and beating drums, but the mayor of Summerville refused permission. We did show black and white shorts of our trip to Africa." Gertrude became an active supporter of lowcountry arts and conservation groups.

During a 1984 renovation, workers discovered old brick walls stamped with the Hyrnes family coat of arms, making clear that the house had been built in 1704 or 1705, when Edward and Elizabeth Hyrnes owned the property, rather than earlier, as Mrs. Martin claims. The previous building had burned to the ground and was replaced by the Hyrneses' much smaller structure.

Gertrude Legendre, once an avid hunter, became a wildlife enthusiast and preservationist. She gave two perpetual conservation easements on the land of Medway: the plantation house and its surrounding buildings and grounds (eighty-three acres) to the Historic Charleston Foundation; and the remaining land, approximately six thousand acres of forests and wetlands, to the Ducks Unlimited Foundation.

# Mepkin

Mepkin, historical old plantation in Berkeley county, has been owned since about 1912 by J. W. Johnson, of New York, manufacturer of surgical bandages and supplies. Recently, it is understood, Mr. Johnson has made this property, which contains 6,534 acres, over to his daughter, Mrs. Helen Rutgers, of New York.

Mepkin is located on the eastern side of Cooper river and although the old plantation house has long since fallen into decay and only a comparatively inexpensive one erected in its place, this is one of the very loveliest locations on the Cooper river.

The house, which Mr. Johnson remodeled from the one which he found there, making it into an attractive, two-story shingle house, painted white, faces immediately upon the river. The grounds are extensive and are very rolling. A terraced walk leads down to the boat landing, which is most picturesque. From the landing, the ground rises again sheerly to a little Hill, at the top of which rests a square of gray granite without markings of any kind. It is beneath this simple, unmarked square that rest the ashes of Henry Laurens, also known as "Tower" Laurens, long-ago owner of Mepkin.

Henry Laurens is said to have bought Mepkin as his country home from the John Colleton estate in 1762. The entrance gates now used at Mepkin are said to be the original gates.

Henry Laurens was a native of Charleston and was a large merchant. He received his training in London and at one time lived there and also in Paris. The story goes that in 1779 he was commissioned to go to Europe and his ship was captured by the British while off the coast of Newfoundland. He carried some valuable papers, which he threw into the water in an effort to destroy them. However, they were found and used against him and he was committed to the Tower of London on a charge of high treason. He was released in 1782 and was then appointed peace commissioner to Paris.

Henry Laurens ordered that his body be cremated at his death. It is said he was led to make this request because of the fact that his young daughter had a narrow escape from being buried alive. The young girl had supposedly died, and was laid out in a room

Original title: "Mepkin, Henry Laurens Plantation. New York Manufacturer Reclaims Home Site Whose Grounds Roll Down to Picturesque Boat Landing on Cooper River." Publication date: May 17, 1931.

J. W. Johnson's house at Mepkin. *Photograph courtesy of the South Carolina Historical Society*

with windows open. A storm came up and rain beat into her face. She was later revived and lived to be an old lady.

Down a steep Hill at one side of the house is an old family burying ground, where, on time-moulded stones, may be read the names of Laurens, Pinckney and others. One tomb is marked 1782 and another 1812.

Native shrubbery has been used wherever possible on the grounds, a unique feature being a long border of holly. ✎

In all the Carolina lowcountry, no land surpasses in natural beauty the high ground above the Cooper River where Henry Laurens established himself in 1762. His first house was burned by the British, and its successor was destroyed sometime later. When J. W. Johnson bought Mepkin in 1916, he renovated an old dwelling built in 1906, giving it a New England appearance with shingle siding. It served as the Rutgers family house as well.

The father of Helen Johnson Rutgers (wife of Nicholas G. Rutgers), James Wood Johnson (1856–1932), was president of Johnson and Johnson, the surgical manufacturing company, until illness forced his retirement. He and his brother Edward established the business in New Brunswick, New Jersey, in 1885. A third brother, Robert, joined the firm later, and eventually it grew to be the largest company in its field in the world. During World War I the Johnsons, in support of the war, offered the federal government the use of their manufacturing plant, at the sacrifice of their own profits.

James Johnson, hoping to regain his health after a long illness, acquired Mepkin for the serenity and natural beauty of the land. At Mepkin he, a widower, married the nurse who had cared for him in his years of declining health. The couple were on their way home from a trip to Scotland when Johnson died aboard the liner *Majestic* in September 1932.

Though Mrs. Martin does not seem to have been particularly impressed with the architecture of the Mepkin house in 1931, her reaction to the next developments probably would have been even more severe. Henry and Clare Boothe Luce bought the seventy-two-hundred-acre property in 1936 from Helen Rutgers for $150,000 and had the Johnson house taken down. The Luces were sophisticated people; he was the publisher of *Time*, *Fortune*, and *Life* magazines, and she was a successful playwright, a U.S. congresswoman, and ambassador to Italy. Though, according to her biographer Sylvia Jukes Morris, Mrs. Luce "often dressed as a Southern belle, in full-skirted, turquoise tafetta, with short, puffed sleeves, pearls or lapis lazuli jewelry and velvet bows in her hair," the couple wanted no reproduction of a southern plantation house. Instead they sought something modern and efficient.

Their architect was Edward Durell Stone, who with Philip Goodwin was working in the international style and at the time building the Museum of Modern Art in Manhattan (1939). Stone designed for the Luces a low set of brick cubes, with the main residence on one side and three small guest units on the other, connected by a walkway. Writing of them, a contemporary reporter stated, "The casual visitor might gain the impression that the buildings resembled smart shops at a beach resort." In truth, this severe composition had an uncomfortable relationship to the site. Loutrel Briggs of Charleston planned the landscaping of the grounds.

Mrs. Luce joined the Catholic Church in 1946, two years after the death of her daughter, Ann, in a car accident. She and her husband gave Mepkin to the Trappist order in 1949. Eventually Stone's work was taken down, and over time several handsome ecclesiastical buildings have gone up, including a chapel, all fully in harmony with the topography. Several members of the Luce family are buried at Mepkin.

# *Mulberry Castle*

(also South Mulberry)

Mulberry, known to some as Mulberry Castle, is one of the most famous of the low-country plantations. This old place, located four or five miles from Moncks Corner, comprises several old ante-bellum plantations, among them being Polly and Salt Point. The entire property, containing more than twenty-five hundred acres of land, has been owned by C. W. Chapman since about 1914.

The house at Mulberry was built in 1714 by Thomas Broughton. The architecture is one of the most imposing and unusual of any of the homes in this entire section. It is of brick, built two stories high with a Dutch roof and dormer windows. The most unusual features of the structure are the four towers or flankers standing one at each corner of the house. These towers are semi-detached from the rest of the house and were said to have been used by the women and children of the surrounding country as a refuge from attacks of Indians.

Mulberry remained in the Broughton family until there were no sons bearing the name. A daughter married Thomas Milliken and it then became the property of the Millikens. Then a Milliken married a Barker and Theodore Barker came into possession of the estate eventually.

## Plantation Divided

While it was still in the hands of the Broughtons, however, Mulberry was divided and the new division came to be known as South Mulberry and became the property of Philip Broughton's son, Alexander Broughton.

Dr. John B. Irving in his "A Day on Cooper River," printed in 1842, has the following to say concerning Mulberry: "Mulberry, on the left as we ascend the river (owned by Mr. Milliken) has a very imposing looking house on it built by Gov. Broughton. . . . It

Original title: "Mulberry Castle, Built in Indian Days. Chapmans, Owners since 1914 of This Cooper River Plantation in Berkeley, Have Developed Gardens but Have Changed Famous House Little, Continuing Even to Light with Lamps and Candles." Publication date: July 26, 1931.

Mulberry Castle. *Historic American Buildings Survey, photograph # SC, 8-MONCO. V. 5-3*

was long known as Mulberry Castle. . . . It has or had loop holes in its walls for musketry with bastions at the four corners of the building. Mulberry Castle was used formerly as a garrison for the purpose of defending the settlers in the vicinity against the invasion of the Indians. An old cannon, the relic of by-gone days, may still be seen in the yard upon an ancient mound, doubtless an old fortification."

And at another place in this same volume: "On the west side of the Cooper river is Mulberry built in 1714. The land on which this house stands was purchased by Lieutenant Governor Thomas Broughton from Sir John Colleton. . . . "

The two old cannons, spoken of in this book, are still to be seen at Mulberry although unmounted. The Chapmans are very proud of them and are on the lookout for appropriate mountings. These cannons, which, it is thought, were on the plantation before the Revolution, were given by Major Barker, the last Broughton descendant, to the Stoney family at Medway. When this plantation was sold, the Stoney family returned them to Mulberry.

### Huge Living Room

One enters Mulberry into a tremendous living room with hand-carved mouldings and a great fireplace. This house was in a bad state of disrepair when the Chapmans bought it. Parts of the ceilings and floors were gone and, with the exception of these replacements and the addition of baths, which were put into some of the numerous large closets about the house, there have been no changes in the house. The mouldings and mantels are all original.

There are twelve rooms in the house. One of the towers or flankers has been fashioned into a breakfast room, another is a gun room. The furnishings are exquisite and thoroughly in keeping with the atmosphere of the house itself. The Chapmans have not even run electricity into the house, preferring to light it with lamps and candles. Mrs. Chapman has a unique collection of old lamps.

The walls of the towers are very thick, and there are heavy old wooden doors, which still have the original bolts and hinges. There are entrances into the cellar on the east and west sides and four oddly picturesque old iron weather vanes on each flanker bearing the date 1714.

Just how Mulberry got its name does not seem to be clear, although there are many mulberry trees on the place.

There are those who say that Mulberry used to have an underground passage to the river, but Mrs. Chapman says no evidence of this passage was found when repairs were made to the house, although she believes it is possible that the passage could have been filled in long since.

## Gardens Are Developed

Mulberry is situated immediately on the Cooper river and its grounds are rolling and spacious. There was no evidence of a former garden at Mulberry when the Chapmans bought it, but Mrs. Chapman is sure there must have been. She herself has what might be termed a series of gardens. Immediately to the right of the house is a small evergreen garden of miniature shrubbery. Down a grassy slope from this is a magnificent garden of rare beauty and charm. Here azaleas, japonicas, bulbs of various sorts, magnolias, beautifully shaped cedars, shrubbery and live oaks grow in thick profusion. There is a path which runs the length of the garden parallel with the river. This garden is entered by means of a terraced brick walk. Between the gardens and the river is a canal with a picturesque boat house straddling it. At the back of the gardens is an unusually high bank which has been planted to yellow jasmine and ivy.

Besides these two gardens, there is a new one which is laid out farther up the river to the side and in front of the house. This is in the shape of a natural amphitheater and has a handsome iron entrance gate and grill brought from England and an outdoor piazza or flagged place to sit. Along one side is a tier of brick seats. The garden itself has been planted to shrubbery. Beyond the garden are the rice fields and the river.

Mrs. Chapman, having completed these three gardens, is now planning a water garden a little beyond.

All of the gardens together comprise about 20 acres. On the other side of the house is a stretch of rolling green.

## Entrance through Forest

Mulberry is approached through a high gate, at which is the gate keeper's cottage, and thence over a long winding country road through a magnificent virgin forest.

The Chapmans make Mulberry their winter home and are there throughout the entire season.

South Mulberry has been owned by F. A. Dallett of New York for about fourteen years. Mr. Dallett's holdings include, besides South Mulberry, Farm and Harry Hill plantations, a total of 4,540 acres. The house is an attractive, modern-appearing, three-story frame building set on a high basement. This place has been remodeled and modernized by the Dalletts.

In her book *Historic Houses of South Carolina*, Harriette Kershaw Leiding says regarding South Mulberry, "the chief charm of the place being the garden filled with rare shrubs cultivated by Dr. Sanford Barker, who married Christina Broughton, of North Mulberry. Dr. Barker was a botanist who failed to record his scientific achievements, but one who loved to botanize, and with whom many noted scientists also botanized on long visits to South Mulberry extending over many months at a time." ✤

About 1800 the Charleston artist Thomas Coram produced a number of small oil paintings of Mulberry, including a famous image of the main plantation house and two rows of one-room, thatch-roofed slave quarters. The marvelously detailed painting is now among the collections of the Gibbes Museum of Art in Charleston.

Maj. Theodore Barker, of whom Mrs. Martin writes, was a person of note in nineteenth- and early twentieth-century Charleston and Flat Rock, North Carolina. His family came into the Mulberry property in 1820 through his mother. The major trained as a lawyer but was also a successful rice planter, both on the Cooper River and at Pon Pon. He attained military distinction in the Civil War under Gen. Wade Hampton at the Battle of Manassas in 1861. Young Henry Middleton, writing to his mother after the engagement, noted, "Theodore behaved splendidly. His conduct was beyond praise—it was glorious."

In her edited version of Irving's *A Day on Cooper River*, Louisa Cheves Stoney gives a handsome account of the major and his wife, Louisa Preston King, who was the daughter of Judge Mitchell King. Of Major Barker she writes that he was "a man of marked intellect, of great wit and distinguished presence." The Barkers did not marry until October 1875, when he was forty-three, and they had no children, but they surrounded themselves with relatives and friends. They were so agreeable and pleasant that they never wanted for company, particularly among the young. The major lived until 1917, his eighty-fifth year. His stone in the churchyard of St. John in the Wilderness at Flat Rock proudly states that he was "By birth and residence a citizen of South Carolina."

Loutrel Briggs, in *Charleston Gardens*, writes that Mr. Clarence Chapman, whom he describes as "among the first of numerous Northerners to appreciate and possess a low country plantation," bought Mulberry in 1915. Mr. Briggs drew the plan for the garden at Mulberry in 1930. E. T. H. Shaffer, the author of *Carolina Gardens*, says of the gardens that "for beauty of location . . . and perfection of execution I have found no finer garden anywhere."

Mr. Chapman, like so many of the northern plantation owners, made his fortune on Wall Street. He was a member of the New York Stock Exchange from 1900 until his retirement in 1936, his firm being in later years Chapman, Carson, and Company. While in South Carolina he joined Yeamans Hall in North Charleston.

In 1947, less than a year before Mr. Chapman died at age eighty-six, he and his wife sold Mulberry, then twelve-hundred acres, to preservationist Lawrence A. Walker Jr. of Summerville. The property went through various owners, the price rising from Walker's "in excess of $100,000" to more than $2.3 million, until, almost forty years later, Walker again became involved. By then, in 1987, he was serving as president of the Historic Charleston Foundation, and his group grew concerned that the property would be developed. So the foundation purchased Mulberry and its eight-hundred acres, placed protective easements on the house and surrounding grounds, and resold it all less than a year later to S. Parker Gilbert, a New York City investment banker. It remains in private hands.

South Mulberry was also part of the Broughton tract, separated about 1835 from Mulberry Castle to the north when a daughter of the family married Dr. Sanford Barker, a cousin of the major. Dr. Barker was born in Charleston in 1807. He studied medicine at the Medical College of South Carolina and went into practice in St. John's Berkeley, establishing himself there also as a planter. For thirteen years, beginning in 1850, he represented his parish in the state senate. Dr. Barker died at age eighty-four.

When Mrs. Martin wrote her article, Frederick A. Dallett (1869–1948), the owner of South Mulberry, was serving as president of his family's Red "D" merchant shipping line, one of the oldest in America. He held this office from 1917 to 1937. The company, founded in 1820 by Dallett's ancestors, was also known as Bliss, Dallett, and Company and as Dallett and Son. The firm's original business was bringing Venezuelan coffee to the American market; passenger service between New York and the Caribbean was later offered. The Red "D" was sold to the Grace Line in 1937.

# *Pimlico*

Pimlico plantation in Berkeley county was formerly the property of the Balls, but is now owned by G. D. B. Bonbright, of Rochester, N.Y.

The handsome new home which occupies the site of the old plantation home was erected about four years ago by Mr. Bonbright, the old house having been in such a bad state of repair, it was considered best to build over entirely.

The front of the new home is like that of the original house. It is a large white two-story frame building, approached over a curving avenue bordered by tall oaks. There is a stately white entrance gate. The estate was in a great state of dilapidation when it was purchased by Mr. Bonbright and he has worked wonders with its appearance. The grounds have been made lovely with grass, flowers and shrubbery. Japonicas, roses, violets and other plants are numerous.

The house itself is of rather unusual appearance. The main part of the building has a long, curving wing at one side and back. It has green blinds and a gray painted roof. The wing has both an upstairs and a downstairs porch, with vines trailing up its rails.

## Borders Cooper River

Mr. Bonbright's holdings comprise about three thousand acres of land, including both Pimlico and Point Comfort plantations. The Cooper river winds around it, only a few feet away.

Mr. Bonbright has a sea plane, a sea sled and a Chris-Craft, all of which he keeps for his pleasure and that of his guests while at Pimlico.

The Bonbrights with their three children make Pimlico their winter home and enjoy it thoroughly. The wooded lands belonging to the plantation afford good hunting, mostly quail, doves and ducks. In addition, the game keeper and manager of the estate, W. G. Butler, has about 150 turkeys on the plantation. Mr. Butler and his wife occupy a small white bungalow beyond the "big house."

Original title: "New Yorker Reclaims Pimlico. Rochester Man Replaces Old Berkeley Plantation House with Handsome Two-story Frame Building and Beautifies Grounds with Grass, Flowers and Shrubbery." Original date: May 24, 1931.

Pimlico, 1970. *Photograph courtesy of Robert B. Cuthbert*

An oddly picturesque feature about the approach to the house is the curving brick wall to one side of the winding avenue. This wall has the effect of giving balance to the picture, being on the opposite side from that of the long wing to the house.

### Pimlico Plantation

Mrs. Harriette Kershaw Leiding in her book "Historic Houses of South Carolina" has this to say of Pimlico plantation, quoting, also, from the Ball Book: "one of Alwyn Ball's brothers, Hugh Swinton Ball (1808) married 'Miss Anna Channing, daughter of Walter Channing of Boston. They had several children, all of whom died very young. His wife and himself both perished in a wreck of the steamer Pulaski, on their way from New York to Charleston. The boiler exploded on the night of 14th of June, 1838; the vessel was blown to pieces, and many of the passengers were lost. Soon after their death, a lawsuit, which lasted several years, arose about the property. As the survivor was to inherit the bulk of it, the question was, which one was the survivor—a question not easily decided after a scene of such confusion and terror. The court finally decided in favor of the plaintiffs—Mrs. Ball's family—the evidence (as I have heard) showing that Mrs. Ball's voice had been heard calling in the darkness for Mr. Ball; and the presumption was, that, had he been living at the time, he would have answered her. By this decision, not only his wife's property, which was considerable, but more than half of his own, went to the plaintiffs. His intention had been to leave his plantation Pimlico to his nephew, Elias Nonus Ball, son of his brother Elias Octabus; but the plantation and the negroes had to be sold for division. His nephew, however, found himself in possession of a very comfortable property on coming of age.' After the sinking of the Titanic in 1914 this case was cited in court . . . the plantation itself was among the grants made to the three sons of Sir John Colleton. . . . "  ✦

Three historic properties—Mepshew, Kecklio, and Pimlico—were brought together by Elias Ball in 1809 to form Pimlico plantation. It totaled 2,248 acres in 1810. The Ball family owned the place until the deaths of Hugh Swinton Ball and his wife in the sinking of the *Pulaski* in 1838.

The steam packet *Pulaski* set out from Savannah on the morning of Thursday, June 13, en route to Baltimore. After a stop at Charleston to pick up additional passengers the ship headed to sea again the next morning. By 11:00 P.M. it was off the coast of North Carolina when it encountered high winds and rough seas. The captain, trying for a record time for the voyage, called for a maximum increase in steam pressure to compensate for the storm's resistance. In the confusion the water in one of the two boilers was allowed to "boil off." While the tank was being refilled, the cold water ran over the heated copper, causing the tank to explode with "tremendous violence." One of the ship's decks was blown off and the forward bulkhead stove in. The ship careened and settled as the heavy engine broke free and sank. As it did, the boat began to split in two. Many of the passengers were thrown into the water; those who were able reached for any bit of floating debris they could find or pulled themselves onto the two sections of the boat that had separated and were above water.

The next morning two small boats, retrieved from the *Pulaski,* with six strong men, all good swimmers, headed for shore in search of help. The exhausted crew reached shore that evening, but they landed in an unpopulated area of the coast, so not until the next day was the alarm given in Wilmington. Because of the intensity of the storm and the lapse of time since the explosion, public officials concluded that there could be no chance of survivors, and no search was undertaken.

The two sections of the wreckage drifted apart at sea and were lost to one another. Survivors on one of the sections sighted ships and sails in the distance, but their frantic signals went unnoticed. Not until Tuesday, June 18, did a ship sailing from Philadelphia to Wilmington come upon the group of desperate victims and bring them aboard. They reported that for several days they had seen a low mass, indistinguishable in the distance but moving parallel to them, and urged that a boat be sent to investigate, hoping it might be the other section of the *Pulaski.* A boat was sent and returned with 20 dispirited men and a boy, the last to be saved. Exposure, dehydration, and shock had taken many lives. The Balls were not seen after the night of the explosion. Of the 131 passengers thought to have been aboard (the numbers are uncertain), 54 persons were saved and 77 lost. Five members of the Parkman family of Palmetto Bluff, Beaufort County, were also among the casualties.

The Ball estate was settled in 1844, when Pimlico was sold at public auction to Gov. Thomas Bennett for forty thousand dollars. Bennett sold the property to James Gadsden in 1852, and at Gadsden's death six years later the property was acquired by James Poyas. In 1883 the 1,779-acre plantation was conveyed to Francis William Heyward (1844–1907) of Wappaoolah. It was owned by several timber companies in the early twentieth century until 1925, when it was purchased by Mr. Bonbright, as discussed by Mrs. Martin.

The old Ball family dwelling, although in poor condition, was still standing when Mrs. Leiding visited Pimlico prior to 1920. She described it as a "hipped roof wooden house. . . . Inside the house a cultured atmosphere of fine Colonial days is immediately restored by the presence of exquisitely finished, hand-carved woodwork on the windows, wainscoting and mantels. The stairway, a perfect example of its kind, rises from the rear of a long entrance hall, adjoining which are two large, perfectly proportioned rooms." The new owners found the old house beyond repair, but they salvaged much of the interior woodwork for the house that Albert Simons of Charleston designed for the site, a design that was modified in the final building.

Mr. Bonbright and his brother Irving were stockbrokers in Rochester, New York, also headquarters of the Eastman-Kodak Company. As a friend and adviser, Mr. Bonbright had suggested that George Eastman, head of the company, invest in the motion picture industry, then in its infancy, and gave similar advice about technicolor. Mr. Eastman could see no future in either, passing up a fortune.

Mr. Bonbright died at his summer home on Nantucket in 1939 at the age of sixty-four. His widow sold Pimlico in 1941 to Powel Crosley Jr. of Cincinnati. Crosley was an industrialist and inventor with business interests ranging from radio and household appliances to the development of an inexpensive automobile that bore his name. Today he is best remembered as the co-owner with his brother Lewis of the Cincinnati Reds baseball team and the ballpark in which they played, Crosley Field.

Mr. Crosley sold the plantation in 1942, and it is supposed that he never lived there. The South Carolina Public Service Authority, known as Santee Cooper, bought the land and several other properties along the Cooper River to forestall almost certain lawsuits resulting from the flooding and destruction of old rice fields highly valued by plantation owners for duck shooting. The hydroelectric plant on Lake Moultrie at Moncks Corner went into operation that same year, releasing a heavy flow of water downstream. When Santee-Cooper resold these places, the new deeds reserved to the seller "the right to themselves to flow the property without accountability."

P. O. Mead Sr., the timberman whose name appears on a number of other lowcountry plantation deeds, was the next owner of Pimlico. The family lived there until 1948. The

Pimlico shortly before it was destroyed, circa 1993. *Photograph courtesy of Robert B. Cuthbert*

property passed through several owners until it was sold to Reeves Broadcasting Corporation in 1956. This company, headed by Drayton Hastie of Charleston, operated under different corporate names, though it was essentially the same entity. It began laying out plans for a residential development known as Pimlico Plantation in 1959 or soon thereafter. The Bonbright house and four acres were kept together until 1993, when the house, which had been badly damaged by Hurricane Hugo in 1989, was taken down.

# *Wappaoolah*

Wappaoolah, in Berkeley county, formerly the home of the Heywards, is a charming country estate. The plantation, which is now the joint property of W. H. Barnum and Owen Winston, of New York, has, of course, been considerably improved since it was purchased by these men in 1927.

The house is a typical old-fashioned coastal plantation home. It has two stories with a brick-floored, flat open veranda in front with over-hanging eaves. The second story has no porch. The new owners of this property have made no changes on the exterior appearance of the house with the exception of the addition of two wings at the back, so as to give more room and also to balance the house. The interior has been done over and freshened considerably, as the house was much in need of repair when purchased.

There is a large entrance hall, from which a graceful staircase leads to the second story. To the right is the large, spacious living room and to the left of the hall the attractive, formal dining room. The furnishings of the house are exquisitely simple and thoroughly in keeping with the architecture.

The grounds are spacious and green and the columns of the sunny veranda are twined with yellow jessamine and roses, which in springtime make it an alluring spot in which to sit and dream.

The building of this house, which is of black cypress, is credited to both a Mr. Lucas and a Mr. Pogson. It is better known, however, as the home of Frank Heyward, who married Fannie Ferguson. Slave labor is said to have been used in building it.

The plantation includes about nine hundred acres of land. Both Mr. Barnum and Mr. Winston are fond of hunting and they come down throughout the hunting season with their families, thoroughly enjoying the quiet and beauty of Wappaoolah. Mr. Barnum is intrigued by the Indian name Wappaoolah, which, he says, means "Sweet Waters."

The house combines simplicity with dignity and charm and this type of architecture, modified, seems to have been popular with old plantation owners along the Cooper river. ✄

Original title: "Wappaoolah, Berkeley Country Estate. Two New Yorkers with Their Families Come to Cooper River House throughout Hunting Season to Enjoy Sport of Place Whose Indian Name Means 'Sweet Waters.'" Publication date: March 22, 1931.

Wappaoolah, 1930. *Photograph courtesy of the South Carolina Historical Society*

In the annotated edition of Dr. Irving's *A Day on Cooper River,* Louisa Cheves Stoney tells us that the old house at Wappaoolah was put up by the Reverend Mr. Pogson, minister of St. James Goose Creek Church, sometime before 1808. She says he bought the frame of a barn and made it the skeleton of his house. However, Wappaoolah is generally known as a Heyward place.

It was at Wappaoolah that the Charleston watercolor artist Miss Alice Ravenel Huger Smith was first introduced to plantation life, particularly the rice plantation, which would be a popular subject for her for the rest of her life. A friend since childhood of Marie Heyward, Miss Smith often spent several weeks in the spring and again in the fall with the Heywards. While she was there, a party of young people would set off through the countryside in an old buggy, going sometimes as far as Mulberry Castle, with Miss Smith observing and sketching. A number of watercolors in her *A Rice Plantation of the Fifties* were based on drawings that she made at Wappaoolah.

Mr. Owen Winston, one of the two men who bought the house from the Heywards, joined Brooks Brothers in 1905 and rose to the position of vice president before he retired in 1949. He died the next year. William H. Barnum, the co-owner, was one of the investors who organized the Continental Mortgage Guarantee Company, and he served as its president for a number of years. He died in 1963. Both men also owned Grove plantation at the conjunction of the Dawhoo and Edisto rivers and were members of Yeamans Hall, the North Charleston club frequented by many northerners.

A number of Heyward family members, deeply attached to their old home place, said that Wappaoolah was later pulled down because a tragic death had occurred there. In the years after Winston and Barnum sold the property, the new owners were unwilling to occupy a house with that dark association. Apparently this was a reference to the suicide of Anthony J. Drexel III, who bought Wappaoolah after selling Callawassie Island in Beaufort County in 1947.

# BIBLIOGRAPHY

RESEARCH FOR THIS VOLUME was conducted at the South Carolina Historical Society in Charleston, the Charleston County Public Library, the College of Charleston's Addlestone Library, the Beaufort County Library, the South Carolina Department of Archives and History, the South Caroliniana Library at the University of South Carolina, and a number of government offices in the five counties (especially the Registers of Mesne Conveyance).

Among many other publications, the following were especially useful for a great many of the plantations: Robert Mills, *Atlas of the State of South Carolina* (Baltimore: F. Lucas, 1825); Lawrence S. Rowland, Alexander Moore, and George C. Rogers, *The History of Beaufort County, South Carolina, Volume I, 1514–1861* (Columbia: University of South Carolina Press, 1996); the *New York Times* (especially obituaries); the *Charleston News and Courier* and its descendant, the *Charleston Post and Courier;* the *Dictionary of American Biography;* and the five-volume collection of *South Carolina Historical and Genealogical Magazine* articles entitled *South Carolina Genealogies* (Spartanburg, S.C.: Reprint Co., 1983). In the list of sources of information for specific plantations, short titles are used for the following volumes, which are cited often:

*Colleton County South Carolina: A Pictorial History.* Walterboro, S.C.: Colleton County Historical and Preservation Society, 1994.

Cross, Jay Russell. *Historic Ramblin's through Berkeley County.* Columbia, S.C.: R. L. Bryan, 1985.

Hilton, Mary Kendall. *Old Homes & Churches of Beaufort County, South Carolina.* Columbia, S.C.: State Printing, 1970.

Irvin, Willis. *Selections from the Work of Willis Irvin: Architect, Augusta, Ga.* New York: Architectural Catalog Co., 1937.

Irving, John B., M.D. *A Day on Cooper River.* 1842. Enlarged and edited by Louisa Cheves Stoney. Columbia, S.C.: R. L. Bryan, 1969.

Iseley, N. Jane. *Beaufort.* Beaufort, S.C.: Historic Beaufort Foundation, 2003.

Iseley, N. Jane, photographs, and William P. Baldwin, text. *Lowcountry Plantations Today.* Greensboro, N.C.: Legacy, 2002.

———. *Plantations of the Low Country: South Carolina, 1697–1865.* Greensboro, N.C.: Legacy, 1985.

Linder, Suzanne Cameron. *Historical Atlas of the Rice Plantations of the ACE River Basin—1860.* Columbia: South Carolina Department of Archives & History for the Archives and History Foundation, Ducks Unlimited, and the Nature Conservancy, 1995.

Lowcountry Council of Governments. *Historic Resources of the Lowcountry: A Regional Survey of Beaufort County, S.C., Colleton County, S.C., Hampton County, S.C., Jasper County, S.C.* Yemassee, S.C.: Lowcountry Council of Governments, 1979.

McTeer. J. E. *High Sheriff of the Low Country.* Beaufort, S.C.: Beaufort Book Co., 1970.

Perry, Grace Fox. *Moving Finger of Jasper.* N.p., n.d. Copy at South Carolina Historical Society, Charleston.

Porcher, Richard Dwight, and Sarah Fick. *The Story of Sea Island Cotton*. Charleston, S.C.: Wyrick, 2005.

Rocz, Ron Anton, photographs, and Nina Burke, text. *Plantations of St. Bartholomew's Parish, South Carolina*. Walterboro, S.C.: Colleton County Historical and Preservation Society, 2005.

Stoney, Samuel Gaillard. *Plantations of the Carolina Low Country*. Charleston, S.C.: Carolina Art Association, 1938.

Todd, John R., and Francis M. Hutson. *Prince William's Parish and Plantations*. Richmond, Va.: Garrett & Massie, 1935.

**Belfair**

*Charleston News and Courier*, January 18, 1931.

McTeer, J. E. *High Sheriff of the Low Country*. Beaufort, S.C.: Beaufort Book Co., 1970.

**Bindon**

*Charleston News and Courier*, November 23, 1930; October 16, 1932.

Goldberg, Robert, and Gerald Jay Goldberg. *Citizen Turner: The Wild Rise of an American Tycoon*. New York: Harcourt Brace, 1995.

Todd and Hutson. *Prince William's Parish and Plantations*.

**Bluff**

*Charleston News and Courier*, September 27, 1931.

Heyward, Duncan Clinch. *Seed from Madagascar*. Chapel Hill: University of North Carolina Press, 1937.

Linder. *Historical Atlas of the Rice Plantations of the ACE River Basin*.

Lowcountry Council of Governments. *Historic Resources of the Lowcountry*.

Rocz and Burke. *Plantations of St. Bartholomew's Parish*.

Wallace, David Duncan. *The History of South Carolina*. New York: American Historical Society, 1934.

**Bonny Hall**

*Charleston News and Courier*, December 19, 1930.

Cheves/Middleton Collection, South Carolina Historical Society, Charleston.

King, Edward. *The Great South*. 1875. Baton Rouge: Louisiana State University Press, 1972.

Linder. *Historical Atlas of the Rice Plantations of the ACE River Basin*.

Lowcountry Council of Governments. *Historic Resources of the Lowcountry*.

Middleton, Alicia Hopton. *Life in Carolina and New England during the Nineteenth Century*. Bristol, R.I.: Privately printed, 1929.

Morgan, Ted. *Maugham*. New York: Simon & Schuster, 1980.

Todd and Hutson. *Prince William's Parish and Plantations*.

**Bradley Estate**

*Charleston News and Courier*, March 8, 1931.

Coulter, E. Merton. *George Walton Williams: The Life of a Southern Merchant and Banker, 1820–1903*. Athens, Ga.: Hibriten Press, 1976.

Craver, Charles, and Jeanne Craver. "The Forgotten Man: Peter Bradley's Role in Early American Breeding." *Arabian Horse World* 24 (July 1984), www.geocities.com/Heartland/Estates/3095/TheForgottenMan.html?200723 (accessed October 28, 2008).

**Bray's Island**

*Beaufort Gazette*, April 29, 1929; August 29, 1963.

*Charleston News and Courier*, December 9, 1930; May 12, 1947; February 22, 1959.

Lowcountry Council of Governments. *Historic Resources of the Lowcountry*.

Porcher and Fick. *The Story of Sea Island Cotton*.

**Brewton**

*Charleston News and Courier*, November 23, 1930.

Hochman, Todd. "Joe Frazier & Mama's New House," *Philadelphia Daily News*, January 28, 1972.

Todd and Hutson. *Prince William's Parish and Plantations*.

Wolfe, Gerald. *New York: A Guide to the Metropolis*. New York: McGraw-Hill, 1983.

**Buckfield**

*Charleston News and Courier*, April 12, 1931.

**Callawassie Island**

Behan, William A. *A Short History of Callawassie Island, South Carolina: The Lives & Times of Its Owners & Residents, 1711–1985*. Lincoln, Neb.: iUniverse, 2004.

———. *Exploring the Sullivan Tabby Point Ruins, Callawassie Island, South Carolina*. Columbia: South Carolina Institute of Archaeology and Anthropology, 2007.

*Charleston News and Courier*, May 10, 1931.

Rowland et al. *The History of Beaufort County, South Carolina, Volume I, 1514–1861*.

**Castle Hill**

Cawley, Sherry J. *Around Walterboro, South Carolina.* Charleston, S.C.: Arcadia, 1998.

*Charleston News and Courier,* November 23, 1930.

Irvin. *Selections from the Work of Willis Irvin.*

Irvin. *Selections from the Work of Willis Irvin.*

Todd and Hutson. *Prince William's Parish and Plantations.*

**Cat Island**

Baxandall, Lee. "Baring Witness: America's First Nudist Colony Had a South Carolina Address," http://www.scpronet.com/point/9509/s03.html (accessed October 28, 2008).

*Charleston News and Courier,* May 8, 1932; October 1, 1933; September 2, 1934.

McTeer, J. E. *High Sheriff of the Low Country.*

*Sea Island Sanctuary: Mile Square Semi-Tropic Island Resort.* Port Royal, S.C., n.d. Copy at South Caroliniana Library, University of South Carolina, Columbia.

*Seacroft: A Workers' Educational Community.* Port Royal, S.C., 1935. Copy at South Caroliniana Library, University of South Carolina, Columbia.

**Cheeha-Combahee**

*Charleston News and Courier,* February 15, 1931.

Emmet, Richard S. "Memories of Cheeha Combahee Plantation, 1929–1991." *Carologue* (South Carolina Historical Society) 15 (Autumn 1999): 18–22.

Rocz and Burke. *Plantations of St. Bartholomew's Parish.*

**Chelsea**

*Charleston News and Courier,* June 7, 1931.

Iseley and Baldwin. *Lowcountry Plantations Today.*

Lowcountry Council of Governments. *Historic Resources of the Lowcountry.*

Perry. *Moving Finger of Jasper.*

"Portrait of John Heyward (1807–1839)." Chelsea Plantation file (30-25-58), South Carolina Historical Society, Charleston.

**Chisolm Island**

*Beaufort Gazette,* November 25, 1926.

*Charleston News and Courier,* July 19, 1931.

Sanford, Marshall C., Jr. "The Progression of Coosaw Plantation into the 20th Century." Copy at Beaufort County Library.

**Clarendon**

*Beaufort Gazette,* February 11, 1932.

*Charleston News and Courier,* January 24, 1932; March 31, 1935.

Irvin. *Selections from the Work of Willis Irvin.*

Stockwell, Charles. "Clarendon Plantation Game Preserve." *Beaufort, Land of Isles* (February 1974).

**Clay Hall**

*Charleston News and Courier,* December 7, 1930.

Cheves/Middleton Collection. South Carolina Historical Society, Charleston.

Linder. *Historical Atlas of the Rice Plantations of the ACE River Basin.*

Todd and Hutson. *Prince William's Parish and Plantations.*

**Coffin Point**

*Charleston News and Courier,* December 14, 1930.

Dabbs, Edith M. *Sea Island Diary: A History of St. Helena Island.* Spartanburg, S.C.: Reprint Co., 1983.

Hilton. *Old Homes & Churches of Beaufort County.*

Johnson, Guion Griffin. *A Social History of the Sea Islands.* Chapel Hill: University of North Carolina Press, 1930.

Lowcountry Council of Governments. *Historic Resources of the Lowcountry.*

McTeer. *High Sheriff of the Low Country.*

Pearson, Elizabeth Ware. *Letters from Port Royal, 1862–1868.* New York: Arno Press, 1969.

Rose, Willie Lee. *Rehearsal for Reconstruction: The Port Royal Experiment.* Indianapolis: Bobbs-Merrill, 1964.

Rosengarten, Theodore. *Tombee: Portrait of a Cotton Planter.* New York: Morrow, 1986.

Rowland et al. *The History of Beaufort County, South Carolina, Volume I, 1514–1861.*

Towne, Laura M. *Letters and Diary of Laura M. Towne: Written from the Sea Islands of South Carolina, 1862–1884.* 1912. New York: Negro Universities Press, 1969.

**Combahee**

*Charleston News and Courier,* September 27, 1931.

*Colleton County South Carolina: A Pictorial History.*

Linder. *Historical Atlas of the Rice Plantations of the ACE River Basin.*

Lowcountry Council of Governments. *Historic Resources of the Lowcountry.*

Rocz and Burke. *Plantations of St. Bartholomew's Parish.*

Wallace, David Duncan. *The History of South Carolina.* New York: American Historical Society, 1934.

**Cotton Hall**
*Charleston News and Courier,* December 2, 1930.
Goldberg, Robert, and Gerald Jay Goldberg. *Citizen Turner: The Wild Rise of an American Tycoon.* New York: Harcourt Brace, 1995.
Heyward, James Barnwell. *Heyward.* 1931. Copy at South Carolina Historical Society, Charleston.
Todd and Hutson. *Prince William's Parish and Plantations.*

**Cuthbert Point (Pleasant Point)**
*Beaufort Gazette,* March 27, 1930; April 29, 1955; March 3, 1993.
*Charleston News and Courier,* January 11, 1931.
Pearson, Elizabeth Ware. *Letters from Port Royal, 1862–1868.* New York: Arno Press, 1969.
Spieler, Gerhard. "Pleasant Point Has Rich History." *Beaufort Gazette,* March 3, 193.

**Cypress Gardens (Dean Hall)**
*Charleston News and Courier,* July 19, 1931.
Cross. *Historic Ramblin's through Berkeley County.*
Irving. *A Day on Cooper River.*
Iseley. *Beaufort.*
Lowcountry Council of Governments. *Historic Resources of the Lowcountry.*

**Dataw Island**
*Beaufort Gazette,* May 16, 1935.
Bennett, Helen Christine. "Kate Gleason's Adventures in a Man's Job," *American Magazine,* October 1928.
*Charleston News and Courier,* November 30, 1930.
"Kate Gleason," http://winningthevote.org/KGleason.html (accessed October 29, 2008).
Rowland et al. *The History of Beaufort County, South Carolina, Volume I, 1514–1861.*

**Delta**
*Charleston News and Courier,* January 20, 1931.
Iseley and Baldwin. *Lowcountry Plantations Today.*
Lowcountry Council of Governments. *Historic Resources of the Lowcountry.*
Perry. *Moving Finger of Jasper.*
Rowland, Lawrence S. "'Alone on the River': The Rise and Fall of the Savannah River Rice Plantations of St. Peter's Parish, South Carolina." *South Carolina Historical Magazine* 88 (July 1987).

Rowland et al. *The History of Beaufort County, South Carolina, Volume I, 1514–1861.*
Sawyer, Angus C. "History, Historical Archaeology, and Cultural Resource Management: A Case Study from Jasper County, South Carolina." Master's thesis, Department of Sociology and Anthropology, Georgia Southern University, 2008.

**Foot Point**
*Charleston News and Courier,* August 2, 1931.
Edmunds, Emma. "Slouching towards Bluffton." *Atlanta Weekly,* June 27, 1982.
Marscher, Fran Heyward. *Remembering the Way It Was at Hilton Head, Bluffton and Daufuskie.* Charleston, S.C.: History Press, 2005.
Smith, Henry A. M. *The Baronies of South Carolina.* Spartanburg, S.C.: Reprint Co., 1988.

**Fort Fremont**
*Charleston News and Courier,* December 21, 1930.
Gooch, Barry. "Fort Fremont–Lands End, St. Helena Island, South Carolina," http://www.sciway.net/hist/fort-fremont-st-helena-island.html (accessed October 28, 2008).
Lowcountry Council of Governments. *Historic Resources of the Lowcountry.*
Spieler, Gerhard G. "Ft. Fremont: An Enigma after 268 Years." *Beaufort Gazette,* November 23, 1972.

**Good Hope Camp**
*Charleston News and Courier,* December 22, 1928; October 4, 1946.
Fox. *Moving Finger of Jasper.*
Lowcountry Council of Governments. *Historic Resources of the Lowcountry.*

**Gravel Hill**
*Charleston News and Courier,* April 5, 1931.
Lawton, Thomas O., Jr. *Upper St. Peter's Parish and Environs.* Garnett, S.C., 2001.

**Green Point**
*Charleston News and Courier,* December 7, 1930, July 5, 1931.
Cheves/Middleton Collection. South Carolina Historical Society, Charleston.
Linder. *Historical Atlas of the Rice Plantations of the ACE River Basin.*
Todd and Hutson. *Prince William's Parish and Plantations.*

**Gregorie Neck**

*Charleston News and Courier,* February 8, 1931.

Irvin. *Selections from the Work of Willis Irvin.*

Iseley and Baldwin. *Lowcountry Plantations Today.*

Lowcountry Council of Governments. *Historic Resources of the Lowcountry.*

Perry. *Moving Finger of Jasper.*

Todd and Hutson. *Prince William's Parish and Plantations.*

**Hilton Head Island**

*Beaufort Gazette,* November 14, 1889; April 26, 1928.

*Charleston News and Courier,* January 12, 1931; February 7, 1932.

Conant, Jennet. *Tuxedo Park: A Wall Street Tycoon and the Secret Palace of Science that Changed the Course of World War II.* New York: Simon & Schuster, 2002.

Danielson, Michael N. *Profits and Politics in Paradise: The Development of Hilton Head Island.* Columbia: University of South Carolina Press, 1996.

Hilton. *Old Homes & Churches of Beaufort County.*

Holmgren, Virginia C. *Hilton Head: A Sea Island Chronicle.* Hilton Head Island, S.C.: Hilton Head Island Publishing Co., 1959.

Lowcountry Council of Governments. *Historic Resources of the Lowcountry.*

Porcher and Fick. *The Story of Sea Island Cotton* [Coggins Point].

Rowland et al. *The History of Beaufort County, South Carolina, Volume I, 1514–1861.*

**Hobonny**

*Charleston News and Courier,* December 19, 1930.

Linder. *Historical Atlas of the Rice Plantations of the ACE River Basin.*

Lowcountry Council of Governments. *Historic Resources of the Lowcountry.*

Todd and Hutson. *Prince William's Parish and Plantations.*

**Honey Hill Battleground**

*Charleston News and Courier,* December 22, 1928.

Fox. *Moving Finger of Jasper.*

Hudson, Leonne M. "A Confederate Victory at Grahamville: Fighting at Honey Hill." *South Carolina Historical Magazine* 94 (January 1993).

Lowcountry Council of Governments. *Historic Resources of the Lowcountry.*

**Hope**

*Beaufort Gazette,* December 22, 1927.

Cawley, Sherry J. *Around Walterboro, South Carolina.* Charleston, S.C.: Arcadia, 1998.

*Charleston News and Courier,* March 1, 1931.

*Colleton County South Carolina: A Pictorial History.*

Linder. *Historical Atlas of the Rice Plantations of the ACE River Basin.*

Lowcountry Council of Governments. *Historic Resources of the Lowcountry.*

**Lady's Island**

*Charleston News and Courier,* November 25, 1934.

Verdier, Eva L. *"When Gun Shoot": Some Experiences While Taking the Census among the Low Country Negroes of South Carolina.* N.p., 1932.

**Laurel Bay**

Barnwell, Stephen B. *The Story of an American Family.* Marquette, Mich., 1969.

*Charleston News and Courier,* January 24, 1932.

Porcher and Fick. *The Story of Sea Island Cotton.*

**Laurel Spring**

*Beaufort Gazette,* October 27, 1927.

*Charleston News and Courier,* January 25, 1931.

*Colleton County South Carolina: A Pictorial History.*

Doar, David. *Rice and Rice Planting in the South Carolina Low Country.* Charleston: Charleston Museum, 1936.

Foner, Eric. *Nothing but Freedom: Emancipation and Its Legacy.* Baton Rouge: Louisiana State University Oress, 1989.

Linder. *Historical Atlas of the Rice Plantations of the ACE River Basin.*

Lowcountry Council of Governments. *Historic Resources of the Lowcountry.*

**Long Brow**

*Charleston Mercury,* June 21, 1863.

*Charleston News and Courier,* March 29, 1931; April 26, 1936.

Linder. *Historical Atlas of the Rice Plantations of the ACE River Basin.*

Rocz and Burke. *Plantations of St. Bartholomew's Parish.*

**Mackay Point**

*Charleston News and Courier,* December 25, 1930.

Iseley and Baldwin. *Lowcountry Plantations Today.*

Lowcountry Council of Governments. *Historic Resources of the Lowcountry.*

Perry. *Moving Finger of Jasper.*

Todd and Hutson. *Prince William's Parish and Plantations.*

**Maurene**
*Charleston News and Courier,* July 14, 1931.

**Medway**
Beach, Virginia. *Medway.* Charleston, S.C.: Wyrick, 1999.
*Charleston News and Courier,* April 26, 1931.
Coté, Richard N. "Medway Plantation, Back River: An Historical Outline, 1684–1993." Researched by Agnes Leland Baldwin for Gertrude S. Legendre. Goose Creek, S.C., July 1993.
Cross. *Historic Ramblin's through Berkeley County.*
Irving. *A Day on the Cooper River.*
Iseley and Baldwin. *Lowcountry Plantations Today.*
———. *Plantations of the Low Country.*
Legendre, Gertrude Sanford. *The Time of My Life.* Charleston, S.C.: Wyrick, 1987.
Stoney. *Plantations of the Carolina Low Country.*

**Mepkin**
*Charleston News and Courier,* May 17, 1931; January 24, 1938.
Cross. *Historic Ramblin's through Berkeley County.*
Irving. *A Day on Cooper River.*
Yuhl, Stephanie E. *A Golden Haze of Memory: The Making of Historic Charleston.* Chapel Hill: University of North Carolina Press, 2005.

**Mulberry Castle, South Mulberry**
Briggs, Loutrel. *Charleston Gardens.* Columbia: University of South Carolina Press, 1951.
*Charleston Evening Post,* August 25, 1988.
*Charleston News and Courier,* July 26, 1931; November 8, 1946; February 10, 1953; July 18, 1987.
Cross. *Historic Ramblin's through Berkeley County.*
Hamilton, Elizabeth Verner. "Mulberry." *Charleston Museum Quarterly* 2, no. 1 (1932).
Irving. *A Day on Cooper River.*
Iseley and Baldwin. *Lowcountry Plantations Today.*
———. *Plantations of the Low Country.*
Leiding, Harriette Kershaw. *Historic Houses of South Carolina.* Philadelphia: Lippincott, 1921.
Shaffer, E. T. H. *Carolina Gardens.* Chapel Hill: University of North Carolina Press, 1939.
Stoney. *Plantations of the Carolina Low Country.*

**Myrtle Grove**
*Beaufort Gazette,* January 27, 1927.
Cawley, Sherry J. *Around Walterboro, South Carolina.* Charleston, S.C.: Arcadia, 1998.
*Charleston News and Courier,* May 31, 1931.
Heyward. *Seed from Madagascar.*
Heyward, James Barnwell. *Heyward.* N.p., n.d.
Linder. *Historical Atlas of the Rice Plantations of the ACE River Basin.*
Lowcountry Council of Governments. *Historic Resources of the Lowcountry.*
Rocz and Burke. *Plantations of St. Bartholomew's Parish.*

**Nieuport**
*Charleston News and Courier,* December 7, 1930.
Cheves/Middleton Collection. South Carolina Historical Society, Charleston.
Larson, Kate Clifford. *Bound for the Promised Land: Harriet Tubman, Portrait of an American Hero.* New York: Ballantine, 2004.
Linder. *Historical Atlas of the Rice Plantations of the ACE River Basin.*

**Okeetee Club**
*Charleston News and Courier,* May 3, 1931.
Kilgo, James. *Pipe Creek to Matthew's Bluff: A Short History of Groton Plantation.* Chelsea, Mich.: Book Crafters, 1994.
Lowcountry Council of Governments. *Historic Resources of the Lowcountry.*
Perry. *Moving Finger of Jasper.*

**Old House**
*Charleston News and Courier,* December 22, 1928.
Rowland et al. *The History of Beaufort County, South Carolina, Volume I, 1514–1861.*

**Orange Grove, Seaside**
*Charleston News and Courier,* December 15, 1930.
Dabbs. *Sea Island Diary.*
Hilton. *Old Homes & Churches of Beaufort County.*
Iseley. *Beaufort.*
Iseley and Baldwin. *Lowcountry Plantations Today.*
Johnson. *A Social History of the Sea Islands.*
Rose, Willie Lee. *Rehearsal for Reconstruction: The Port Royal Experiment.* Indianapolis: Bobbs-Merrill, 1964.
Towne. *Letters and Diary of Laura M. Towne.*

**Palachucola Club**
*Charleston News and Courier,* February 22, 1931.
Davis, John E. "The Plantation Broker." *South Carolina Wildlife* 50 (November–December 2003).

**Palmetto Bluff**

*Charleston News and Courier*, December 28, 1930; February 25, 1932; January 13, 1935.

Fletcher, Joshua N., Carol J. Poplin, and Eric C. Poplin. *"Let Me Tell You about the Very Rich": Archaeological Data Recovery at 38BU1804 and 38BU1788, Palmetto Bluff, Beaufort County, South Carolina.* Charleston, S.C.: Brockington and Associates, 2004.

Inglesby, Edith. "Plantations of the Low Country: Palmetto Bluff." *Islander*, April 1967, June 1967.

Kennedy, Patricia Richards. *A History of Palmetto Bluff.* Bluffton, S.C.: Palmetto Bluff LLC, 2005.

**Paul and Dalton**

*Charleston News and Courier*, March 15, 1931.

*Colleton County South Carolina: A Pictorial History.*

Iseley and Baldwin. *Lowcountry Plantations Today.*

Linder. *Historical Atlas of the Rice Plantations of the ACE River Basin.*

Lowcountry Council of Governments. *Historic Resources of the Lowcountry.*

Rocz and Burke. *Plantations of St. Bartholomew's Parish.*

**Pillot Hunting Club**

*Charleston News and Courier*, December 31, 1930.

Lee, Clermont Huger. *The Joseph Alston Huger Family.* Richmond Hill, Ga.: Gordon Gardner, 2002.

Perry. *Moving Finger of Jasper.*

**Pimlico**

*Charleston News and Courier*, May 24, 1931.

Irving. *A Day on Cooper River.*

Norris, Ann Shreve. *Pimlico Plantation: Now and Long Ago.* N.p.: Published by the author, 1984.

**Pine Island**

*Beaufort Gazette*, December 19, 1935; April 9, 1936.

*Charleston News and Courier*, December 20, 1931.

McGowan, Pierre. *The Gullah Mailman.* Raleigh, N.C.: Pentland Press, 2000.

**Pineland Club**

*Charleston News and Courier*, February 1, 1931; June 28, 1936.

Lowcountry Council of Governments. *Historic Resources of the Lowcountry.*

Perry. *Moving Finger of Jasper.*

**Polawana Island**

*Charleston News and Courier*, March 15, 1929; November 30, 1930.

Dabbs. *Sea Island Diary.*

Lowcountry Council of Governments. *Historic Resources of the Lowcountry.*

Towne. *Letters and Diary of Laura M. Towne.*

**Retreat**

Barnwell. *The Story of an American Family.*

*Charleston News and Courier*, November 30, 1930.

Hilton. *Old Homes & Churches of Beaufort County.*

Lowcountry Council of Governments. *Historic Resources of the Lowcountry.*

Rowland et al. *The History of Beaufort County, South Carolina, Volume I, 1514–1861.*

Walker, Emmeline Dabney Greene. "The Walkers of South Carolina" (Beaufort County Library).

Way, John. "Retreat Plantation." *Beaufort: Land of Isles*, Spring 1975.

**Rose Hill**

Behan. *A Short History of Callawassie Island, South Carolina.*

*Charleston News and Courier*, November 13, 1932; January 23, 1938; February 26, 1939.

Hilton. *Old Homes & Churches of Beaufort County.*

Iseley and Baldwin. *Plantations of the Low Country.*

Lowcountry Council of Governments. *Historic Resources of the Lowcountry.*

Porcher and Fick. *The Story of Sea Island Cotton.*

**Spring Hill**

*Charleston News and Courier*, December 29, 1930.

Hine, William C. "Thomas E. Miller and the Early Years of South Carolina State University," *Carologue* (South Carolina Historical Society), Winter 1996.

Lowcountry Council of Governments. *Historic Resources of the Lowcountry.*

Perry. *Moving Finger of Jasper.*

**Spring Island**

Baldwin, Agnes. "History of Spring Island." Unpublished, 1966.

Behan. *A Short History of Callawassie Island, South Carolina.*

*Charleston News and Courier*, January 4, 1931; March 31, 1935.

Hays, Lucile Walker. *Spring Island Plantation: A Remembrance.* Beaufort, S.C.: Coastal Villages Press, 2004.

Rowland et al. *The History of Beaufort County, South Carolina, Volume I, 1514–1861.*

**Strawberry Hill**
*Charleston News and Courier,* April 19, 1931.
Perry. *Moving Finger of Jasper.*

**Tomotley**
Cawley, Sherry J. *Around Walterboro, South Carolina.* Charleston, S.C.: Arcadia, 1998.
*Charleston News and Courier,* November 23, 1930; September 6, 1931; March 29, 1932.
Linder. *Historical Atlas of the Rice Plantations of the ACE River Basin.*
Lowcountry Council of Governments. *Historic Resources of the Lowcountry.*
Stoney. *Plantations of the Carolina Low Country.*
Todd and Hutson. *Prince William's Parish and Plantations.*
Way, John. "Tomotley: Aristocracy in Carolina." *Beaufort: Land of Isles,* Fall 1975.

**Twickenham**
*Charleston News and Courier,* December 19, 1930.
Linder. *Historical Atlas of the Rice Plantations of the ACE River Basin.*
Lowcountry Council of Governments. *Historic Resources of the Lowcountry.*
Todd and Hutson. *Prince William's Parish and Plantations.*

**Wappaoolah**
*Charleston News and Courier,* March 15, 1930.
Irving. *A Day on Cooper River.*

Severens, Martha, ed. *Alice Ravenel Huger Smith: An Artist, A Place, and a Time.* Charleston, S.C.: Carolina Art Association, Gibbes Museum of Art, 1993.
Stoney. *Plantations of the Carolina Low Country.*

**White Hall (Colleton County)**
*Beaufort Gazette,* April 5, 1928.
*Charleston News and Courier,* March 15, 1931.
*Colleton County South Carolina: A Pictorial History.*
Linder. *Historical Atlas of the Rice Plantations of the ACE River Basin.*
Lowcountry Council of Governments. *Historic Resources of the Lowcountry.*
Rocz and Burke. *Plantations of St. Bartholomew's Parish.*

**White Hall (Jasper County)**
*Charleston News and Courier,* December 2, 1928.
Heyward. *Heyward.*
Lowcountry Council of Governments. *Historic Resources of the Lowcountry.*
Rowland et al. *The History of Beaufort County, South Carolina, Volume I, 1514–1861.*

**Woodward**
*Charleston News and Courier,* January 24, 1932.
Barnwell, Stephen B. *The Story of an American Family.* Marquette, Mich., 1969.
Porcher and Fick. *The Story of Sea Island Cotton.*

# INDEX

# ABOUT THE EDITORS

**ROBERT B. CUTHBERT,** a native of Summerville, attended Clemson University and graduated from the College of Charleston. He has served on the staff of the U.S. Vegetable Lab at Charleston for more than forty years. An active member of the South Carolina Historical Society, he has an avid interest in researching the history of the South Carolina coast.

**STEPHEN G. HOFFIUS** is a freelance writer and editor in Charleston and the former director of publications for the South Carolina Historical Society. He is coeditor with Angela D. Mack of *Landscape of Slavery: The Plantation in American Art.*